# Achieving Student Success

## Effective Student Services in Canadian Higher Education

Edited by
DONNA HARDY COX AND
C. CARNEY STRANGE

D0103157

McGill-Queen's University Press
Montreal & Kingston · London · Ithaca

ISBN 978-0-7735-3621-0 (cloth)
ISBN 978-0-7735-3622-7 (paper)

Legal deposit first quarter 2010
Bibliothèque nationale du Québec

Printed in Canada on acid-free paper that is 100% ancient forest free
(100% post-consumer recycled), processed chlorine free
Reprinted in paperback, 2011

McGill-Queen's University Press acknowledges the support of the Canada Council
for the Arts for our publishing program. We also acknowledge the financial
support of the Government of Canada through the Canada Book Fund for
our publishing activities.

The authors graciously acknowledge the Canadian Association of College
and University Student Services, the Student Affairs and Services Association,
and the Educational Leadership Foundation of the American College Personnel
Association for their generous support of this project.

**Library and Archives Canada Cataloguing in Publication**
Achieving student success: effective student services in Canadian higher education /
edited by Donna Hardy Cox and C. Carney Strange.

Includes bibliographical references and index.
ISBN 978-0-7735-3621-0 (bnd)
ISBN 978-0-7735-3622-7 (pbk)

1. College students – Services for – Canada. 2. Student affairs services – Canada.
3. Universities and colleges – Canada – Administration. I. Cox, Donna Gail Hardy,
1961– II. Strange, Charles Carney

LB2342.94.C3A34 2010          378.1'940971          C2009-904565-6

Typeset in Sabon 10/12
by Infoscan Collette, Quebec City

# Contents

# Foreword

*Achieving Student Success: Effective Student Services in Canadian Higher Education* – what lofty goals and what a timely focus for Donna Hardy Cox and Carney Strange in their first collaborative book! The title itself captures the primary value of this book and the commitment of the authors and of the profession on which they are focusing: the success of students. But this volume is much more than the sum of its chapters and the collective wisdom of its authors. In its presentation of both the evolution and the current state of the profession of student services in Canada and the celebration of its roots, this book utilizes an approach that is near and dear to the hearts of most student services professionals – campus ecology.

Briefly, the ecological approach emphasizes the importance of the interactions among all aspects of the environment – physical, human, organizational, and constructed – on the behaviour, experiences, and learning of that community and on the *relationships* among these various components that can help or hinder learning, growth, and development.

In this book, Donna and Carney set the stage for the descriptions of services for students by giving us a synopsis of the underlying historical, philosophical, and theoretical foundations of our work. Only by knowing how our profession evolved in Canada, and the unique forces that shaped it, can one fully appreciate Canadian student services. Somehow it seems right that this book is co-edited by Canadian and American educator-professionals, since much of our own recent professional history has been informed and supported by our USA colleagues. Some of the "pioneers" of student services in Canada, including Paul Gilmor, Doug Eaton, Fred Nichols, Elspeth Baugh, Bill Stewart, and George McMahon, introduced their campuses to the writings of American academic experts in the newly developing theory about students. By inviting some of these experts to be keynote speakers at our national professional conferences in the 1980s, they provided the opportunity for others to learn what they had discovered in their own professional learning – that there was exciting and instructive new information available that could inform and enhance our work with students. Then, in the 1990s, the Canadian Association of College and University Student Services (CACUSS) sponsored Student Affairs Institutes, an annual series of professional education events that also featured renowned US experts, such as Bob Rodgers, Jim Banning, Susan Komives, Elizabeth Whitt, and Gary Hanson, to further enrich our profession and our colleagues. For the first time in our history, there was support and recognition for professional development, for credentials, and for knowledge-based practice about students and student services. The knowledge "environment" of the student affairs profession was changing in Canada, and these changes and the support that followed them stimulated the development and education of our profession.

As I look at the authors of the various chapters in this book, I am struck by the era they are from – an era that was grounded in this new knowledge base and in the professional credentials that emanated from the work of the original pioneers and the generation of professionals and educators who worked with and informed them. The environment for student services on college and university campuses in Canada and the student services profession changed forever in the 1980s. That change and the people who were shaped by it are now in turn educating others. Some of these authors contribute knowledge about their functional or service areas, while others look more broadly at the connections of student services with their institutional missions and in the various educational contexts in which students learn. Some of the more recent structural connections and collaborations for student services in Canada are also examined – enrolment management and judicial affairs. Professionals in these areas, who also value and support our students and their learning, are welcome additions to our student services family.

Finally, the co-editors view the practice settings and forms through the lens of strategies and principles for good practice, a theme that connects us all. This order of presentation also parallels the history of the provision of services for students in post-secondary settings in Canada, a history that saw our practice and focus move from separate functional areas to a more central and coordinated connection with our institutional missions and to others in our educational communities. Like our USA colleagues we are refocusing and reshaping our methods and aligning with the commitments and approaches described so well in *Learning Reconsidered* (Keeling 2004) and *Learning Reconsidered 2* (Keeling 2006), and we are taking our rightful place as knowledgeable partners in post-secondary education.

So, as we learn from our colleagues about the structures and strategies important to student success, may we also, as Donna and Carney remind us, remember and honour the roots of this knowledge and the value of sharing it with others. This book does just that. As you read it, bear in mind that it also holds the keys to understanding the future of our profession in Canada, a future which honours and builds on our own ecology and our past accomplishments, and which encourages us to look ahead to discover new models, approaches, and practices. It is exactly this commitment to sustaining our profession and our knowledge that will be required for the 21st century.

To Donna, Carney, and all of the authors of this book, thank you and congratulations. A new era has begun!

Dr Peggy Patterson
Professor, Higher Education Leadership
University of Calgary, Alberta
CACUSS President 1992–94

# Preface

In recent decades, the degree of professionalization has significantly increased in those student services personnel who support student success in Canadian higher education. In terms of both standards for staff performance and expansion of the knowledge base and understanding required to support its work on campus, the student services field has emerged as a primary contributor to the quality and outcome of the Canadian post-secondary experience. While some of this has occurred over time, arguably in response to provincial/territorial and consumer mandates for accountability and efficiency, much of this improvement can also be attributed to the natural evolution of a profession of student services educators intent on achieving its mission of supporting student learning and development as full partners in the academy.

Student services began as a modest focus in the Canadian post-secondary system, identified mostly with a loosely connected group of counsellors and administrators committed to helping students on campus in any way deemed appropriate. The goal from the beginning was student success – or the completion by students of the goals they set out to achieve in our institutions. Student services on Canadian campuses today are provided by a more highly sophisticated group of professionals who bring expertise from any number of specialties. Some, for example, are versed in creating a positive learning experience for incoming students, in the form of effective orientation and first-year experience programs. Some specialize in engaging students through leadership and service opportunities in student unions, organizations, and societies. Still others understand the complexities of career decisions, the nature of community life in residence, and the varying needs of an increasingly diverse student population. Thus, like their predecessors, they all serve to promote various dimensions of student success.

The student services field in Canada has benefited greatly in recent years from these gains and in response has generated a strong professional community and the beginnings of graduate-level professional preparation. The Canadian Association of College and University Student Services (CACUSS) now stands as the premier professional organization for some 1,000 members who gather at annual and regional conferences to develop new understandings of the Canadian post-secondary experience and to promote best practices in serving students. The first curriculum for formal preparation of student services administrators and practitioners has been established at Memorial University of Newfoundland, in the form of accessible (Internet-based or in-class) training at the master's level. Doctoral programs, too – for example, at the University of Calgary – are turning their attention to questions of student services leadership. In addition, rising interests have created new agendas for research and practice in the field that promise to further transform the institutions they serve.

All of this suggests that time and opportunity are ripe for identifying and distilling the developments and contributions of student services to the Canadian post-secondary enterprise. This book is a contemporary response to the need for a comprehensive understanding of student services and the various roles its professionals serve in effecting student success.

There is a growing consciousness throughout Canadian higher education that student services is a critical partner in fulfilling the promises and enhancing the outcomes of the post-secondary opportunity. This volume articulates the purposes, histories, practices, and issues that underlie the functions of student services in Canadian colleges and universities. Our intent is to inform the profession, the academy, consumers, and public policy-makers of the breadth and depth of our work, and to suggest the range of issues and barriers that challenge higher education as it continues to respond to Canada's needs for the development of its citizens' talents.

This book divides the topic of student services into three sections. Part One focuses on the historical, philosophical, and theoretical foundations that frame the organization of post-secondary services in support of student success; Part Two reviews the various campus-based functions and forms of student services that support student success; and Part Three considers the integration of student services within different institutional types, missions, and delivery systems. The book concludes in Part Four with some observations on what might constitute principles of best practices in the field and directions for development of student services in the future.

The authors of this volume incorporate a wide range of experiences in Canadian higher education, especially in student services. Among them are four former presidents of CACUSS, those who have completed their doctorate and hold faculty or other professional appointments at Canadian colleges and universities, and those who serve in senior student services leadership positions in a variety of Canadian post-secondary institutions. Collectively, these authors have contributed extensively to numerous professional development opportunities, as practitioner-scholars and scholarly practitioners, with many holding positions of executive leadership in a range of student services organizations. The perspectives they bring to this topic come from not only their years of hands-on experience but also their appreciation for the emerging literature that is beginning to inform their practice. Each offers a synopsis of his or her respective student services area, with an invitation to join in the conversation about the issues and concerns contained therein.

So we begin and end our introduction with the two questions that have framed this volume from the outset: What is the status of student services in Canadian higher education? and How might these services contribute to the success of students enrolled in the Canadian post-secondary system? We hope that this initiative is a useful start in developing an emerging identity among Canadian student services professionals who are poised to make a real difference in the lives of Canadian post-secondary students. As the experiences recounted here infuse the Canadian student services field with a useful critique of its status and suggest new possibilities for its future, we welcome the dialogue and input this work will engender.

Donna Hardy Cox
C. Carney Strange

We dedicate this edition to the memory of

*Michel Ouelette (1955–2009)*

a passionate advocate for student success.

ACHIEVING STUDENT SUCCESS

# PART ONE
# Historical, Philosophical, and Theoretical Foundations of Student Services

The story of any field is a history of persons, events, and situations that in hindsight seem to connect in a sequence of antecedents and consequences, as if destiny and purpose were its guides. While underway, though, it is more often the case that causes are elusive and outcomes are unpredictable. Any description of history is necessarily a slice of understanding in time, limited by current perspectives and shaped by selective experiences and contacts of the authors.

Chapter 1 begins this exploration of the role of student services in the success of Canadian post-secondary students with a recall and description of the events and persons who have contributed to its development through various associations and institutions, from those first established to the most recent. Clearly, those who were part of this evolution will recognize the moments and times that shaped who we have become and the principal ideas that constitute what we espouse. Some sixty years ago the student services field in Canadian higher education was a loosely connected division of institutional offices whose function on most campuses was to dispense their respective services to those who came in the door. Today it continues those same services, but with a more proactive and collective professional sense of its mission and central role in effecting the success of students pursuing the post-secondary experience. An emerging professional identity and a commitment to a common purpose distinguishes the current status of this field, with an expectation among its ranks that it will continue as an integral partner in the enterprise of higher learning in Canada. Such expectations are also grounded in an evolving set of ideas that constitute the beginning of a theory that can explain both the developmental paths of students as they progress toward their goals and the influence of educational environments that support this experience.

A distinctive sign of an emerging field is the sense among practitioners of carrying forward and improving upon a tradition as new experiences intersect with better ideas and explanations. A collective wisdom is honed and shared by members while setting new standards and shaping best practices. Thus, another mark of a maturing field is the existence of a theoretical knowledge that informs practice and offers a conceptual framework for considering its designs and aims. In chapter 2, the rudiments of such a knowledge base are described in response to two core questions essential to the aims of student success: How do students learn, develop, and grow? and How can the post-secondary experience enhance that process? Drawing from a wide range of socio-behavioural disciplines, the constructs explained therein constitute the core of "student development theory" that frames the work of student services in the post-secondary setting.

In summary, this section introduces the foundations of the field of student services in Canadian higher education, with reference to its principal events and to key understandings of the phenomena to which it applies its expertise.

# 1

# Foundations of Student Services in Canadian Higher Education

## DONNA HARDY COX AND C. CARNEY STRANGE

The contributions of student services to Canadian higher education extend deep into the history of an enterprise that is both evolutionary and multi-faceted. Beginning with a people intent on preserving a monarchy and its inherent sense of order, the first settlers of North America brought with them desires that were civil as well as practical. On the one hand they depended on the skills of builders and crafters to survive the challenges of a vast wilderness; on the other hand they also sought to develop a society with a vision of decency and civil participation that spoke of their European roots. All of this required a system of education that would preserve heritage, generate new understandings, and prepare leaders to guide an emerging polity. Thus, higher education evolved in Canada, from east to west, following the paths of explorers and community-builders who saw its goals as both necessary and inspirational.

## CANADIAN HIGHER EDUCATION

The origins of Canadian post-secondary education are traced to the middle of the seventeenth century, with the early vocational offerings of the Collège des Jésuites (1635) "for men who might become priests or enter the professions" (The Canadian Encyclopedia). Soon thereafter Monseigneur François de Laval established the Séminaire de Québec (1663), which was eventually granted a Royal Charter as Université Laval in 1852, the first French-language institution of higher education in North America. A century later came the Provincial Academy of Arts and Sciences (1785) in Fredericton, subsequently chartered as the University of New Brunswick in 1859 and claiming status as the oldest English-language public institution of higher learning in Canada.

Concurrent with these initiatives was the work of Anglican Loyalists who, on the heels of the American Revolution, moved to Nova Scotia and founded the University of King's College (1789) in Halifax (now part of Dalhousie University). This was the first university in English Canada and remains the oldest English-speaking Commonwealth University outside Great Britain. Also instrumental in the generation of these first Canadian institutions were a number of religious foundations, such as the Jesuits, which provided technical education (e.g., training pilots, explorers, ship's captains, and surveyors) in the first decades of the eighteenth century and, in the nineteenth century, established St Mary's University (1802), St Michael's College (1852), St Francis Xavier University (1853), and St Dunstan's College (1855) (now the University of Prince Edward Island).

Development of Canada's post-secondary system received further impetus in the late nineteenth and early twentieth centuries from increased governmental involvement and passage of several key legislative acts. For example, the British North America Act (1867) made provinces responsible for a system of public institutions (i.e., colleges, university colleges, and universities), and to support provincial efforts the federal government provided funding through further legislation (e.g., agricultural grants in 1912, Technical Education Act of 1919). Meanwhile, by the early 1900s, Canadian university presidents recognized the need to exchange information and discuss common problems and, in 1917, established the National Conference of Canadian Universities as "the voice and conscience of Canada's institutions of higher learning" and predecessor of the present-day Association of Universities and Colleges of Canada (AUCC) (1965). By the latter decades of the twentieth century, additional legislation (e.g., Adult Occupational Training Act in 1967, Canada Student Loans Act in 1964, and National Training Act in 1982) spurred further growth in the system and also resulted in the emergence of a provincially/territorially controlled college sector addressing the technical, diploma, and certification needs of a greatly expanded society. In 1972, the Association of Canadian Community Colleges (ACCC) was incorporated and currently represents some 150 community colleges, institutes of technology, CÉGEPs, and university colleges in over 900 locations across Canada.

In 2009, Canadian higher education supports approximately 785,000 full-time and 270,000 part-time university students across 90 campuses and 900,000 full-time and 1.5 million part-time learners enrolled in over 900 colleges and institutes. In total, these institutions are served by more than 67,000 faculty members. Canadians have come to expect much of their premier system of colleges and universities in terms of quality, accessibility, affordability, relevance, and responsiveness to changing societal and economic needs in a knowledge-intensive age (Sontag 1999). Paramount to their concerns is a demand for post-secondary structures that support students' aspirations for success. This is a goal that has long involved the integral contributions of practitioners and administrators known collectively as campus "student services personnel" or "student affairs professionals."

Woven into the tapestry of Canadian higher education are a history of student services and the tireless work of a range of professional staff who enthusiastically support the goals of student success in the academy. Once "house mothers," matrons, dons, nurses, coaches, and deans of men or women, and now vice-presidents, deans of students, directors of housing, residence managers, and coordinators of student development, leadership, and wellness, these individuals inform, orient, advise, challenge, support, and guide students through a myriad of decisions during the post-secondary years. Whether it be questions about financing education, selecting majors, making new friends and living in community, learning how to lead, or taking steps toward self-direction, student services professionals have come to assume a major role in such concerns while facilitating students' transition, matriculation, and program success.

The field of student services (or student affairs) shares a common history with Canadian post-secondary education (Jones 1997), evolving over the past century through four overlapping phases: (a) the early years, when services were rudimentary and extended from a philosophy of *in loco parentis;* (b) a period of professional identities and roles, when the emergence of the first formal organizations spurred the rapid development of professional expertise and affiliation; (c) an era of specialization, when generalist professionals evolved into various kinds of specialists directly linked to changing societal needs and an increasingly diverse student body; and (d) an age of professional preparation and skill, when standards and expectations of professional preparation for student services roles were codified for the first time in Canada at the graduate level.

## EVOLUTION OF STUDENT SERVICES IN CANADA

Over the years, the student services field in Canadian higher education has evolved into a cadre of administrative service professionals who bring a breadth of understanding and scope of institutional responsibility to shaping the post-secondary student experience. In the beginning, however, practitioners tended to respond to student needs only as they arose.

### Early Years

The earliest history of student services as a recognized function in Canadian higher education spans roughly seventy years, from the final two decades of the nineteenth century to about the middle of the twentieth century. This was a seminal time in student services development as various administrative personnel took it upon themselves to closely monitor the behaviour of their student charges. Although most encounters back then involved mischief of one sort or another, were it not for the 1875 date on the following incident report issued by Queen's University, the characters and tensions of these events could perhaps have happened on any campus just yesterday.

> They had cut both chapel and classes to go to a hotel downtown where each, it is reported, quickly drank two glasses of brandy. They then returned to classes where they had the misfortune to encounter Principal William Snodgrass in the corridor. He noticed their condition and promptly brought the matter before the senate, where the two were found guilty of "an offence against moral propriety and good discipline" and suspended from their rank as undergraduates. They might continue to attend classes, but must not wear gowns and could not sit for any exams for the duration of their sentence. Their fellow students thought the punishment too harsh, and petitioned for a remission of the sentence. When they received no reply, most refused to go to classes. In less than a week they sullenly backed down, however, when Snodgrass replied that the senate could not change its decision and that any further absences would be punished by expulsion (Queen's Encyclopedia n.d.)

Although the gist of this incident might ring true to anyone managing disciplinary measures on campus today, the difference may lie in how it was resolved. Unlike current practices, in earlier days the prevailing paradigm of student services was one of *in loco parentis* ("in place of parents"), wherein campus personnel were expected to play an authoritative role in students' lives, with close monitoring and careful regulation being the order of the day. Regardless, such an approach was well-meaning and purposeful (if not paternalistic), as reflected in the following president's comments: "In respect of student social events some care must be exercised, for there are in St. John's, in my opinion, too many things which tend to distract young persons of studious purpose" (Paton 1927).

Also during this period, rudimentary understandings of various services requiring attention from institutions first emerged. For example, the roots of the residential option are apparent in President Paton's (1926–27) reflections that, "Our outport students are scattered in lodgings. They have none of the advantages of the collegiate life, the closer intercourse in which angles are rubbed down, mind is whetted by contact of mind, and soul grows in contact with soul ... A corporate life needs a recognized habitation" (Paton 1927). Even the significance of wellness services was anticipated as early as the 1930s when President Hatcher commented: "Not everyone realizes the close relation between health and efficiency in studies. A pallid and nervous bookworm is by no means our ideal of a successful student"

(Hatcher 6 June 1939). In addition, students were thought to have benefited from the same degree of engagement prized today, as President Paton (1925–26) again observed in his annual report:

> From the very beginning we have associated the students themselves with the organization of the social life and the games, and with the control of discipline. Four Representatives, two men and two women, were elected. These met the Staff regularly each week and brought forward any matter that had arisen in the week touching College management. These discussions were quite frank and always friendly. A form of constitution for the Students' Representative Council has been drafted.

The importance of co-curricular involvement during this era was also noted by another president who reported that, "Each student is required to engage regularly both in some cultural activity outside the regular 'academic' courses and also in some form of games. Organized games form a part of the health programme of teachers-in-training" (Hatcher 1938).

Finally, in these early decades of student services, the value of specialized appointments on behalf of students was recognized, initially in response to the perceived special needs of women. Thus, following a movement begun in the 1890s at Queen's University, Caroline McNeill became the first dean of women in 1918, a position that later became one whose occupant:

> lived in residence with women students and supervised them directly, making and enforcing rules about such things as curfews, late-leaves and visitors. The Dean also made rules for women who lived off-campus, supervising how they dressed ... and their choice of housing (no unsupervised apartments, no boarding houses with men, no boarding houses that had not been personally approved by the Dean)(Queen's Encyclopedia n.d.)

Other institutions soon followed suit, for example, with Mary L. Bollert appointed dean of women at the University of British Columbia in 1921, Monnie G. Mansfield at Memorial University of Newfoundland in 1943, and Marion Stillwell Bates at McMaster University in 1946. By the end of this period, some institutions had come to appreciate the contributions of those dedicated to such service and moved to formalize and define their roles more broadly, as happened at Memorial University of Newfoundland in 1939, when a faculty committee had "taken steps to improve certain conditions under which our undergraduates do their work" (Hatcher 6 June 1939). A sense of student services as a sound dimension of post-secondary education had arrived. During the transition to the subsequent period of professional identity, however, events of global proportion intervened, spurring campus services personnel to affiliate more closely and benefit from a collective approach.

## Professional Identities and Roles

If the early period of student services tended to feature protective measures and humanistic processes, this second period of professional identity and practice, spanning the middle decades of the twentieth century until about the early 1970s, emphasized applications of professional methods and associations. Five events are significant in that development, corresponding to the foundation of each of five professional organizations relevant to the delivery of student services on Canadian campuses. First came the establishment of the University Advisory Services (UAS) in 1946, then the University Counselling and Placement Association (UCPA) in 1952, the Canadian Association of University Student Personnel Services (CAUSPS-1) in 1953, the Council of Associations of University Student Personnel Services (CAUSPS-2) in 1961, and finally, in 1971, the Canadian Association of College and University Student Services (CACUSS). Each occasion represented the coming together of like-minded practitioners who saw the need for a more systematic approach to their work, including an understanding of its underlying principles and values.

This movement toward professionalization of student services was first precipitated by concerns arising from a sudden, large enrolment of men and women discharged from the Canadian Armed Forces following the Second World War. As a result of the Veterans Rehabilitation Act (1945), which provided for a university education, including tuition and family and living allowances, Canadian campuses swelled to accommodate war veterans who would comprise nearly one-quarter (21 per cent) of all enrollees by the 1949–50 academic year. Usually older and married with children, these new learners challenged common assumptions about services designed for traditional students and raised expectations for the practical payoff of their efforts, most specifically in terms of career goals and gainful employment once finished. Thus, the University Advisory Services (UAS) was established to represent the veterans' counsellors who offered students personal and financial counselling, as well as placement advice (Hoskin, Melhuish, and Wagner 1969). In 1947, at its second conference, Dr A.J. Cook, University of Alberta, expressed a hope that "services set up for student veterans might become permanent and available to all students" (Hoskin, Melhuish, and Wagner 1969, 27). Two years later at its conference in Halifax (1949), UAS decided to encompass other areas of "student personnel work," and so invited additional like-minded colleagues, such as registrars and deans of men and women, to join the effort (Hoskin,

Melhuish, and Wagner 1969). Within three years of this shift to extend its purview, UAS evolved into the University Counselling and Placement Association (UCPA) (1952), offering further opportunity "for any person involved in student personnel work at a member university or college" to become a member (Hoskin, Melhuish, and Wagner 1969). By 1958 UCPA had embraced personnel in financial aid, orientation, international student advising, and student housing and residence life, as well as associate members from industry, business, and government. This broader base led to a redefining of student personnel services to include those engaged in "counseling on academic progress, admission requirements, elective studies, employment, finances, health, personal matter, 'personality deviations,' religious matters, social behavior and vocational plans" (Hoskin, Melhuish, and Wagner 1969). It was during this period that institutional roots were first established within Canadian colleges and universities to formally acknowledge both a "student personnel" student services role on campus and the importance of external partnerships with industry and government.

Organizational expansion during this period also generated momentum for a professional identity that embraced the education of students as the core of student services work, although it also raised concerns about the ability of a single comprehensive structure to meet all the needs of a diverse membership. Consequently the Canadian Association of University Student Personnel Services (1963) chartered three autonomous divisions, identifying them respectively as the Canadian Student Affairs Association (CSAA), the University Career Planning Association (UCPA), and the University Counselling Association (UCA). This was a time when attempts to stabilize a seemingly disjointed organization – such as by introducing *The Journal,* sponsoring annual conferences, accommodating constitutional revisions, and focusing on a common purpose – fell short of the goal, leaving the door ajar for further developments, including a name change to the Council of Associations of University Student Personnel Services (CAUSPS-2). This decision signalled the formation of yet another assembly with the benefits of centralized membership and divisional autonomy. The Canadian Student Services Association (CSSA), the Canadian University and College Counselling Association (CUCCA), and the Canadian College Health Services Association (CCHSA) federated in 1961 to achieve common purposes, albeit absent the University Career Planning Association (UCPA), a charter member that by then had decided to proceed in its own direction.

Unfortunately, while calls increased for greater integration of student services on college and university campuses, challenges to the umbrella structure of CAUSPS-2 soon erupted from a fractious organizational culture that had pitted divisional strengths against common membership. Ultimately, a solution was sought in a reconstitution of the organization in 1971 as the Canadian Association of College and University Student Services (CACUSS).

During this period of professionalization, CACUSS showed steady growth, reaching a membership of over 1,000 student services personnel across five divisional associations by the time of its silver anniversary in 1996. Throughout its first several decades CACUSS succeeded, for the most part, in affirming its structure with a full-time secretariat, a balance of divisional autonomy and centralized services, a national publication – *Communiqué* – professional development activities such as the Canadian Institute on Student Affairs and Services (CISAS), and annual conferences regularly drawing 400 to 800 participants. To date, CACUSS has remained the premier comprehensive organization of student services professionals in Canada even though various divisions have disaffiliated and joined over the years (e.g., the Canadian Association of Student Financial Aid Administrators (CASFAA) sought independence in 2001, and divisions responsive to Aboriginal students – National Aboriginal Student Services Association (NASSA), students with disabilities – Canadian Association of Disability Service Providers in Post-Secondary Education (CADSPPE), and issues of academic integrity and judicial affairs – the Canadian Academic Integrity and Student Judicial Affairs (CAISJA) emerged within the organization in recent years). CACUSS continues to address concerns across the spectrum of institutional missions in Canadian post-secondary education and in collaboration with other higher education organizations (e.g., the Association of Universities and Colleges of Canada and the Council for the Advancement of Standards in Higher Education).

## Specializations

These developments in Canadian student services paralleled an increased consciousness of regional differences and needs, a perspective quite compatible with the historical provincial/territorial grounding of the higher education system. Accompanying this trend was a shift from a general focus on professional competence in the field to the value placed on specialized expertise. Consequently, this period of development also featured a flourishing of various professional associations and activities that were more regionally established or specifically committed to the needs of particular student groups and the exercise of particular professional skills.

### REGIONAL GROUPS

Due to geographic distance and culture, regional efforts have always characterized development of professional student services communities in Canada. First as informal gatherings of personnel from nearby institutions and then later as formal meetings with planned agendas and elected officers, regionalized associations in Canadian student services evolved almost immediately from the start. Notable examples are those established in the Atlantic provinces – the Atlantic Association of College and University Student Services/Association des Services aux Étudiants des Colleges et Universités de L'Atlantique (AACUSS/ASEUCA), serving Newfoundland and Labrador, Prince Edward Island, Nova Scotia, and New Brunswick; Ontario – Ontario Committee on Student Affairs (OCSA); and the Western provinces – Western Student Affairs Administrators (WESTSAA), serving Manitoba, Alberta, British Columbia, and Nunavut. Both OCSA and WESTSAA serve principally senior student services officers within their respective regions, while AACUSS/ASEUCA tends to address a full range of institutional needs and personnel.

The AACUSS/ASEUCA was among the first to organize on a regional basis. Formed in 1956, just after UCPA, as the Association of Atlantic Universities Deans of Men and Women, its members met twice a year to discuss issues of mutual concern, as well as to renew friendships and enjoy one another's company. The informal genesis of this group evolved, by 1975, into a fully constituted association committed to: (a) evaluating the needs of Atlantic colleges and universities as they relate to student services; (b) providing a medium for exchange, review, and evaluation of information among members, students, and other interested groups; (c) interpreting the role of student services in universities and colleges; (d) encouraging and developing programs directed at the professional enhancement of its members; (e) developing, encouraging, and supporting professional and ethical standards in student services; and (f) serving as an effective arm of the Atlantic Association of Universities (Atlantic Association of College and University Student Services). Some thirty years later ACCUSS/ASEUCA, the longest established regional student services organization in Canada, continues to honour its history and serve as a forum for exchange, review, and evaluation through professional development, establishment of standards, and discussion of regional concerns, and as a venue for informal interaction and the development of good relationships among student services professionals in Atlantic Canada. As additional institutions sought to capitalize on the expertise of their neighbours, other regional organizations have followed suit in attending to the local student services needs of their own constituents.

SPECIALIZED GROUPS
The recent few decades have also witnessed the emergence and further development of a number of specialized professional organizations in student services. Some have evolved around particular functions within student services, e.g., career and employment services, and others have focused on the needs of particular student populations, e.g., Aboriginal students. Examples of associations responding to the need for greater depth of expertise relative to various functional specializations include the Canadian Association of Student Financial Aid Administrators (CASFAA) and the Canadian Association of Career Educators and Employers (CACEE). In

2001, following twenty-two years of affiliation, CASFAA declared its independence from CACUSS and proceeded on its own to represent financial aid administrators and awards officers in colleges, universities, and institutes across Canada. CASFAA continues as an important liaison with the federal government, service providers, financial institutions, and various other stakeholders in student financial aid; advocates on behalf of members by providing input on student financial assistance programs and policies; and provides professional development opportunities for members, including an annual conference. In recent years CASFAA has played a leadership role with the Canadian federal government, lobbying for a comprehensive student aid program and advising on new federal scholarship programs, e.g., the Canadian Millennium Scholarship.

The Canadian Association of Career Educators and Employers' (CACEE) roots date to the earlier formation of the University Advisory Services (1946), created to assist returning veterans in Canada's colleges and universities. In the 1970s it affirmed its organizational identity, and over the ensuing decades it expanded its services and constituencies to achieve a membership, by 2000, of 800 professionals representing every Canadian university, many colleges, and over 300 employers across Canada. In the 1990s CACEE was instrumental in assisting the transition of Canada Employment Centres to institutional career centres, a move that has placed career development at the core of the Canadian post-secondary experience.

Organizations responding to the needs of particular student populations include, for example, the Canadian Association of Disability Service Providers in Post-Secondary Education (CADSPPE) and the National Aboriginal Student Services Association (NASSA). CADSPPE emerged as an independent organization within CACUSS in 1998 and by mission is "committed to the creation of accessible, equitable, and inclusive learning environments for students with disabilities" (Canadian Association of Disability Service Providers in Post-Secondary Education). Its student development and learning core services include transition support, academic accommodation advising, adaptive technology, learning disability assessment, learning strategy support, disability related counselling and coaching, student development, and exam accommodation.

ACCESSIBILITY AND EQUITY

Services related to these aims encompass advocacy, training, education, staff selection and retention, and liaison with campus stakeholders and external agencies. NASSA, one of the more recent associations to form on behalf of a targeted population, affirms as its mission, "to empower institutions of higher learning to become welcoming environments where Aboriginal Peoples can successfully pursue educational goals while maintaining their cultural identities" (National Aboriginal Student Services

Association). Among its goals are to promote Aboriginal cultural awareness/participation within all areas of post-secondary institutions; increase abilities of all student services providers to effectively respond to the needs of Aboriginal peoples; and develop a national network of Aboriginal post-secondary student services providers. Sharing their voice in the 1990s, these population-specific student services organizations have been leaders in promoting and securing dedicated personnel at Canada's colleges and universities.

### Professional Preparation and Skills

The most recent leg in the journey of student services in Canadian higher education comes in the form of a growing understanding of the complexities of the post-secondary experience, the need for greater responsiveness to students, demands for greater accountability in the service transaction, and the desire to achieve a higher standard of professional preparation and competence. Such presses, some within and some external to the field, have created further impetus for development, generating additional professional networks, assessment initiatives, and the first programs at the graduate level to prepare student services professionals.

Historically, the student services field has been a baccalaureate profession in Canada, with many practitioners ascending from undergraduate leadership experiences and positions to full-time administrative or service appointments at their alma maters. This remains a frequent pattern, especially in areas such as residence life, student leadership and organizations, admissions and enrolment, and orientation. Additionally, it is not uncommon for senior level positions in student services to be occupied by faculty who have transferred from various disciplinary homes to contribute their skills on an institution-wide basis. However, there are signs that such status quo will no longer be sufficient to address the challenges that lie ahead for Canada's post-secondary system. Indeed the success of students themselves will depend increasingly on the capacity of student services professionals to design and implement policies and practices of the highest standards that facilitate student success as effectively and efficiently as possible.

Contributing to this increased press toward encouraging student success has been a rising accountability movement in Canadian post-secondary education, honed in on questions of whether specialized services are achieving their intended outcomes and institutional expenditures are realizing appropriate returns. The 1990s in Canada saw a groundswell of national interest around performance indicators (PIs) and links to resource allocations, leading to initiatives such as the establishment of the Canadian Undergraduate Survey Consortium (CUSC)(Hardy Cox et al. 1998; Smith 1991), which has been called the Canadian University Survey Consortium since 2007. Based on the assumption that institutions need to know what students are thinking in order to provide the level of service they expect, the goal of this consortium was to create reliable, up-to-date information about students, their experiences on campus, their plans, and their aspirations for the future. The purpose of CUSC was to produce cost-efficient comparative data for assessing campus programs and services. Through a centralized research effort, principles of institutional input, ownership, and control of data were affirmed – that is, aggregate data were owned collectively, composite reports were prepared and shared among members, and institutional identities were kept confidential. Consortium members also controlled their own institutional data for further local analysis. The first such study conducted by CUSC was the *National Perception Data – Benchmarking Student Life* (1994). This was followed by studies, for example, on the *Undergraduate Experience at Eight Canadian Universities* (1994), a *Survey of the Undergraduate Experience at 10 Canadian Universities* (1996), a *Graduating Student Survey at Nine Canadian Universities* (1997), and the *Survey of First Year University Students at Nineteen Canadian Universities* (1998)(Canadian Undergraduate Survey Consortium; Hardy Cox et al. 1998). Overall the continuing focus on outcomes assessment in Canadian higher education has challenged student services to demonstrate its leadership and coordinating role in the implementation of such activities, a mandate that is being linked increasingly to provincial/territorial funding and competitive rankings (e.g., Maclean's). Consequently this most recent era in Canadian student services has demanded even more sophisticated levels of expertise, implicating the timely need for graduate-level preparation.

The goal of dedicated graduate-level training for student services administrators in Canada was first approached at Memorial University of Newfoundland, where an online Master of Education in Post-Secondary Studies program was initiated in 1996. This advanced degree offered a special focus in student services, within the broader context of post-secondary education, and featured coursework options in leadership and human resource development; foundations of instructional design; issues and trends in administration; administration of student services; and student development theory, services, and programs. Completion of this degree anticipated and continues to prepare professionals for positions at the associate and director levels within student affairs.

Professional development opportunities for practicing student services providers have also expanded during this period. The field now includes, for example, doctorate-prepared practitioners in counselling, housing, career, health, disability, student development, and Aboriginal student services, and professional education continues to evolve through conferences, journals, research, and credit and non-credit courses and programs. Increased opportunities for professionals to share innovations through formal study, professional development, journals and newsletters, resource clearinghouses, and professional associations all indicate the growing recognition of student services as an integral component in the success of Canadian post-secondary students.

## CONCLUSION

The student services field has evolved considerably since its beginnings as a diminutive but supportive partner in Canadian higher education. Following several decades of recent developments it can be argued that the field has emerged as a solid presence in the post-secondary enterprise and has become a significant instrument in creating institutional environments that nurture student success on campus. Evidence of this status is perhaps best reflected in the work of its professional associations, most particularly the Canadian Association of College and University Student Services (CACUSS). The achievements of this broad-based group offer a useful measure of the field's activities to date.

In their Maturation Model for Professional Associations, Johnson and Stamatakos (1991) proposed that the maturation of a professional association can be examined through six variables: (a) organizational structure, (b) ethics and standards, (c) membership, (d) public relations, (e) fiscal policies, and (f) services and publications. Advancement in these dimensions signals movement of an association through a sequence of stages, from birth to survival and stability, then toward reputation, uniqueness, and contribution. Accordingly, the organizational structure of a mature association would have moved from one of freewheeling leadership with fluid strategies and tactics toward one where basic policies have been established, periodic restructuring has encouraged additional involvement and the reevaluation of goals and objectives, long-range planning is in place, and internal auditing of resources reflects a delegation of power and improved communication to members. Likewise, professional ethics, standards, and preparation goals are routinely examined; professional affiliation is prized; contributions to society are apparent; sufficient revenues are generated to support additional initiatives; and a full range of products and services support the professional development of its members. Insofar as its achievements are mirrored in this analysis, the student services field in Canada has reached a point of maturity in recent decades that is impressive. Its educational commitments to the primacy of institutional mission, the quality of the teaching and learning community on campus, the worth, dignity, and respect due each student, the aims of holistic development, and the desire for partnership with students, staff, administrators, and faculty suggest that student services will continue to shape in significant ways the achievement of student success in Canadian post-secondary education for years to come.

# 2

# Theoretical Foundations
# of Student Success

## C. CARNEY STRANGE

The concept of student success is complex and multi-dimensional. From the perspective of a student it might be the achievement of a specific, short-term academic goal, such as sitting successfully for an exam, writing a term paper, or completing a challenging course. The view of a parent might include an expected level of independence exhibited by a daughter as she negotiates the many decisions of a university experience. And for those who plan and implement the various services of a post-secondary institution, student success is most often reflected in successful enrolment numbers, program retention rates, and degree completion figures. Whatever the case, success implies both a goal of some sort that has been reached and the steps taken to reach it.

In recent decades, higher education and student services professionals have focused on how they can support the developmental processes already underway in students. Drawing from a wealth of models and theories of student development, they have mapped out various progressions of learning, growth, and development during the post-secondary years. This body of literature has reframed and given rich insight to the concept of student success, while influencing and reshaping institutional designs to promote it. Further, these new understandings have accompanied a transformation of the field in recent years, focusing greater attention on student learning and development as the proper measures of student success (American College Personnel Association 1994) and on out-of-class opportunities as potential contributors to such outcomes (Kuh, Schuh, Whitt, and Associates 1991). Tenets that comprise this knowledge base have also guided the implementation of many campus policies and practices (Strange 1994) and have challenged educators at all levels to reconsider the nature and design of campus learning environments (Strange and Banning 2001).

Grounding these new understandings are two domains of concepts informing, respectively, the nature of student development and the impact of post-secondary educational environments on the factors that influence that development. Within the first domain – student development – are three lines of inquiry in the literature, attending to each of three fundamental aspects: psychosocial identity formation; the evolution of cognitive-developmental meaning-making structures; and the emergence of personal preferences, styles, and types. From the second domain – campus environments – has come a range of concepts focusing on the natural and synthetic physical features of a college or university; the effects of various human aggregate groupings; the impact on functioning of different organizational designs; and the nature of socially constructed aspects of institutional press, social climate, and culture. These streams of thought have contributed significantly to an understanding of the processes of human development and maturation during the post-secondary years, and the potential of educational institutions to influence these processes. Thus, these concepts are helpful in examining the goals of student success and the practices of student services professionals to support them.

Although this literature has emerged almost exclusively from research in USA post-secondary institutions, the dynamics identified by these models and frameworks also inform the Canadian context, in that issues and patterns of young adult growth and development are likely to parallel closely across the two cultures, while reflecting differences of specific influences and factors. For example, the importance of autonomy, as a marker of maturity in one culture, might be attenuated in the other culture due to its respective emphasis on collective association and identity. As a shaping feature, this latter dynamic might lead to differing developmental expectations for maturity, although achieving independence remains nonetheless an important measure. Likewise, when considering the stages of critical thinking outlined in some of these schemes, for example, the structures themselves are not likely to differ significantly from one context to another, although the factors that influence the degree and rate of change might alter the quality of the developmental path experienced. In this literature, the insights about the learning, growth, and development of post-secondary students lean more toward the universal rather than the particular. Adaptation of such constructs to the Canadian context nonetheless requires sensitivity to the cultural tenets that define the Canadian post-secondary experience and shape the progression of these developmental changes and environmental dimensions.

## STUDENT DEVELOPMENT THEORY

The body of research known as *student development theory* has attended to questions about: (a) how students' psychosocial identity formation evolves across the lifespan, (b) how students make meaning of their experiences through advancement of cognitive-structural development, and (c) how students acquire a consistency of approach through development of personal preferences, styles, and types. "Success" from these perspectives might entail resolution of certain developmental tasks (psychosocial development), advancement toward more complex forms of meaning making (cognitive-structural development), and identification and consistency of a personal style (typological development). In concert, such changes are recognized as arti-facts of maturity, the goal of any institution intent on human development.

### Lifespan and Psychosocial Identity Formation

Lifespan and psychosocial identity models chart human development through sequential cycles of stability and transition, with particular attention to the dynamics of individuation and attachment. These models further identify age-appropriate developmental tasks reflective of maturation at various points in the lifespan. The works of Levinson and Levinson (1996) and Chickering and Reisser (1993), for example, address human development from such a perspective.

Levinson and Levinson (1996) have constructed the human lifespan across four age-linked eras, each a period of approximately twenty-five years: Childhood and Adolescence, Young Adulthood, Middle Adulthood, and Late Adulthood. These eras overlap, with the developmental work of each period commencing, culminating, and forming a point of transition for the next. For example, one transition starts around age eighteen and continues until about age twenty-three, marking both the end of the Childhood and Adolescence era and the beginning of the Young Adult era. What precedes and follows any given period of transition is a period of stability. It is this alternating between stability and transition that creates the dynamic quality of the lifespan, as one's life structure (comprised of myriad decisions about relationships, occupations, goals, and expectations) is affirmed or changed according to the tasks of the period. During periods of stability (typically six to ten years) the essential tasks are to make firm choices, rebuild one's life structure, and pursue goals. In contrast, periods of transition (usually four to five years) are structure-changing, beginning with terminating the current life structure and accepting concomitant losses, proceeding with a review and evaluation of the past – deciding which aspects to keep or reject, and then exploring possibilities for the future while initiating new life structures to support them. Consequently the qual-ity of any period of stability is most often intentional and committed, whereas a period of transition is fundamentally tentative and open. There are periods of major transition throughout the lifespan, separating each era, as well as lesser transitions within any given era. For example, a common transitional experience within the Young Adulthood era occurs typically between ages twenty-eight and thirty-two when decisions about life structure, made when entering this era, are adjusted (e.g., change of career choice or dissolution of a relationship) in order to construct a more satisfactory life structure to carry one through completion of this particular era.

The import of this lifespan view of human development is that individuals often seek formal educational opportunities during periods of transition in their lives, whether in anticipation of an impending transition, in the midst of a transition, or at the point of completing a transition. This connection between learning and living has been institutionalized in our culture for the transition between Childhood and Adolescence and Young Adulthood. In fact, in our society, the expectation for advancing to university or college has become practically embedded in the rites of passage between these two eras. In addition, with the recent emergence of returning adult learners in our institutions, we are beginning to understand that the formal structures and supports of post-secondary learning are also facilitative of other periods in the lifespan as individuals move into, through, and out of various transitions (Schlossberg 1981), for example, from Young Adulthood to Middle Adulthood, or Middle Adulthood to Late Adulthood.

In many ways the vast store of resources available in most post-secondary institutions today, for example, related to advising and career counselling, make universities and colleges ideal settings within which to experience and negotiate a life transition. Perhaps therein lies the clearest connection to student success. From such a perspective, success entails the effective resolution of appropriate developmental tasks in each student's life period, the details of which are contained in other theories of student development, such as the psychosocial vector model of Chickering and Reisser (1993).

In *Education and Identity,* Chickering and Reisser (1993) focused primarily on the transition between Childhood and Adolescence and Young Adulthood, suggesting that post-secondary education can be a powerful force in the resolution of seven thematic tasks or "vectors of development" associated with this transition: developing competence, managing emotions, moving through autonomy toward interdependence, developing mature interpersonal relationships, establishing identity, developing purpose, and developing integrity. Each of these vectors contains an expected agenda of achievement at this stage that also offers appropriate learning goals for the college or university experience. For example, the first vector – developing competence – contains tasks related to intellectual, interpersonal, physical, and manual competence, and an overall sense of competence. Accordingly, resolution of this vector entails developing the critical skills of advanced reasoning and communication around one's ideas; acquiring a facility for relating to others in various roles; honing one's strength, fitness, and self-discipline; and establishing an integrated degree of confidence about one's level of effectiveness in all of this.

The university or college experience is a rich arena for many as they approach these challenges. From assignments and examinations in the curriculum to opportunities for involvement and leadership beyond the classroom, the whole of this experience has great potential for contributing to the achievement of these developmental goals in students' lives. Collectively these vectors suggest tasks that could form a student development framework for these years.

The focus of these lifespan and psychosocial models is on the achievement of identity as a manifestation of success. However, a number of complementary theories on select aspects of this question have emerged in recent years, focusing on the context of various group identities as they are shaped, for example, by characteristics of gender (e.g., Josselson 1987), culture-ethnicity (e.g., Atkinson, Morten, and Sue 1983; Cross 1995; Helms 1993) and sexual orientation (e.g., Cass 1979). These theories suggest that the further layering of psychosocial development with the dynamics of minority status results in an intertwining of a healthy self-concept with a positive cultural identity. Since concepts and assumptions of "normalcy" are inevitably extensions of the dominant culture, individuals who do not participate fully in that culture, nor share its values, are challenged most by a press to conform within two disparate cultures: one (a subculture), that acknowledges and supports their identities as members of a minority group (e.g., LGBQT students); and another, the much larger dominant group, that challenges their identities for their failure to match common expectations and norms (Strange and Banning 2001). Neglect of the subculture removes an important source of support for these individuals; neglect of the dominant culture might result in barriers to achievement. In effect, for these individuals, success often entails a double consciousness (DuBois 1903), capable of sustaining simultaneously both the minority and dominant cultures. Consequently, issues and tasks of development are almost certainly accompanied by additional degrees of complexity, as personal identity emerges in response to hegemonic forces. Thus, these models typically begin with a description of the individual in a naive stage, oblivious to the dynamics of the dominant culture. This stage gives way to a consciousness of distinction and difference, in response to either positive or negative encounters with the dominant culture, followed by a stage of immersion, as dominant forces are rejected in favour of relevant differences (e.g., gender, sexual orientation, race, ethnicity). Completion of the sequence culminates in an integrated stage where a balance of self and otherness is achieved in a comfortable mix of identifiers as the relative salience of different aspects of identity shift.

The success implicit in these models is that students achieve a workable state of identity that incorporates the distinction of difference in which their identity is grounded. Most important for student affairs educators, then, is to incorporate explicit recognition of these sources of identity (e.g., gender, sexual orientation, race, and ethnicity) in the design and delivery of various programs and services.

## Cognitive-Structural Development

Beyond the question of personal identity, success at university or college also involves advancement in various forms of meaning making or thinking as described in theories of cognitive-structural development. The characteristics of such advanced forms correspond closely to the goals of post-secondary education.

The literature on cognitive-structural development maps out patterns of meaning making that individuals bring to life experiences. Exemplifying this perspective, for example, is the seminal theory of Piaget (1950) or more recent theories that focus on charting these increasingly complex patterns (e.g., Baxter Magolda 1992; Gilligan 1982; King and Kitchener 1994; Kohlberg 1969; and Perry 1970). According to these models, individuals progress through a stepwise hierarchy of stages or positions, with each succeeding level reflecting greater complexity and different assumptions about how things work with respect to a given domain. Early simplistic assumptions ("Dualistic," "Pre-Conventional," or "Received Knowing," depending on which theory is used) are gradually replaced by more advanced assumptions ("Relativistic," "Principled," or "Contextual Knowing") as individuals seek new and more sophisticated meanings for the events and experiences in their lives. For instance, in the domain of intellectual reasoning, individuals progress through increasingly complex forms (or stages) of reasoning as they learn to resolve "ill-structured" problems – those with multiple answers and resolutions with reference to experts in the field, to the compelling quality of the available evidence, and to established rules of inquiry (King and Kitchener 1994). Thus, a person holding assumptions characteristic of early stages of reasoning might argue that the "truth value" of one point of view is established unquestionably by the endorsement of an authority, or simply because one "believes it to be so," believing that all points of view are equally valid since "no one knows for sure." At more advanced stages, individuals begin to acknowledge differences between facts, opinions, and interpretations, and convey a more complex understanding of inquiry as an inherently fallible process of critical review over a period of time, involving many sources of input from many individuals and yielding solutions that only approximate truth.

Figuring prominently in these cognitive-structural descriptions of student development is the role of external power, authority, and expertise. Successful progression through advancing stages of meaning making is dependent on the capacity to move beyond the simple stability of certainty toward a comfort with the complexity of ambiguities and unknowns. By definition this involves rejection along the way of external sources of knowing, as a prelude to the development of a sense of self-authorship (Baxter Magolda 1992). Student success from this perspective requires the acquisition of advanced capacities, such as critical consideration, decision-making, and conceptual understanding.

These models suggest a role for student services professionals in structuring opportunities for students to encounter differences of perspective and to assume responsibility for judgment-making and the management of complex tasks. Such strategies (whether within or beyond the classroom) serve to engage students in the kinds of challenges that can replace earlier simplistic cognitive structures with those that accommodate a more complex and subtle view of the world. Such advanced structures reflect nicely the goals of almost any program of liberal studies.

### Personal Preferences, Styles, and Types

The literature on personal preferences, styles, and types suggests that maturation is influenced by and expressed through relatively stable patterns that characterize how individuals approach and resolve the various tasks and challenges of learning, growth, and development during the post-secondary years. These theories underscore the importance of concurrent differences among individuals and how such differences reveal themselves in consistent ways. Models that illustrate this idea describe styles or patterns of behaviours with respect to a variety of dimensions in students' lives, such as their vocational interests (Holland 1973), personal styles (Myers 1980), and learning orientations (Kolb 1983). From these perspectives individuals appear somewhat predictable, as others recognize their "usual way of doing things." For example, we learn from this line of inquiry how various "Myers-Briggs types" exhibit preferred ways of using "their minds, specifically the way they perceive and the way they make judgments" (Myers 1980, 1). Some perceive primarily through the senses, whereas others rely upon intuition; some use a logical process of thinking to arrive at judgments, whereas others judge out of their appreciation and feelings for the event or situation. According to the model, either kind of perception can team up with either kind of judgment. Furthermore, depending on individuals' relative interest in their outer world (extraversion) or inner world (introversion), as well as their preference for a perceptive versus a judging attitude, a variety of combinations emerge reflecting "different kind[s] of personality, characterized by [differing] interests, values, needs, habits of mind, and surface traits" (Myers 1980, 4). Collectively these characteristic combinations offer important clues as to the compatibility of various experiences and opportunities for any given type.

Similarly these assumptions can also be applied to the decisions students make about academic majors and careers. For example, according to Holland

(1973), there are six personality-vocational types, each distinguished by a particular combination of interests, skills, values, and attitudes: Realistic, Investigative, Artistic, Social, Enterprising, and Conventional. Thus, Realistic types are competent in manual and technical areas, value power and status, are practical, and are drawn to occupations involving physical, outdoor activities. In contrast, Social types prefer working with people to educate and inform, using their interpersonal strengths and reflecting the value they place on co-operation, empathy, and tact. Congruence in the type characteristics of the individual and the characteristics of an experience or opportunity results in the benefits of a person-environment fit. From a student's perspective it might be the realization that "I've found the right major!" Congruence results in satisfaction and stability of choice; incongruence leads to potential dissatisfaction, risk, and attrition.

An important insight of these perspectives is that individuals develop relatively stable and consistent styles of performance over time that benefit from becoming engaged in experiences that reinforce those preferences. Also implicated in this understanding is the idea that individuals can benefit from developing an expanded and complementary range of styles or preferences, as this adds to their adaptability to a greater variety of circumstances. Thus, student success from this view entails both the exploration and clarification of one's own style, as well as development of a range of complementary alternatives. Student services professionals informed by these ideas will consider the variety of styles and types among the students with whom they work, supporting their development with opportunities that reflect these preferences as well as experiences that challenge them.

In summary, these human development theories portray college and university students as persons who are engaged in a variety of age-related developmental tasks, who construct meaning from and approach challenges of learning in characteristic patterns or styles, and who must resolve issues of individuation within the dynamics of gender, ethnicity, sexual orientation, and other identifying characteristics. Definitions of student success that take into account these developmental dynamics suggest service designs and programs that can enhance achievement of that success.

## CAMPUS ENVIRONMENT THEORY

An important contribution of student development theory is the notion that student success is only partially a function of students' developmental characteristics. To complete this understanding, it is helpful to explore the literature that informs the design of the institutions in which students encounter these developmental opportunities. This requires examination of the concepts of educational environments, beginning with the premise that behaviour is a function of both the person and the environment (Lewin

1939). Having addressed the former in the previous section with a review of student development theories, this section examines the latter.

The body of research known as *educational environment theory* (Strange and Banning 2001) attends to questions about the effects of the natural and synthetic features of educational settings; the influence of human aggregate groupings on select behaviours; the outcomes of functioning related to various organizational structures and designs; and the manner in which campus environments, as mediated through participants' social constructions, shape their attraction, satisfaction, and stability in a setting. Collectively, these features comprise the major components of any college or university environment designed to support the learning, growth, and development of students. As Moos (1979) contends, the "arrangement of environments is perhaps the most powerful technique we have for influencing human behavior ..." and as Dewey (1933) observed long ago, "Whether we permit chance environments to do the work, or whether we design environments for the purpose makes a great difference." I suggest in this model (Strange and Banning 2001) that educational purposes are served best when we include, secure, involve, and invite students into the learning community of higher education.

## Environmental Components

### PHYSICAL DIMENSIONS

The physical dimensions of educational environments, either natural (e.g., climate and terrain) or synthetic (e.g., interior layout and colour schemes), shape students' attitudes and influence the quality of their experiences in powerful ways (Stern 1986; Sturner 1973; Thelin and Yankovich 1987). These dimensions serve both functional and symbolic ends. Functionally, they define space for activities and events, thereby encouraging some phenomena while limiting others (Michelson 1970). For example, a classroom with flexible seating might facilitate small group discussions more readily than one with furniture fixed to the floor. Physical components also send symbolic, non-verbal messages. To further illustrate, a teaching podium placed twenty feet from the first row of seats might signal the formal nature of a classroom experience. Physical artifacts (e.g., signs, art work, posters, and graffiti) placed on campus to direct, inspire, or warn (Banning and Bartels 1993) also send strong non-verbal messages about campus culture that are often seen as more truthful than written or verbal messages (Mehrabian 1981). The best outcomes result when physical components, both functional and symbolic, support desired behaviours (Wicker 1984).

### HUMAN AGGREGATES

Human aggregates include the collective characteristics of people within any environment. Whether demographic (e.g., sex, age, or race) or psychosocial (e.g., personality types or learning styles), human aggregate characteristics create features in an environment that reflect varying degrees of differentiation (i.e., type homogeneity) and consistency (i.e., type similarity) (Holland 1973; Smart, Feldman, and Ethington 2000). An environment inhabited mostly by individuals of one characteristic or type is said to be highly differentiated and consistent. This would be the case in a class where all students share the same major, or a residence hall where residents are of the same gender. An environment dominated by a single and consistent type accentuates its own characteristics over time (Astin 1985), attracting, satisfying, and retaining individuals who share the dominant features. Thus the quality of anyone's experience is a function of his or her congruence, or degree of "fit," with the dominant group. If placed in an incompatible environment, an individual is less likely to be reinforced for preferred behaviours, values, attitudes, and expectations, and the risk of that person leaving the environment increases. The experiences of cultural minorities on historically white campuses reflect these dynamics as Aboriginal students, for example, struggle to accommodate the preferences, values, attitudes, and expectations of the majority.

ORGANIZATIONAL STRUCTURES

Organizational components arise from the myriad decisions made about environmental purposes and functions. Who is in charge? How will resources be distributed? By what rules, if any, will those in the environment function? What must be accomplished and how quickly? How will participants be rewarded for their accomplishments? Getting organized is a typical response to such questions, generating various arrangements or structures that define the organizational characteristics of an environment. For example, concentrating decision-making power within a few individuals in the environment yields a high degree of centralization (Hage 1980); likewise, a decision to enforce numerous explicit rules implies a high degree of formalization in the setting (Price 1972). These organizational structures are important since they converge to create characteristic organizational designs, reflecting a continuum of flexibility (Hage and Aiken 1970). At one end are dynamically organized environments: flexible in design, less centralized, and informal; at the other end are static environments: rigid, centralized, and formal. These designs, in turn, affect the four performances of any successful organization: (a) innovation, (b) efficiency, (c) quantity of production, and (d) morale (Hage 1980). Like all organized environments, colleges and universities must innovate, produce efficiently, and maintain a modicum of satisfaction among those who participate in them. Whether an environment is able to achieve these performances, or not, is influenced by the degree to which it can maintain a dynamic quality and by how well it can mitigate the effects of organizational size. In general, the larger the organization the more challenging it becomes to succeed at these goals.

CONSTRUCTED FEATURES

Socially constructed components reflect the subjective views or social constructions of environmental participants. This perspective assumes that
environments are understood best through people's collective perceptions
of them, as manifested in environmental presses, social climates, and cultures. These perceptions, in turn, influence behaviour in the environment
(Stern 1970). A distinctive press is evident in any consensus of perceptions
about particular behaviours or expectations in an environment. For example,
perceptions that the majority of students on a particular campus work
diligently in the library between classes and on weekends imply the presence of a press toward academic achievement. Environments can also be
described in terms of their personalities, or social climates, composed of
relationship, personal development and growth, and system maintenance
and change dimensions (Moos 1968, 1979). Personalities of two classroom
environments can differ dramatically, for example, in the degree to which
students are perceived to support one another – a relationship dimension;
the goals and expectations of the course – a personal growth and development dimension; or the extent to which innovation and creativity are
encouraged – a system maintenance and change dimension (Moos and
Trickett 1974). Last, the culture of any environment reflects an amalgam
of assumptions, beliefs, and values that inhabitants use to interpret or
understand the meaning of events and actions (Schein 1992). Environmental
culture forms a distinctive character usually known only to members, but
impressive to outsiders as well.

In summary, an understanding of any educational environment begins
with the identification of its essential features: its physical components and
design; its dominant human characteristics; the organizational structures
that serve its purposes; and participants' constructions of its presses, social
climate, and culture. These components create a variety of environmental
conditions on campus, and enhance or detract from student learning and
success (American College Personnel Association 1994).

## Environmental Design Purposes

Learning entails a progression of increasingly complex steps in identity
formation, meaning making, and self-understanding. This requires both the
acquisition of new information as well as opportunities for the exercise of
new skills, competencies, and ways of thinking and acting. Whole learning
merges personal identity, values, beliefs, knowledge, skills, and interests
toward fulfillment and human actualization (Maslow 1968).

What qualities and features are present in an environment designed to
achieve self-actualized learning? Strange and Banning (2001) posited a
hierarchy of environmental purposes wherein the inclusion and safety of

participants must be attended to first, followed by structures that promote involvement and then conditions of community. Colleges and universities must offer inclusive and secure environments for all students. Without a sense of belonging in an institution, free from threat, fear, and anxiety, attempts at other goals of learning are likely to fail. Thus, the first step for campus administrators is to assure that the physical, human aggregate, organizational, and socially constructed components of various campus environments create such conditions and serve such purposes.

Inclusion and safety are not the end points, though. If campus environments are to serve educational purposes they must also engage students in significant learning experiences by inviting them into active and meaningful roles. Without environmental structures of involvement, students risk detachment from any investment in or responsibility for their own learning, key requisites for powerful educational outcomes (Astin 1985). Finally, while inclusion, safety, and involvement are necessary conditions for the achievement of educational purposes, they are insufficient for assuring an integrated whole learning experience. This requires a third level of investment, in a complete experience of *learning community,* wherein goals, values, structures, people, and resources come together in a seamless experience for purposes of learning and fulfillment.

Conditions of learning community become evident as students assume significant roles over time and contribute to the very ethos and culture of the setting. Such levels of membership and involvement create a synergy of experiences in a specific time and place that are unique and memorable to those who have been part of them. Whether in the form of a student organization accomplishing special feats during a particular academic year, or an experience of an especially memorable class, communal environments sustain members in a bond that leaves lasting impressions in the cultural and historical evolution of a setting. This is best achieved when space is available for a group of individuals who share common characteristics and interests; when flexible organizational designs invite participation, role taking, and decision-making; and when artifacts of culture extend and support community visions and purposes (Strange and Banning 2001). These conditions compel individuals to engage one another creatively in the achievement of specific goals and outcomes, and this is the framework, when sustained across time, that is thought most powerful for the pursuit of learning (Carnegie Foundation for the Advancement of Teaching 1990; Palmer 1987; Strange 2003).

## THEORY AND PRACTICE IN STUDENT SERVICES

While the relationship between theory and practice in any applied field is often a loosely connected link, the framework generated by these concepts of student development and educational environments, if understood and used, becomes a distinguishing characteristic of a student services professional at work. Unlike amateurs, professionals (a) are able to reasonably explain the phenomenon they purport to address; (b) are aware of the validity of their explanations as supported in the research; (c) can use these explanations to guide their actions, through application of standards and models of practice; (d) can demonstrate the effectiveness of their applications; and (e) have a clear idea of the ends toward which their efforts are directed. In short, professionals use *theory, research, practice,* and *evaluation* as tools to carry out what they understand to be important work, framed in a coherent set of professional and personal *values.* Our expertise includes student development in post-secondary education and the myriad concepts and ideas that inform each of the functional areas we serve. To be an effective student services professional is to access a knowledge base that, in addition to framing the particulars of one's specific service function, describes how students learn, develop, and grow, and how the components of educational environments can serve those ends. Therein lays the connection between what we do as student services practitioners and the goals of student success. From this knowledge base we draw insights about not only the end point of student success but also the steps and processes to achieve such a goal.

The theoretical foundation to student services introduced in this chapter offers an important conceptual framework for considering the construction of policies and the design of educational practices intended to promote student success. As Lewin (1951) averred, "there is nothing so practical as a good theory." Rather than through a direct link, however, this theoretical framework serves to tune our ears to the critical concerns and questions in students' lives and the potentials of the educational settings we shape to respond to their needs. It is out of this mix that student success is achieved, less a matter of chance than the planned intent of educators who understand the purposes of higher learning and the pathways to them.

As student services professionals in Canadian higher education continue to design strategies and apply practices to support student success, knowledge of students' development and the dynamics of campus environments become critical tools for increasing the effectiveness of the college and university experience. An additional mandate is to consider such concepts and frameworks as they search for indigenous explanations that speak more directly to the Canadian context.

## PART TWO

# Forms, Functions, and Practices: Structuring Services for Student Success

This section sets the context for the diverse functions that support students in Canadian post-secondary education, identifying common services and practices in a variety of areas that connect to student success. Each chapter introduces an area of student services, describing basic functions, and linking them to the broader history and philosophy of higher education. Each also considers significant issues (both evolutionary and emergent) that shape the organization and practice of this service, while benchmarking practices and protocols that would usually support this area and discussing challenges and opportunities for further development and research in this domain.

The chapters have been grouped according to three distinctive service missions of any post-secondary institution: (a) the matriculation of new students;(b) their accommodation, engagement, and involvement; and (c) the support and adjustment of all students. The Matriculation section looks at those services designed to effect admission to an institution, offer instrumental support, and guide and establish an early foundation for achievement and success. Thus, chapter 3 provides an overview of enrolment management, admission, and registrar services in relation to student success; chapter 4 focuses on programs and services related to financial assistance, including a discussion of governmental, institutional, and personal funding issues; and chapter 5 overviews the status, as well as the history and evolution, of orientation services provided to first-year students.

The second section – Accommodation, Engagement, and Involvement – overviews those services designed to engage students in the living, leadership, and learning environments of colleges and universities. Chapter 6 examines student housing and residential living programs in relation to student success; chapter 7 focuses on the direction of student leadership and service learning and volunteer programs on campus; and chapter 8 addresses the evolution of services to support students relative to academic integrity issues, education, and policy in Canada.

Support and Adjustment, the third group of chapters, surveys those programs and practices designed to assist students with personal and academic challenges related to the affective dimensions of students' adjustment to post-secondary life and decisions about personal wellness and health, as well as services that assist students in preparing for the adult world of work following graduation. Specifically, chapter 9 overviews the range of counselling services provided to support student success; chapter 10 describes student wellness programs and student health services in relation to student success; and chapter 11 reviews the development of career and employment services on college and university campuses. Chapter 12 considers, in broad strokes, those services that support the success of students from diverse cultures or with varied histories and needs, emphasizing the underlying principles that inform all such initiatives.

Concluding Part Two, chapter 13 outlines the challenges of leadership in an integrated portfolio of student services. Included is a presentation of models that guide the administration and delivery of student services on campus, with special emphasis on the managerial role of the senior student services officer and on the critical nature of various aspects of delivery to supporting student success.

# 3

# Enrolment Management, Admissions, and Registrar Services

## BONNIE NEUMAN

This chapter examines the office of the registrar, its historical roots in Canadian higher education, and the complex set of functions it manages while supporting the academic mission of the institution it serves. From enrolment management through examination and course scheduling, student record keeping and intra-institutional liaison, the registrar's world today is one of increasingly sophisticated technology in the delivery of services. Registrars now play a significant role on most Canadian campuses as initiators of information technology development. Rising expectations related to enrolment planning and management, institutional marketing, and student engagement and satisfaction have elevated this position to one of strategic importance within most university senior administrative teams.

The complexity of issues facing today's Canadian registrar suggests the need for multi-dimensional leadership skills in this position. Contemporary registrars must oversee a comprehensive administrative portfolio, combine a campus-wide vision with the traditional registrar's attention to detail, and lead a team of professional staff who are managing both changing external trends and new internal demands from students, faculty, and senior administration.

The role of the registrar in Canadian higher education is based on the Oxford-Cambridge post-secondary model. Its importance is normally recognized through inclusion in the legislated list of required officers specified in the provincial/territorial government acts that establish most Canadian universities. The academic support services provided by the office of the registrar are key components of every post-secondary institution. Viewed as a member of the senior administration and on a par with the deans, the registrar generally carries one of the few administrative votes in the academic senate (sometimes called general faculties council) and is typically responsible for both recruitment/admissions and course scheduling/student records.

Although not quite as senior in status as in the original British model, the Canadian registrar is usually seen by the faculty as having considerable status and influence on campus. In addition to student records, the role of some also includes serving as "university secretary," supporting the academic senate and keeping the official records for institutional academic policy, in addition to student records. Although some Canadian institutions (e.g., York University and the University of Toronto) feature a centralized approach, wherein a senior admissions officer/enrolment manager may report to a vice-president (students) and student records are relegated to another office, an integrated organizational structure is more common, where the roles of recruitment and admissions are combined with the scheduling, record-keeping, and information systems functions of an office of the registrar. Nevertheless, common interests of both areas are recognized in the constitutional mandates and membership of the two key North American professional organizations: the Association of Registrars of the Universities and Colleges of Canada (ARUCC) and the American Association of Collegiate Registrars and Admissions Officers (AACRAO).

Thus, in Canada, while the senior student affairs officer is viewed as the administrator responsible for addressing issues of student life and behaviour and providing support services for students, the registrar is often a more visible campus senior administrator who engages more frequently with other senior academic administrators (vice-president (academic), deans, department chairs) on a daily basis. However, at subordinate levels, the situation is reversed and registrar's office staff may still be viewed as primarily clerical whereas student affairs staff may position themselves as more senior "professional" staff, based on their counselling roots and the increasingly common practice of having student affairs staff teach in first-year University 101 transition courses.

## ESSENTIAL FUNCTIONS AND SERVICES

The core registrar roles centre on bringing in and registering each student class; providing the systems, records, and clerical support to schedule classes and exams, and document students' academic progress; and making available and certifying students' records to those within and external to the institution. An overview of these basic functions suggests that the registrar's office profoundly impacts the quality of students' everyday academic lives and ultimately students' success as they pursue their studies.

The essential functions and services of the office of the registrar are often organized into the following categories of activities. The first two are at the policy level and require personal involvement of the registrar, in concert with the vice-president (academic), the deans, and various senate committees:

• Enrolment management policy and decision support
• Academic policy and decision support

The remaining functions are generally carried out by staff teams reporting to senior managers with the title of associate registrar or director, under the general direction of the registrar:

• Publications, student information, and communications
• Recruitment and admissions
• Scholarships and financial aid
• Scheduling
• Student records
• Information systems business analysis and data reporting

All of these require extensive automated systems to collect and store information for analysis and decision-support and to meet certification and reporting needs. The registrar works in close partnership with the senior information officer or head of the administrative systems unit and staff. The technical expertise and business analysis expertise of staff in each area provide not only the office of the registrar but the entire campus with the systems support for the university's core teaching and learning functions.

## Enrolment Management Policy and Decision Support

"Enrolment management," now a high strategic priority and a status-infused position title, was practically an unknown term on Canadian campuses twenty years ago. Since then, a transformation has occurred in the attention given to marketing activity directed at prospective students and their key influencers. This substantive shift, from a passive "build it and they will come" approach to aggressive competition among Canadian institutions, resulted from the intersection of several factors in the 1990s:

• Continued government funding cutbacks prompted institutions to look for increased revenues through both enrolment and fee increases.
• The first Canadian popular rankings were published, weighting both institutional reputation and admissions data heavily (*Maclean's* magazine).
• Ranking lists and publications, national and international, increased as media outlets realized their potential for new advertising revenues and collection vehicles for the university demographic market (e.g., *Globe and Mail* partnership with www.awards.com).
• Competition from American schools intensified, with offers of significant scholarship support to high-achieving Canadian students.
• A new emphasis on students as consumers with choice was reinforced by increased openness to transporting scholarships across provincial/

territorial boundaries, media publicity for popular rankings, and high-profile events such as the Ontario Universities' Fair every September.

- Ongoing competition for the best students, reinforced by the heavy weight on merit indicators in popular rankings, escalated marketing activity (and costs) across the post-secondary sector.
- Decreases in international applications from areas of traditional supply (e.g., Malaysia, Taiwan, and Hong Kong) and periodic hits on other sources, due to local conflicts or currency fluctuations, decreased the reliability of these markets just as they became increasingly important to institutions that had introduced hefty "differential fees" for international registrants.

In the 1980s, most institutions still had "directors of liaison" within their admissions or external affairs departments who saw their role as primarily information delivery. Using the word *marketing* was considered bad taste and training or experience in marketing was not required. However, small liaison/recruitment budgets were seen as expendable and to reduce costs recruitment efforts were generally confined to provincial/territorial borders or local areas (with the exception of a few "national schools" such as Queen's University, McGill University, and University of Toronto).

By the late 1990s, a convergence of factors had its impact: the words *recruitment* and *marketing* began to appear frequently in job titles, most schools had relocated recruitment activities (from external relations to the registrar's admissions unit), differential athletic scholarship practices between western and central Canadian schools heated up a presidential debate over the appropriate use of financial aid, many colleges and universities initiated major international recruitment activities, and increased funding supported a new level of professionalism in recruitment. In the early twenty-first century, additional factors have raised the enrolment management stakes even higher for Canadian institutions:

- Governments approved college-based applied degree programs (in Alberta, British Columbia, and Ontario) and elevated some colleges to full university status, blurring perceptions, among prospective enrolees, of any difference between colleges and universities in Canada.
- Demographic shifts in the Canadian population refocused institutional growth on the traditional, direct-entry university profile, especially within the Greater Toronto Area in Ontario and, to a lesser extent, the Lower Mainland of British Columbia. Outlying rural areas are experiencing significant downturns across Canada, with Atlantic provincial forecasts projecting up to a 20 per cent decrease in this profile group by the year 2020. In Saskatchewan and Manitoba, further

demographic projections have refocused universities on the challenges of engaging higher proportions of the Aboriginal population.

Recruitment is now perceived clearly as the business of working "the admissions funnel." From making one's campus more visible in the marketplace to attracting and converting applications into accepted offers of admission and subsequent registrations, the leadership of the registrar is critical in the achievement of an institution's enrolment goals. Ontario schools, with the largest population to cover and a great number of competing institutions – and still reeling from an early 1980s enrolment drought and a heavy government intervention to manage the grade 12 and 13 double cohort in 2003 – have probably invested the most in domestic recruitment. Atlantic provinces have also engaged a number of eastern schools in attracting students from across Canada and, in particular, from Ontario.

Many institutions have strategically targeted the international sector and budgeted for international recruitment accordingly. Early leaders included the University of Windsor and Seneca College in Ontario; Memorial, Saint Mary's, and Acadia Universities in eastern Canada; and the University of Victoria and Malaspina College (now Vancouver Island University) in British Columbia, to name a few. In previous decades the use of professional international agents to extend the reach of an institution's recruitment effort was virtually unheard of. Now, compensating international agents with a percentage of the first-term fees of the students they deliver to an institution's programs is standard best practice. Initially colleges, and increasingly now universities, look for opportunities to negotiate with other governments for cohort admission groups or to partner with institutions with 2 plus 2 transfer and other arrangements. A number of Canadian colleges and universities have established "branch" operations in key international destinations in China, India, and the Middle East. Although at this point the majority of Canadian institutions see increasing international enrolments as a key thrust in their enrolment management strategy, a closer look at the history of international recruitment in Canada sends up warning flags that such goals may encounter numerous unexpected barriers. Among these challenges are inevitable currency fluctuations, effects of war and conflicts, economic uncertainties, new competitors (e.g., UAE universities; expanding targets in the UK and USA), and expanding local options in India, China, and the Middle East.

Increased institutional attention to enrolments has dramatically altered the role and functions of the office of the registrar. First, it has had a significant impact on organizational structures. In Canada, admission authority generally resides with the faculty, and the vice-president (academic) is charged with negotiating the enrolment plan with the deans, while the registrar monitors, projects, and informs the process, making offers of admission only on the basis of delegated authority. However, more and more Canadian institutions are adding to the university registrar the title of associate vice-president (enrolment management), with related responsibility for enrolment outcomes and leadership in admissions policy, but under the continuing oversight of the faculty and academic senate who approve such policies.

Setting enrolment targets in Canadian institutions is increasingly a professional, data-driven process. Early initiatives in this regard negotiated consensus between institutional representatives (e.g., the vice-president (academic) and the registrar) and the deans of the faculties, through "marketplace wishful thinking," with the registrar inserting tempered advice regarding its feasibility. Genuine enrolment management begins with serious discussions of numbers wanted and data-driven program analyses of what the market can provide (demand for programs as well as demographics). Such considerations are also linked to institutional capacity analyses and a willingness to shift teaching resources and to open or close programs in response to fluctuations of student or faculty interest.

The registrar and senior admissions staff are central players in designing and implementing admissions policy and recruitment activity to attract larger and higher quality applicant pools, to convert more applicants to first choice, to increase admission offer conversion rates, and to advise and collaborate with the faculties regarding faculty recruitment initiatives. However, as the portion of institutional budgets funded by student fees has edged upward and enrolment management has increased in importance, the management of these sets of campus relations has become fraught with potential pitfalls and power differentials, demanding from the campus registrar/enrolment manager even greater patience and wisdom. Ultimately, enrolment shortfalls or windfalls require steady leadership to conclude that perhaps fault lies in poorly judged targets in the academic community rather than inadequate performance by the admissions office.

ACADEMIC POLICY AND DECISION SUPPORT
The registrar in Canada is a key administrator, sitting ex officio on academic senate committees that develop academic policy and regulations. Historically, it has often been registrars and their senior staff who carry out preliminary background research on policy, evaluating student attrition and retention impacts, and suggesting new and alternative campus policies for consideration. The registrar establishes the academic schedule, generally five to ten years into the future, for submission to the academic senate for final approval. A registrar spends a good deal of time advising academic colleagues in the early stages of faculty proposals to influence admissions requirements and student academic progression regulations, identifying potential problems and ensuring feasibility and passage of the proposals through appropriate university committees while they are still in the formative stages.

The registrar, as keeper of institutional data on student performance, is uniquely positioned to partner with faculty colleagues, academic senate committees, and the vice-president (academic) in the critical examination of school policies as they affect students. It is often the registrar who takes the lead in institutional reviews to standardize (or maintain uniformity across faculties for) grading policy, tuition fees, and academic progression. In the absense of strong leadership of a registrar, there is a risk that critical assessments of retention results emerging from an institution's regulations and academic policies may not be maintained, and thus the capability to trace patterns of behaviour to their policy roots or to project unintended consequences of new regulations or admission requirements could potentially be forfeited. Ultimately, it is the registrar who makes it possible for a college or university to initiate proposals for change and revision and to improve the experience of students as they interact with institutional bureaucracy.

PUBLICATIONS AND STUDENT INFORMATION
The constant press for recruitment offices to deliver their school's offer of admission to applicants first, more visibly, and in a "more personalized" manner (often with the use of the most sophisticated software) has yielded a plethora of initiatives, ranging from the good (e.g., plain language edits of correspondence) to the bad (e.g., rock concerts and bars at campus open houses) to the ridiculous (e.g., university presidents hand-delivering offers of admission to the homes of out-of-province scholarship winners). Nevertheless, academic administrators now understand that the "university brand," reflected in current students' perceptions of student satisfaction, university reputation, and graduation and employment rates, strongly influences applicants' choices. As the source of the majority of publications sent to prospects and current students and the manager of the most frequently accessed part of the institutional website, the registrar is a key leader in the implementation of a university's public messaging, and consequently should be the leader in any institutional initiatives to standardize brand image for maximum public impact.

The enrolment management–focused registrar avers that the responsibility for recruitment goes beyond the admissions and recruitment office, and is shared across campus to ensure that the student experience is of highest quality, both in and outside the classroom. The following are core communications of the office of the registrar:

- calendar/course catalogue publications
- website communications for students
- prospective student information
- current student information
- information for individual faculties

The registrar's publications staff work with the teaching departments, faculties, and academic senate to produce authorized, up-to-date information in the annual Calendar. As with most services of its kind, the annual Calendar has evolved in both print and online versions, with some institutions converting entirely to an online format to save on costs and improve reliability of information.

Just as it is the institutional "custodian" of students' official records, the registrar is also seen as the key "user/owner" of the navigation design and contents of the majority of website data for prospective and current students (exclusive of all the other information developed and owned by individual teaching departments, the library, and various student affairs/services units). However, recognition of the registrar's role as a content "editor-in-chief" working in concert with the technical team that hosts the institutional website (similar to the registrar's role vis-à-vis the official Calendar) generally results in a more audience-focused, functional, and up-to-date institutional website, hosting and connecting both information and transactional services online.

Prospective student information is now considered a critical component of the publications produced by an office of the registrar and will consume the greatest portion of its overall publication budget. In print, university view books, program handbooks, faculty-specific view books, recruitment posters, and recruiters' presentations – along with input on recruitment advertising media and content – all fall under the registrar's recruitment and admissions function. These are normally developed in conjunction with a campus marketing and communications group, and in the case of key recruitment pieces, are usually outsourced to professional marketing designers, who carefully manage both the graphics and content of the university brand to achieve maximum effect; it is also generally the job of the registrar to convince faculty colleagues of the value of brand consistency to the success of their program enrolment outcomes.

University websites are now the most important source of information for prospective applicants, and the registrar's role in the development of their content and design is critical to successful enrolment management outcomes. Information for current students includes website information, regulations in the Calendar, brochures, and transaction forms regarding any of the functional areas for which the registrar is responsible. Best practices in recruitment advertising have moved away from traditional print and television spots to newer media where students are found – on the Internet and in movie theatres; every school hopes for a "viral marketing hit" in the virtual world.

While not always publications per se, the registrar's office also produces numerous information brochures and notices to inform individual faculty of academic regulations and parameters related to their teaching role. In addition to individual class lists and grade reporting instructions, these might include information and advice regarding academic policy on diverse matters such as institutional grading policy, grades collection, "unofficial" registrants, auditors, rules for changing individual classes or exam times, deferred and supplemental examination procedures, and lists of referral services available for faculty when students present problems beyond the parameters of classroom content.

Similarly, the registrar's office is also the source of administrative information to assist teaching departments and faculties in their leadership roles relative to teaching, from course demand analysis to grade allocation patterns to multi-year performance and student persistence patterns, as well as regularly scheduled admissions and registration statistics. Essentially, the systems staff in the office of the registrar act as knowledgeable intermediaries between these various campus users and the campus IT department. The business/application analysts in the registrar's systems unit must be "bilingual," so to speak, effectively communicating in the day-to-day operational language of the academic world as well as the technical language of the administrative computing unit.

Continuously evolving technologies create additional channels for communication with students and the campus, but also escalate student and parental expectations regarding the number of communication channels and the quality and frequency of contact. A number of online communities have emerged as important components of students' online presence, from Facebook, YouTube and Flickr to Second Life and Wikipedia. The only certainty is that students' use of technology in the future will continually change as new platforms develop. This constant evolution and proliferation of online communication will continue to increase both the workload and the potential for misinformation, as well as present new opportunities for those registrars with creative vision for it all.

RECRUITMENT AND ADMISSIONS RESPONSIBILITY

While the individual registrar and the senior staff in recruitment and admissions actively engage in enrolment management policy and strategy directions for the university, admissions officers on staff turn those policies and strategies into registered new students every fall through a variety of functions:

- Mail management (posted and email): incoming and outgoing; often for the entire registrar's office; and large outsourced mailings
- Responses to prospective applicant queries that come online and by mail and fax
- Organizing and running in-person campus activities for prospective applicants; open houses, campus tours, and connecting with faculty as requested

- Maintaining prospect and liaison contact databases
- Application systems and processing (paper and online formats for application forms, document collection)
- Application status monitoring systems, accessible by applicants to determine progress/decisions, as well as systems to monitor workload, file completion, and decision-making
- Prospect and admissions communications (email, letters, offer of admission packages, telephone, text messaging), by individual and by selective groups
- Electronic data interchange (EDI) (e.g., automated update of high school grades and transcripts between institutions)
- Admissibility assessment, ranking and automated decision systems, particularly for direct entry students from high school
- Transfer credit articulation systems for courses taken at other institutions
- Event management (recruitment open houses, receptions, scholarship events, offer confirmation activities/open houses)
- Application processing and ranking
- Admissions committee support (professional and limited enrolment programs)

In carrying out these roles, the staff members in admissions maintain key partnerships and integrated procedures with the external relations/marketing and communication departments, the vice-president (academic) and his/her associates, and the deans and associate deans of the faculties. Examples of the latter include the application centres for each university and college admissions office in Ontario and the government agencies responsible for inter-institutional transfer guides in Alberta and British Columbia. The key consideration in all these interconnections is that the registrar's admissions authority is delegated from the faculties, and the degree of support and authority varies by faculty and program. Generally, registrars have full authority for direct entry admission from high school; in professional faculties and graduate studies, where respective admissions committees make final decisions, registrars manage files, collect documents, and convey results to applicants.

SCHOLARSHIPS AND FINANCIAL AID

Increasingly, universities are recognizing the significant relationship between enrolment management and scholarship and financial aid practices (See chapter 4) by realigning these units so they report to the registrar. The linkages are obvious when one looks at their key functions:

- Admission scholarship application processing and ranking
- Admission scholarship committees coordination and support

- Continuing student scholarship assessment and allocation
- Automated ranking/decision-support reports and letter generation
- Student financial need assessment data collection systems
- Bursary application schedules and procedures
- Individual student need assessment and awards
- Links with admission and recruitment systems and procedures
- Student record keeping (e.g., scholarship entries on transcripts)
- Consultation with external relations/fundraising departments regarding new donor scholarship eligibility criteria and implementation
- Coordination with enrolment management and recruitment priorities

Creating seamless convergence between these areas and the registrar's office admissions process remains an ongoing challenge for many institutions. This is in part because some of the major vendors of university student records and enrolment management systems have lagged in introducing Canadian-specific automation modules to support financial needs assessment and systems for student loans, due to the smaller scale of the Canadian market. However, some have been working to redress the gap, and this problem (assuming an institution can afford the upgrades) is dissipating. Any lack of automated support, though, has not stopped Canadian institutions from using scholarships as a key enrolment management strategy in their competition for the best and brightest of Canadian students.

SCHEDULING RESPONSIBILITY

The registrar's scheduling staff tend to be the "unsung heroes" of the campus, working in the background to ensure that the basic course registration infrastructure is in place. This area works extensively with individual teaching departments to provide university-wide services in the following areas:

- Course database set-up and course record changes (e.g., enrolment maxima, registration restrictions, instructor names, pre- and co-requisites, lab/seminar/lecture linkages)
- Timetabling systems (individual class time and room scheduling)
- Registration/course demand monitoring and management in conjunction with teaching departments (e.g., adding new sections to meet strong demand, cancelling low-enrolment courses, combining low-enrolment sections, student notifications of university-generated time-table changes)
- Class lists for faculty at start of each term
- Examination scheduling (e.g., times and locations; schedule conflict management) and examination centre and invigilation coordination
- Special examinations (e.g., credit assessment, deferred exams, supplemental exams, external boards' exam administration, such as TOEFL, GMAT, DAT, MCAT, and LSAT)

Again, with the exception of personal examination invigilation, each of these areas is highly dependent on automation to carry out its functions.

STUDENT RECORDS

In the contemporary office of the registrar, automation of student records is the most common practice. The registrar is the keeper of both the official student record and the official university seal. The latter is used on transcripts, convocation diplomas, and selected other official documents from the office of the president, such as official greetings provided to other institutions at the installation ceremonies for chancellors and presidents. The functional responsibilities of the staff in a student records unit(s) include maintenance of both hard-copy and computerized records, as well as any student transactions with various institutional processes. Examples of these are:

- Student demographic data and status changes (including online opportunities for students to change their own contact data)
- Student registration procedures and systems (now predominantly web-based, online)
- Payment processes for transaction of application fees, tuition and auxiliary fees, and user fees such as for transcripts
- Fees assessment, reassessment, and online payment systems
- Registration status and year of program calculations
- Student registration change policies and procedures
- Grades collection and updating; changes of grade processing
- Degree audit and graduand lists for convocation
- Records certification applications: degree and registration confirmations for employers, registration status and withdrawals for students, official transcripts, unofficial transcripts, degree audit/progress to degree assessments, letters of permission to take a course elsewhere, income tax deduction forms and diplomas/degree parchments printing and replacements
- Encumbrance/hold procedures to withhold certification for students with outstanding accounts, including automatic links between certification systems and the systems that support fees, parking, library, and housing
- Student file management and archiving policy decisions
- Event management (orientation events, convocation and installation ceremonies, ceremonial protocol expertise)

Each of these areas requires specific student records management expertise, extensive knowledge of the particular university culture and academic regulations, and research of other institutions' and systems' approaches for continuous improvement. They also all require a thorough comfort and familiarity with modern technologies, combined with heightened attention to detail and organization.

## INFORMATION SYSTEMS SUPPORT AND DATA REPORTING

The automation of registrar-student transactions, on behalf of the faculties, has evolved into such a comprehensive system of support that some institutions (e.g., University of Alberta) now declare by policy that the computer record, rather than the hard copy, is the official student file. Service delivery for students has also evolved, with additional information and access channels for students that must be developed and maintained by knowledgeable staff: campus websites, event Facebook sites, online kiosks, email, and web applications for 24/7 service support.

Most registrar's offices, particularly for large- and medium-sized institutions, now assign dedicated staff to computer systems to help develop and support every automated transactional service provided. These technicians deliver desktop assistance to office staff and collaborate on specification and testing with systems developers in the IT area. They also provide extensive programming support in response to various data requests from senior administration, the faculties and teaching units across campus, the institutional research office, provincial/territorial governments, and Statistics Canada.

The registrar often assumes a leadership role in moving an institution's course and student systems to a new level of functionality, and as such is a key player in the selection of systems vendors, software suppliers, and technology enhancements. The registrar also evaluates other technologies to facilitate various office functions, including: records storage and camera systems, such as microfilm, microfiche, and digital imaging, used for converting and storing paper records; telephone switchboard and call centre systems; query response systems for email volumes; file management systems for admissions and student records hard-copy files; machines for volume faxing, printing, and envelope stuffing; and editorial/publishing systems for academic calendars, course listings, and registration guides.

The hardware costs to support the development and ongoing maintenance of all technologies, including a sophisticated workstation for every staff member, has greatly increased registrars' capital costs in recent decades. Recruitment and admissions were the last of the registrar's major functional areas to shift from manually driven processing to major technology support. These areas are now at the forefront of innovation with the introduction of sophisticated interactive prospect websites, contact management databases, computer-managed communication systems, and technology-assisted file analysis and decision-making.

## HIGH TECHNOLOGY AND CUSTOMER-FOCUSED SERVICE

This functional analysis suggests clearly that a key best practice for any contemporary office of the registrar is the comprehensive and integrated automation of practically all transactions. Such a standard calls for auto-mated online services infused with a customer-centred, 24/7, "one stop serves all steps" philosophy, compatible with the "ask," "deliver," and online status "report" cycle of users. Accordingly, this would include: online transcript ordering and payment, with multiple address options; immediate online encumbrance checking and payment options for outstanding fines or fees; transcript printing and mailing; online status checking for students/graduates regarding date of mailing; and automated cross-checking follow-up for grade changes and academic progression rulings generating automated reissues and notifications to students.

Best practices also include a "high touch" approach to customer-focused service. The point of automation is not just efficiency, although it has greatly improved service in quantity and quality without corresponding increases in staff. By moving routine work off desks and into computer programs, staff can be called upon to deliver much more personalized problem-solving service to their student clients. As a key point of contact, the registrar's office has a profound impact on the overall service experi-ence students attribute to their institution, for good or ill. Today's human resource challenge for registrars is to recruit, select, and train (or retrain) staff and middle managers to function beyond regulations, to listen for and understand students' unique situations, and to respond with compas-sion and exception when they judge that a situation warrants special intervention. It means moving an entire staff from a traditional clerical approach, where they simply execute procedures, to a more professional approach, where they serve as students' supporters, advisors, and counsel-lors, and know when to refer them appropriately to other resources, such as academic advising and counselling.

This perspective on the dual aspects of technology and service illustrates the increasingly unique and complex professional demands being placed on a registrar and staff. The contemporary office of the registrar can no longer function as a body of clerks handling data, but rather must be a community of service providers focused on the individual needs of constituents.

Finally, another best practice for a registrar's office is to organize front-line services around the student client, rather than around individual admin-istrative functions. This brings services to students rather than sends students scurrying across campus in search of services. It requires the assembly and integration of single-stop service centres and processes, such as that found in the Student Client Services Centre opened at York University in 2003, which assists up to 8,000 student visitors per day in the first week of fall term with enrolment, fees, and financial need. Similarly, Dalhousie University's engineering and architecture campus offers an integrated approach through its Student Services Centre, where students can access enrolment and financial services, the bookstore, and on-site academic advising, financial assistance, study and writing skills assistance, and personal counselling, including time with one of the campus chaplains.

## PROFESSIONALIZATION OF THE FIELD

The role of the registrar in Canadian universities has evolved considerably in recent decades. While long acknowledged as a unique and highly regarded leadership position on campus and a custodian of institutional history and official records, the registrar today is looked to as the key senior administrator whose leadership directs both the institution's enrolment management process and the overall campus service culture. Sixty years ago it would have been common practice for a respected academic from the faculty to assume the role of registrar; today such appointments are rare. Presidents realize the critical nature of this position among their senior administrators, and the search for a candidate rarely proceeds without the assistance of a professional recruitment firm. The challenge is to find an individual who:

- has completed a university education, preferably at the graduate level;
- possesses specific field experience (preferably at multiple institutions) in enrolment management, recruitment and admissions, and student records and scheduling;
- demonstrates solid familiarity and understanding of current technology, preferably in the vendor system of the institution;
- focuses on student service and initiative for improving students' campus experience;
- exhibits superb communication, negotiation, and persuasion skills for interactions with deans, department chairs, and individual faculty; administrative colleagues in student affairs, computing, finance office, and institutional research; as well as parents, alumni, and their respective MPS, MLAS, and lawyers.

Institutional presidents prefer a registrar who is capable of systemic and strategic thinking from a campus-wide perspective; can increase student enrolments and improve student persistence; is detail-oriented and ensures superb organization and accurate execution; actively promotes technological innovation; and communicates superbly, with political sensitivity and an abundance of patience. Furthermore, the successful registrar must be able to persuade reluctant colleagues to compromise local pride, when necessary, for the greater benefit of university-wide branding and academic regulation, and to instill these same traits in an office team, often numbering over a hundred in a large university – and happily rise at 5 A.M. to check email before spending the workday in long consecutive meetings. A frequent search firm recommendation is to add "associate vice-president" to the position title, in order to attract candidates whose experience matches these impressive criteria.

The hierarchy of a typical institution would have the registrar reporting most often to the vice-president (academic). In such cases, the registrar normally interacts with colleagues in at least one associate vice-president (academic) position, who oversees academic personnel issues, and an associate or assistant vice-president or dean of student affairs position, in addition to the deans and institutional librarian. An exception occurs in those institutions where the registrar reports to a vice-president (student services or students), with a close working relationship to the vice-president (academic). This latter approach perhaps advantages the registrar with more opportunities to influence strategy and improve partnerships between the enrolment services and the various student support services on the "student affairs side" of the vice-president's portfolio. Likewise, student affairs staff will have greater interaction and more opportunities to influence the priorities of a registrar who may not yet be skilled in the processes of a service-oriented culture. There are significant areas of overlap between enrolment services and other student services on campus, and the inclusion of the registrar on the senior student affairs management team can have a profound and positive impact on all parties involved. The registrar's forte in technology and data analysis can add an extra dimension to discussions of service development in areas such as counselling, where staff rarely offer such expertise. The registrar's participation in senior councils, particularly enrolment management strategy, can also bring a new understanding and language to student affairs professionals searching for a framework to increase support for the services they provide. As well, it can encourage renewed discipline in collecting service delivery data to support different unit requests for resources.

At both managerial and staff levels, the inclusion of the registrar's office as part of "student services" strengthens personal connections and mutual role understandings for a more seamless experience as students are referred from one unit to another. For example, integrated communication and partnerships between the campus housing department and the admissions office can have a dramatic, positive impact on enrolment conversion rates of offers to registered students. Another area of significant overlap is student discipline, where joint approaches to education about and application of academic integrity regulations and non-academic codes of conduct can contribute to better handling of cases, improved informal solutions, and more consistency in record keeping and communications. Collegial relations between the registrar's financial aid officers and other student services units (e.g., international office, students with disabilities, and counselling) can yield transformative gains in student persistence to graduation. In addition, closer interactions between student affairs units and registrar staff can challenge old stereotypes and increase recognition of their common interests in student success. The power of "being on the same side" within an organization should not be underestimated.

## ISSUES AND CHALLENGES

The world of Canadian higher education is undergoing one of its greatest periods of change in more than half a century. Adding to significant challenges in the form of new technologies, radically different expectations from "millennial" students and families (Howe and Strauss 2000), continual shifts in government support, and demands for institutional accountability are escalating marketing and recruitment pressures, and demographic challenges in recruiting both students and staff that impact campus quality and the student experience.

### Technology Imperative: Build or Buy?

Registrars play key roles in the development and adoption of new administrative technology on campus. Over the last three decades, there has been a major shift from locally developed, custom-built solutions, unique to each institution, to vendor-supplied databases and applications. The collaborative challenge for the registrar and senior information technology officer is to support current service levels for students and faculty while maintaining, refining, and developing applications in accordance with academic policy changes (e.g., degree audit systems). Although some campuses continue on with locally developed systems (e.g., York University and University of British Columbia), with additional vendor applications for recruitment, timetabling, and examination scheduling, most have switched exclusively to vendor-provided systems.

The decision to stay with or redevelop a local system typically rests on two considerations: cost and local culture. In many cases, the cost of replacing existing systems with a vendor-supported one is prohibitive, with some large universities spending in the eight-figure range when all costs for their conversion team are included on top of the vendor price. In other cases, the key factor may be a senior administration decision that the campus culture precludes the adaptive response required by an external system, or that unique needs render the development of a local solution costlier than the value-added promise of a particular vendor system. Many of the current large vendors were established by break-away experts from post-secondary clients and some still recruit heavily from their clients' best staff, especially when they are moving into a new market segment – another worry for any prospective client. Individual institutions' attempts to market locally developed systems generally have not been successful. In fact, the concept that high-cost local solutions should be sold rather than shared may have contributed to the diminished number of viable products in recent years and the escalated costs to purchase vendor systems. At the same time, registrar systems are seen as mission critical and much too valuable to allow experimenting with open source consortia.

Members of the registrars' profession openly share their successes when developing new technology and when collaborating across institutional boundaries. Brigham Young University, for example, was remarkably generous with senior staff time as they researched voice recognition for telephone registration systems through the 1970s. When the University of Alberta introduced Canada's first telephone registration system in 1982, the university hosted numerous visitors from other Canadian institutions interested in seeing the application first-hand. Carleton University also provided leadership to develop Canadian protocols for sharing grades and transcript data for EDI (electronic data interchange). However, it is rare that institutions would share program source code.

### Communication Challenge: Getting Students' Attention

With current students expecting immediate, customized service through email, portals, telephone, fax, in-person, and virtual online communities, the modern registrar's office is poised in the centre of a burgeoning communication web. The successful registrar reacts to this opportunity proactively, planning communication strategies in advance of students' need to know and delivering answers before students become frustrated by the question. The greatest challenge will continue to be getting and holding students' attention long enough for them to absorb the information they need. This is not likely to happen unless it is delivered in customized, plain-language sound bites, in a medium that current students are willing to read, and at the point in time when they need it. Even with these criteria met, fewer and fewer students look to the official messaging of the institution for important information, relying instead on their online social network of peers. This trend is alarming for registrars worried about the accuracy of the information students use to make decisions.

### Dual Roles of the Registrar

As the centre of the administrative support services that facilitate all students' admissions and subsequent registrations at their college or university, the office of the registrar is essential to student success. The position of registrar deals with a duality in its campus culture role. Best practice requires an emphasis on student-focused service and support to facilitate students' academic progress as efficiently as possible. Equally important though is its regulatory responsibility to enforce the institutions' policies, procedures, deadlines, fee collections, and so on, a role less appreciated by students who find themselves in some form of difficulty with the institution and consequently view the registrar's office with a certain resentment and distaste. As the largest front-line service provider on every campus, registrarial managers and staff constantly juggle the demands of both these roles. The degree to which they maintain an appropriate balance between the two directly impacts the professional reputation of the registrar and the office's reputation on campus, as either a service-oriented source of pride and student satisfaction or a student-reviled bureaucracy generating stories of long line-ups and unhelpful staff. Continued balance between appropriate standards and regulation on the one hand and necessary flexibility and support for students and faculty on the other hand is an essential component of the profession.

## Increased Competition and Quality Concerns

The registrar, as a leader in developing a student-focused service culture on campus, is more and more engaged in work related to assessing and reporting on institutional quality, particularly with regard to the student experience. A growing number of colleges and universities are now administering one or several institutional surveys that provide solid diagnostic data on areas of improvement. For example, more than a few Canadian post-secondary institutions are adopting the National Survey of Student Engagement (NSSE), a well-established American survey, as a potential benchmark. While not without its limitations, NSSE offers a third-party, non-government, non-media-authored analysis with sufficient depth to make useful comparisons. Some constituencies, such as the Ontario colleges system, also employ a government-imposed student satisfaction survey as one of several "key performance indicators" for government funding.

The very difficult challenge is forecasting "the tipping point" (Gladwell 2000) at which multiple incremental changes will generate a new perception. Proactive incremental changes for the better do not yield incremental satisfaction responses; in most cases, numerous changes, implemented over several years, must occur before the point is reached where the overall positive impact suddenly is apparent in students' reactions and feedback. On the reverse side, in terms of enrolment changes and budget and service cuts, it is difficult to predict the point where incremental changes induce overload, creating a sudden perceived drastic downturn in students' perceptions of their experience. Any registrar who actively searches for ways to improve students' campus experience and proposes policy changes accordingly may, over time, profoundly improve the campus environment for students and the reputation of the school.

## Professional Continuity and Human Resource Development

A key future challenge lies in the changing demographics of the management personnel in Canadian registrar offices, especially given the number of long-serving baby boomers planning retirements within ten years and future enrolment scenarios that will result in increasing competition for candidates with the requisite skills. Post-secondary institutions in Canada would be wise to focus on development of senior positions in their organizations to cultivate the right mix of experience, skills, and expertise for their needs: marketing knowledge for enrolment management, technology knowledge and vision for operations, the ability to broadly analyze policy impacts from multiple perspectives, intuitive understanding of service cultures, and the courage to stand for professional standards. In a field with long-term incumbency in its leadership positions, this is an ideal opportunity for middle managers in both the registrar's and student services areas to actively seek lateral moves across functional areas for experience in multiple portfolios and development of new skill sets.

## Resources for Registrars and Enrolment Managers

As integrative organizational structures become more common between registrar and enrolment management functions, and between enrolment services and other student affairs units, the need for broad-based leaders creates a significant opportunity for new practitioners. It is a wise career move to participate in a variety of professional organizations, engage in their respective listservs, read extensively in professional literature, and whenever possible, pursue opportunities for site visits to other campuses. Extensive reading of higher education and corporate organization materials, as well as student affairs and enrolment services literature, informs current practice with solid grounding in current research and theory, and provides a vital perspective on wider campus concerns.

The work of Canadian campus registrars is informed by a host of professional organization venues and literature resources. Some are of general interest and address a broad range of issues and strategies of concern to any post-secondary institution, and others apply more directly to the Canadian higher education context and its array of institutional types and regional affiliations. Among those focusing explicitly on post-secondary institutional concerns in Canada are the Association of Registrars of the Universities and Colleges of Canada (ARUCC) (www.arucc.ca) and its regional affiliate groups: Western provinces, (WARUCC) (www.warucc.ca); Ontario University Registrars' Association, (OURA) (www.oura.ca); Atlantic Association of Registrars and Admissions Officers, (AARAO) (www.unb.ca/aarao); Conférence des recteurs et des principaux des universités du Québec, (CREPUQ) (www.

crepuq.qc.ca); and the Ontario-based Committee of Registrars, Admissions and Liaison Officers, (CRALO) (www.cralo.ca). Of particular interest to those in such institutions is the Association of Canadian Community Colleges (ACCC) (www.accc.ca). Regardless of setting, all in the role of registrar would benefit greatly from participating in DocAlert-L, a limited membership listserv (Canadian university registrars and admissions directors) dedicated to informing colleagues of potential cases of document fraud.

The American Association of Collegiate Registrars and Admissions Officers (AACRAO) (www.aacrao.org) is another organization focusing on the broad portfolio of the office of registrar. Although explicit in its focus on the dynamics and particulars of US institutions, it provides an excellent portal to other resources quite useful in the Canadian context. Of special note is its *Guide for Useful Listservs* (www.aacrao.org/useful_links/listserv.cfm), covering a broad range of topics, including community colleges, transfer students, admissions, enrolment management, records and registration, and electronic data interchange. Listservs are one of the best ways to network with colleagues at other institutions, pose questions, share information, and tap into current best practices. AACRAO also features a listserv dedicated to its Canadian members – ARUCC-L (arucc-l@acs.ryerson.ca).

In addition to the annual general conferences and consulting resources (e.g., AACRAO's Strategic Enrolment Management – SEM – Services) sponsored by these professional organizations, libraries of publications and professional journals on relevant topics are accessible to members through respective websites. For example, ACCRAO features a publications webpage (www.aacrao.org/publications/) and issues a quarterly online journal, *College and University*. A sampling of recent resource titles includes those addressing enrolment management and recruitment issues (e.g., SEM *and Institutional Success: Integrating Enrolment, Finance and Student Access*, 2008), admissions processes (e.g., *The College Admissions Officer's Guide*, 2008), student records management (e.g., *Counterfeit Diplomas and Transcripts*, 2008), and the registrar's role in campus leadership (e.g., *Managing for Outcomes: Shifting From Process-Centric to Results-Oriented Operations*, 2007). AACRAO also publishes guides to educational systems around the world to assist admissions officers in credential evaluation. Recent guides include those published for Australia, Brazil, the EU Bologna process, France, Kyrgyzstan, Russia, Taiwan, and United Kingdom.

The nature of its responsibilities necessarily places the office of registrar in contact with a number of other related professional communities. While too numerous to mention all, these might include, the Canadian Association for Co-operative Education (www.cafce.ca/pages/home.php), Canadian Co-operative Association (www.coopscanada.coop), EDUCAUSE (www.educause.edu/node/720?time=1228323481), Society for College and University Planning (www.scup.org), National Orientation Directors Association (www.

nodaweb.org), and the North American Association of Commencement Officers (www.naaco.info). Related international communities can also be contacted at the Association of International Education Administrators (www.aieaworld.org), Council on International Education Exchange (www. ciee.org), NAFSA: Association of International Educators (www.nafsa.org), and World University Service of Canada (www.wusc.ca), to name a few.

Given the integral role registrars play in the data collection and analysis related to campus student enrolment profiles and other institutional information gathering, familiarity with resources that offer such assessments is essential. Toward that end, various subscription surveys and private consultants of interest to enrolment management can be accessed at the Canadian University Survey Consortium (www.cusc-ccreu.ca), National Survey of Student Engagement (nsse.iub.edu), and Academica Group, Inc. (www. academicagroup.com), a private consulting firm specializing in enrolment management support for Canadian universities. Of particular note is an informative blog (www.academicagroup.com/blog/10) maintained by Ken Steele, Academica's Senior Vice-President, Education Marketing.

Collectively, the above references offer a solid base for professionals who wish to supplement personal experience with additional knowledge and study. Through professional meetings, publications, and visits to other campuses (either physical or virtual), they can position themselves well to provide their institutions with the kind of leaders needed in the twenty-first century. Ultimately, through such leadership, students will benefit greatly from the kinds of systems that facilitate their goals and progress toward a successful post-secondary experience.

# 4

# Student Financial Assistance and Scholarship Services

## MURRAY BAKER

Funding post-secondary education has become an increasingly formidable challenge for many Canadian students and their families. Between 1996 and 2004, for example, tuition at Canadian institutions rose at more than three times the rate of inflation (Statistics Canada) and it continues to increase as costs mount and revenues lag. Consequently, through financial aid, colleges and universities have come to play an ever more critical role in ensuring that students are properly funded, not only initially in order to attend their chosen post-secondary institution but subsequently in order to complete their studies without interruption. In total, Canadian institutions spend upwards of one billion dollars annually on scholarships, prizes, and bursaries (Canadian Association of University Business Officers 2008) as financial aid has evolved from an administrative unit for student financial matters to an integral part of students' financial solutions for funding their post-secondary education.

### ROLE AND ORGANIZATION OF FINANCIAL AID

The role of financial aid is twofold: (a) assisting students to access various sources of money to help fund their college or university education (a *service* oriented role), and (b) supporting institutions to attract top academic applicants through merit-based funding (a *recruitment* role). In order to assist students in these ends, financial aid offices are often divided into several functional divisions: (a) a needs-based unit, with access to student loans, bursaries, and in some provinces, work study programs; and (b) a merit-based unit, which handles scholarships, grants, and other awards distributed on the basis of academic performance. Although some institutions merge these two functions into a single entity, others keep them as separate units, usually under the banner of financial aid.

Financial aid reporting structures vary widely among institutions. While frequently linked to student services at many institutions (e.g., University of New Brunswick) – perhaps a reflection of its service mandate – financial aid is more closely aligned at some schools with the registrar's office, recruitment and marketing, or enrolment management services (e.g., Queen's University, University of Manitoba), reflecting a stronger recruitment focus. At still other institutions (e.g., University of Alberta), it is funded by and reports to the students' union, leaving the scholarships and awards unit under university administration.

It is understandable how financial aid could fit under any one of these reporting arrangements, although as the educational and counseling aspects of financial aid grow, its fit within the student services structure also makes increasing sense. Whereas many units, such as counselling, career services, and learning skills, ostensibly deal with students' growth and development, financial aid's role is more indirect – yet equally crucial, given that financial matters are a major stressor for many students during their post-secondary experience.

Institutional financial aid services are often overseen by either a director of financial aid and awards, associate director student financial services and awards, coordinator of scholarships and student finance, or an associate registrar, with specific units within the department reporting to a designated individual in charge of a specific area, for example, scholarships and awards or work study. The department and each unit are often supported by clerical and administrative staff and in many cases trained student-peers. However, the specific arrangement of a financial aid department's administration and staffing is dictated largely by the general administrative structure and size of the institution.

Regardless, the changing role of financial aid necessitates that these offices work with personnel in a range of financial services across the campus, including: (a) Canada and provincial/territorial student loans, bursaries, and scholarship awards and information; (b) educational outreach workshops and orientations on financial matters; (c) emergency loans; (d) work study programs; (e) athletic awards; and (f) information on educational costs. In doing so, financial aid plays a significant role in assisting students with issues that, if not dealt with through sound decision-making, can have a negative impact on their academic performance and their personal health and well-being during their course of studies. Inasmuch as financial barriers are removed and opportunities are created, student success is an extension of effective aid services.

## FINANCIAL AID TRENDS, ISSUES, AND CHALLENGES

In recent decades a number of trends, issues, and challenges that have arisen within financial aid have transformed its policies and practices, as well as the characteristics of those whom it serves. Included among these are shifts in the types of financial aid offered, the burgeoning administrative environment necessitated by changing policies and programs, various dilemmas related to institutional decisions about resource allocation, and challenges of an evolving and increasingly diverse student body.

## Shift in Aid Resources

Since 2000 financial aid in Canada has witnessed a general shift from government subsidy to individual and institutional responsibility in generating funds for post-secondary education. One such trend has been the increased allocation of resources and staffing to scholarships and awards. As governments have cut back on non-repayable sources of funding (i.e., grants) and opted for greater emphasis on repayable loans, colleges and universities are increasingly being forced to pick up the shortfall through institutional-based funding. They have responded with increases in performance-based scholarships.

In light of research suggesting that scholarships might influence students' selection of an institution, but not necessarily students' success (Somers 1993), a major portion of institutional awards (over 80 per cent in the 2001-02 year, for example) are granted to students on the basis of marks (Gucciardi 2004). Furthermore, these same data indicate, an estimated 45 per cent of all such dollars go to first-year students, underscoring once again the growth in importance of institutional funding not only to assist students but more so to attract top candidates.

Also in the mix of shifting resources has been a growing interest in direct student loans. Accessibility to post-secondary education gained a firm position in Canadian culture with the creation, in 1964, of The Canada Student Loans Program (CSLP), established under the Canada Student Loans Act (CSLA). Although funding for the program has shifted between the federal government and banking institutions providing the necessary loan capital, financial aid offices at many post-secondary institutions have remained constant in their front-line contact with students, their confirmation of enrolment, and their role in releasing funds to students whose registration has been confirmed. Although the federal government has been the direct lender for Canada Student Loans since 2000, financial aid offices, along with the National Student Loans Service Centre (subcontracted by the federal government), have played an increasingly integral role in the timely and accurate distribution of these funds to students. While students may access a variety of funding sources from both public (e.g., government and community organizations) and private (e.g., corporations and foundations) sectors, a large portion must be accessed directly from the institutions they attend.

A third funding option that has gained importance is work study programs, which exist in some provinces and are growing in number. Students in need are able to secure a job (usually on campus) and be paid for a set number of work hours per week. However, such programs have proven undependable over time. For example, in 1999, British Columbia discontinued their program though it had once been an integral part of financial aid at many provincial campuses. At some schools (e.g., University of Victoria), similar programs were continued only through the extraordinary funding efforts of the institution rather than the customary provincial government support. However, the dissolution of such programs has not occurred without its own set of issues. Studies suggest that close to half of all students work part-time while attending university, and that a nominal number of hours per week of part-time work (ten to nineteen hours) does not have a detrimental effect on student academic success (Dundes and Marx 2006). That said, a significant number of students work much longer hours while juggling a full-time course load, a scenario that is far more likely to negatively impact students' academic performance as well as their involvement in student life.

With recent changes in government policies, other sources of funding, including non-repayable scholarships and tax deferred savings plans, have also become more appealing. For example, taxation of scholarships moved from a $500 to a $3,000 exemption level in 2000 and was eliminated altogether in 2006. Relaxed plan restrictions on the tax deferred investment vehicle Registered Education Savings Plan (RESP) were also announced by the government in 1998. This, along with contributions of a Canadian Education Savings Grant (CESG), made these much more desirable methods for parents to save for their children's education. Furthermore, in allowing Canadians to borrow from their Registered Retirement Savings Plans (RRSPs) to fund their own post-secondary education, the government has sent a clear message, especially to lifelong learners, that more of the responsibility for financing education is being shifted from government to individual Canadians. Combined with the shift of financing responsibilities to the colleges and universities themselves, this has meant that both schools and individuals are being expected to take on a more proactive role in generating and managing additional resources, resulting in a heightened administrative load for most colleges and universities.

### Growing Need-Resource Gap

The need to increase sources of financial aid, regardless of type, has been precipitated in part by the fact that between 1999 and 2009 post-secondary tuition has increased at a rate far greater than the rate of inflation. Coupled with this trend, increases in family income and student resources have not kept pace during the same period. Exacerbating this problem further are the relatively flat allowable limits to student borrowing under the Canada Student Loans Program; they remained essentially unchanged, fixed at $165 per week, from 1994 to 2004, moving up to $210 in 2009. Consequently, the gap between the amount needed to attend a post-secondary institution and the student and parent resources available continues to widen, in effect contributing to an ever-increasing amount of unmet need for a growing number of students. The college and university financial aid office, at one time established simply to provide emergency funding should a student fall short of resources during the academic year, must now respond to waves of new students often showing up at the *beginning* of the school year already burdened by unmet need. The responsibility to fund such need through institutional financial aid has increased for all colleges and universities, and need, merit, and hybrid resource packages have increasingly become their principal means of response. Interestingly, all of these might still not meet basic needs, compelling some institutions to develop additional resources such as, for example, the University of Manitoba's inclusion of a Food Bank on their financial services website and the University of New Brunswick's Daycare Assistance Finance Program.

### Allocation Dilemmas

Given multiple choices now available, colleges and universities in Canada face a number of challenges regarding allocation of current financial aid funds. Schools must often decide, for example, what portion of their resources is best distributed on a needs basis, how much on the basis of merit, and the amount dedicated to various hybrid packages. An increase in the combined form of aid became more common throughout the 1990s and continued into the subsequent decade. Beyond the question of type of aid is the dilemma of award size. While the distribution of a large number of smaller awards might benefit a greater number of students, fewer scholarships of higher monetary value might be of more benefit to the institution in terms of recruiting the most academically competitive candidates.

The limited and diminishing amounts of funding available to institutions make the job of balancing recruitment goals, through merit-based funding, with accessibility goals, through need-based allocations, more challenging. In the face of increased costs to students, schools are often challenged by the predicament of applicants who lack the resources to attend their institution of choice. Can the school feasibly effect matriculation in light of the financial obstacles these students encounter? Some schools may have sufficient resources, while others may fall far short of providing a competitive level of funding and service. Consequently, the dilemmas of fund distribution are problematic not only for financial aid but for other campus departments as well, including the registrar and development offices, inasmuch as their success depends on the institution's capacity to yield a viable annual enrolment.

Related to this question is the assessment of student financial need. Both federal and provincial governments employ formulas for determining how much students are entitled to in loans and, where applicable, grants. The formula is designed to be fair, although it stands to reason that a one-size-fits-all approach does not necessarily recognize the individual contingencies and circumstances that often complicate students' needs. Therefore institutions must examine how they assist students for whom an unfavorable needs assessment outcome may leave them scrambling for cash. Additionally, many false assumptions exist as to expectations of the various financial aid programs. For example, over 90 per cent of parents expect their child to get government student loans to help pay for college or university, when in fact only 50 per cent actually qualify and access such loans. Likewise, nearly two-thirds of parents believed that their child's education would be at least partially funded through scholarships and awards, when in fact only 31 per cent of students aged eighteen to twenty receive such resources (Anisef and Sweet 2002). Thus financial aid offices must deal with students and parents who may have based their financial strategy on false assumptions. The challenge is to reach students and parents early on, ideally in the high school years, to prevent some of these misconceptions and to minimize the most common errors in the post-secondary financial planning process.

An emerging new twist to this issue is specialized dedicated scholarships, such as those offered for athletic talent. These were traditionally avoided in Canada for fear of falling into a situation where student athletes' accomplishments on the field were not being matched by their in-class performance. However, athletic scholarships have gradually become a part of the Canadian financial aid portfolio as a means of both assisting students financially and attracting students who might otherwise be tempted by athletic dollars available south of the border. Although the numbers and dollar amounts pale in comparison to other systems (e.g., United States), Canadian athletic scholarships have evolved to include the once offside practice of offering athletic financial aid to first-year students. These closely regulated sources of funding are thus becoming an additional option of financial assistance, with administrative responsibility falling to the financial aid office and placing further strain on limited funds. The net impact for most institutions is that student need often outstrips institutional resources, necessitating difficult choices and trade-offs.

## Public Versus Private Good

Like other systems, Canadian higher education was founded on the efforts of private initiatives. Over the centuries, however, it has evolved into a decidedly public resource, as evidenced in the commitments of numerous institutions to their constituents. For example, the University of British

Columbia (UBC), among others, has developed a policy that "No Eligible Student ... will be prevented from commencing or continuing his or her studies at the University for financial reasons alone" (University of British Columbia Board of Governors, 2005), and the Ontario government has developed a statement in the provincial Student Access Guarantee that, "No qualified Ontario student will be prevented from attending our publicly-assisted colleges and universities because of a lack of financial support programs" and ensures that "post-secondary students in financial need have financial aid to cover the cost of their tuition, books and other mandatory fees" (Ontario Student Assistance Program). In effect such commitments have mandated that universities be responsible for bridging any shortfalls in funding for students, and according to some, every shift of funding responsibility to individuals is a potential erosion of an institution's public foundation. Furthermore this tends to disadvantage smaller and newer institutions that may lack a sufficient alumni/ae base from which to derive additional scholarship and need-based resources. As a result, a growing trend is appointment of a designated development officer within the financial aid office to procure monies for such purposes.

## Challenging Administrative Complexities

As education is primarily a provincial concern in Canada, campus financial aid offices must be able to handle policies and programs from all of the provinces and territories, along with those of the federal government. Prior to 2000, the Canada Student Loans Program was supported and administered by a variety of financial institutions. This presented a complexity of problems, from both an administrative and student perspective, since students often subscribed to several federal and provincial loans from different lenders, each with its own particular forms and procedures. Fortunately, since 2000, progress in simplification and uniformity has resulted in only one service provider for the federal student loan program; provincial loan programs are gradually being harmonized with federal specifications, streamlining the process further for administrators and students alike.

However, just as most other administrative units are under pressure to do more, financial aid also grapples with long lineups and workloads that often stretch limited staff and resources. At times this creates a backlog of difficult situations that become even more challenging due to the resource lag, requiring additional measures. Financial aid offices, for example, are increasingly seeing cases that have escalated to serious or dire status prior to any intervention. Action at that stage is at best reactive and palliative, and frequently takes the form of an emergency loan or referral to a student food bank. In an attempt to intervene and educate students, hopefully preventing many of these cases from reaching such a critical level, some schools have initiated educational programs to assist students in how to best access and manage their money. In utilizing tools such as budgeting workshops and information seminars, and drawing upon widely used resources such as the financial survival guide, *The Debt-Free Graduate* (Baker 2008), schools are attempting to educate students earlier in the cycle, ideally prior to their matriculation into a chosen institution. Centennial College, in Ontario, for example, conducts workshops as part of a comprehensive outreach program in local high schools. Other schools capitalize on existing initiatives run by their institutions (e.g., student ambassador programs) or offer online how-to-budget sessions in order to get the financial aid message out.

Recognizing that families are an important financial and support resource for students, some schools (e.g., University of Victoria) have targeted parents together with students in their educational outreach, especially during orientation to university life. Brock University, for example, incorporates a First-Time Borrower financial workshop as part of the loan negotiation process, which students are welcome to access. To facilitate similar programs within the limits of staff and resources, some financial aid offices rely on trained student peer assistants for help. Following this model, Brock University, for example, makes use of peer assistants not only in their seminars but also in their other outreach programs, where students are perhaps best suited to deliver the key messages and information about financial aid.

## Changing Student Demographics

Beyond these logistical challenges, twenty-first-century demographic trends have also had important ramifications on the functioning of campus financial aid offices. As student populations enrolling in post-secondary education continue to diversify, so too do their needs, and so too must the services offered. For example, international students have different needs in terms of their funding and the regulations they must adhere to. Employment limitations and unfamiliar financial practices may require additional staff resources to help such students navigate these challenges. International students have also been found to make much broader use of the financial aid office than do students in general. In response, institutions like the University of Manitoba have initiated bursary programs specifically to support undergraduate international students. Other cases in point include the increasing number of single-parent and graduate students on campus, all requiring specialized and expanded financial services, such as the Sister Eileen McIlwaine Memorial Entrance Bursary for Single Mothers offered at Concordia University. The consequent increased pressure on resources, as well as the diversity of needs met, need to be accounted for in order to provide the support services that these and other emerging groups require.

This of course becomes a much more prominent issue in schools that have a variety of diverse groups within their service populations. Mature students, students with disabilities, Aboriginal and First Nation peoples, and single-parent learners, among others, bring unique needs that will increasingly demand a place in the financial aid resource allocation process.

## PROFESSIONALIZATION OF FINANCIAL AID SERVICES

The evolving nature of financial aid has brought a significant change in the roles, responsibilities, and knowledge expected of professionals serving in such offices. In addition to a strong knowledge of institutional policies and practices as they pertain to financial aid and student services, a broader knowledge of provincial and federal financial assistance is of utmost importance. Increasingly, as institutions recruit internationally and market their programs to new student populations (e.g., lifelong learners and First Nations students), knowledge of specific issues and challenges such students face and any policies in place to assist them is a basic requirement of this work. The financial aid professional is not only a critical administrator for the institution but also an important advocate for students themselves, so multiple skills sets are required. These include policy analysis, writing of briefs and papers, marketing and communication, coordinating public scholarship events, networking and team building, liaison with other administrative units, and financial counselling.

Expanding financial aid roles as educator, broker, advocate, and counsellor necessitate that professionals also come equipped to provide creative educational workshops and online resources addressing issues ranging from application processes to budgeting and responsible loan management. Related to these concerns, since the late 1990s, has been a steady shift by both institutions and government loan providers to move much of their dissemination of information and contact with students to web-based formats, much to the benefit of the process. As a result, financial aid staff members spend less time on basic paperwork or repetitive student contacts and more on other creative, empowering, and proactive tasks. For example, with less time required to provide individual information to students on tasks such as filling out forms and other procedural matters, more time is available for one-on-one service. As the Canada Student Loans Program has moved to a web-based application and information dissemination format, more of the regulatory duties, such as reporting withdrawals, are pushed to the schools themselves. Thus, while the more efficient web delivery of information has not lessened the amount of work for the financial aid office, it has changed the nature and content of the work. There is still much to be done in the implementation of technology and various web applications so as to better handle rudimentary tasks; as well, the level of progress in this regard varies widely, both from school to school and among the various levels of government, resulting in a standard of service that is quite uneven.

In an intermediary role between students and policy, financial aid professionals must also be able to assist with various loan appeals and policy interpretations, as well as the payment of institutional fees. In addition, the emerging role of researcher has informed an understanding of the means by which students finance their education and the impact of these methods on student success. For instance, the Canadian University Survey Consortium has explored the many variables related to financial matters and student success, such as the number of hours students work while attending school and the impact of policy on student accessibility. Financial aid professionals could benefit from basic skills in data assembly, manipulation, and research.

While no particular academic background is critical for preparing professionals in this field, some disciplines lend themselves well to the varied roles of financial aid. Certainly a financial background is beneficial, as is preparation in policy planning, communications, and counselling. However, perhaps most important are the particular talents that an individual can bring to the position. Good analytical and communication skills, for example, are paramount. In addition, knowledge about institutional policy and practices (e.g., experience chairing faculty and staff committees) and about provincial and federal student loans policies and financial institutions is core to the professional delivery of financial student services. Individuals working in this area would also typically be versed in student financial matters on their own campus as well as national and international policies. Such expertise would inform institutional policy on tuition fee rates and advocacy for policy change. All in all, the skills required of a financial aid portfolio entail both a breadth and depth of understanding of the myriad concerns that impinge upon this area of students' lives.

Ongoing preparation and success in this domain of student services is further supported by organizations such as the Canadian Association of Student Financial Aid Administrators (CASFAA). In addition to sponsoring many policy initiatives, this association hosts a national annual conference comprised not only of financial aid professionals from across Canada but also public and private sector stakeholders in the student services and financial aid area – various levels of government, financial institutions, and related companies and organizations – resulting in a growing forum for professional development and discussion of financial aid policy and initiatives. CASFAA leadership plays a significant role in further professionalizing the field while shaping financial aid through its input and direction on governmental policies of funding and taxation. Such efforts are augmented by the work of numerous regional associations (e.g., Ontario Association of Student Financial Aid Administrators, OASFAA) that have similar mandates, including most particularly their focus on provincial policies.

## CONCLUSION

Whereas financial aid was once largely an administrative task, with management of mandated programs imposed externally and adapted to accordingly, it has started to shift increasingly toward assuming an integral role in the policy formation and implementation of these programs. In the last five years, rather than exclusively serving what the menu offers, financial aid has begun more strongly influencing what is actually being featured *on* the menu in the first place. It is also bringing to the table views from student consumers whose experiences are providing critical feedback on the palatability of the fare. In doing so, financial aid has shifted to a stronger advocacy role in support of the constituents it assists.

Although the success of students in the post-secondary experience depends on a host of factors and influences, sufficient funding resources is quickly becoming an essential component in the mix of student supports. Rather than the largely administrative and at times incidental roles they once played in assisting students with nominal costs and expenses, and in disseminating government funds – and in response to forces both within and beyond the institutions they serve – campus financial aid offices now constitute a core component of most student services portfolios.

Changing administrative and programmatic roles, greater demands for proactive education and advocacy initiatives, and an increasingly diverse student population have left most financial aid offices with wider-reaching responsibilities – and consequently increased pressures on their human and financial resources. Nonetheless, if students are to succeed academically and achieve a rich overall post-secondary experience, finding a way to pay for it all is paramount. In that sense the campus financial aid office's role is highly instrumental in assisting students to identify and secure the means for pursuing their goals, for without that, such aims remain only elusive dreams.

# 5

# Orientation and First-Year Services

## ROBERTA MASON

The initial weeks of the first semester are critical for students. Finding one's way on campus, making new friends, and learning where to access various services and how they might be helpful all take on a sense of urgency as students' commitment to this stage in their lives and the new setting they find themselves in grows. Orientation services that support students entering post-secondary education play a significant role in institutional enrolment management and outcome strategies.

This chapter offers an overview of the current functions and practices of orientation services at Canadian colleges and universities. Included is a discussion of the assumptions and principles that underlie such services, the typical nature and kinds of programs, the preparation and skills required of professionals in this field, and issues that continue to shape the design and implementation of orientation services. The chapter concludes with references and resources that can guide student services professionals as they consider orientation policies and programs supportive of their own student and institutional needs.

## EVOLUTION OF ORIENTATION SERVICES

In the not-so-distant past, "orientation" typically consisted of a series of social events seemingly designed to show students a good time before they got into the swing of things academic. Although well meaning, the result was often more *dis*orienting than helpful. In the 1960s and '70s, orientation functions were largely led by student unions and groups wishing to involve students in their many causes – often in reaction to the hierarchical *in loco parentis* practices of university administrators. By the 1980s, the culture had shifted and partnerships with university administrations emerged, delivering more holistic orientation programs that also better managed the risks sometimes associated with such student-run initiatives. In the late

1980s, many Canadian institutions struggled with low retention rates from first to second year. Recognizing the social and economic benefits of keeping the students in whom they had already made the recruiting investment, efforts turned to front-loading services to better support students in the transition to university study and living.

Orientation services in Canadian colleges and universities are now typically much more integrated and expanded, attending to a broader range of issues such as recruitment, retention, academic success, risk management, and performance indicators, while serving a growing diversity of students. Increased co-operation between administrators and students in planning, organization, and implementation has also significantly improved the results. Fundamental assumptions inherent in the planning of orientation services now generally include that students experience normative transitions and ongoing development throughout their university experience, are themselves responsible for their academic and personal success, are often best helped by other students, and that there is a positive correlation between student success and persistence and engagement in the life of the institution.

## ESSENTIAL FUNCTIONS AND SERVICES

Today it is more likely that students will find their first days full of activities strategically planned to help them make the transition to post-secondary study and life. Although orientation services are as varied as the institutions that offer them, most commonly attend issues related to students' instrumental autonomy, such as finding classes, using the laundry machines, and reading university-level texts; negotiation of old and new relationships, including important ties with parents and families, roommates, romances, academic partners, and shifting friendship groups; achievement of balance through managing stress, taking care of one's health and fitness, and managing substance use; and contribution to their communities. Delivery methods may include a mandatory one- or two-day program at the start of a new academic year, such as the University of Calgary's U of C 101; a series of ongoing voluntary activities that begin with an intensive first week and extend over a full semester or the entire first year, such as Yukon College's Orientation Week; credit and non-credit courses, such as Lambton College of Applied Arts and Technology's College Orientation course that is mandatory for most programs – and often a combination of these. They may also feature a variety of support services targeted both to students and their parents, and offer online services to those accessing their education from a distance.

Successful orientation programs are typically founded upon shared strategic, operational, and human resource planning. To define strategy, planning committees comprised of students, faculty, and staff are often convened to determine the goal and objectives and often to determine the program theme. The same committees may also be responsible for coordination of marketing; large event planning; coordination of institutional, academic unit, and student organization activities; and sometimes even budgeting and logistics. The people involved in an orientation program have a tremendous influence on its success, and frequently a good deal of time is spent recruiting and training student staff and volunteers and informing and involving student leaders, faculty, and staff throughout the institution.

While there is no magic formula for orientation program elements, those that achieve institutional and student objectives typically coordinate a mix of cross-institutional, academic program, and student organization activities and services ranging from large-scale events to one-on-one interactions serving mass audiences and specific target groups.

## Centres for Orientation

With growing attention paid in the 1980s to the first-year experience, many institutions created a "centre for new students" for coordination of orientation services. The University of Western Ontario, one of the first to do this, combined student recruitment, orientation, and peer mentor programs. Memorial University of Newfoundland, with the support of a federal grant, developed their Centre for Orientation, Nontraditional, and Commuter Students (CONTACS) in 1990. Typically located in the student affairs portfolio, these units are small but energetic engines that drive activities designed to promote first-year student success. Funding for such centres comes from a variety of sources, including student fees, grants, and university resource allocations.

## University 101 Courses

Many institutions have initiated credit courses – referred to as "First Year Seminar," "University Success," or most commonly, "University 101" – to help first-year students acquire strategies for academic and personal success. Such courses have proliferated in recent years, with over one hundred model course syllabi from sixty different institutions worldwide available in the National Resource Center for the First Year Experience and Students in Transition database.

Canadian post-secondary institutions offer a broad range of such courses. Some, such as Trinity Western University's mandatory University 101, include self-management, learning skills, and academic planning topics. Others, such as the University of Guelph's optional First Year Seminars, are taught by experienced instructors who integrate the interdisciplinary examination of unconventional topics with practical application of cognitive and social skill development. For example, the University of Prince Edward Island, the first in Canada to offer these types of courses, now has a suite of four course options for first-year students, including an online version of its University 100 course and a career and learning portfolio development option.

## Integrated Orientation Support Programs

Increasingly, attention is being paid to supporting the transitions students make *through* and *from* university life and study, rather than a singular focus on their transition *into* an institution. Initiatives such as the University of British Columbia's Tri-Mentoring Program link a first-year student, a senior student, and an alumnus who all share similar career interests, bringing together people at different stages in their own life to learn from one another. At the University of Guelph, students enrolled in large first-year courses can choose to attend small supported learning groups facilitated by seniors who work closely with the instructor to design a group study program, and all first-year students have the option of living in academic clusters in residences, grouped with other students studying in the same academic program and supported by a senior peer leader with a strong background in the discipline who organizes academic enrichment activities bridging class and community. Approaches that address the specific characteristics of a growing number of student target groups are also becoming commonplace.

## Diversity Programs

Understanding the mix of entering students at a given institution is critical to defining successful support strategies. Due to increasing diversity, orientation strategies are now commonly tailored to the specific needs of target groups and, as a result, are typically more effective, and frequently more efficient. The development of international student orientation programs led this trend, which now extends to a wide range of student sub-populations. At Queen's University, for example, international students and their families are welcomed and oriented during five days of specialized programming that precedes the general student orientation activities. The Aboriginal Students' Centre at the University of Saskatchewan offers an Aboriginal Students First Year Experience Program, and includes a Welcome Week Powwow in their orientation events. First-year students at the University of Victoria who have a disability are invited to "Coffeehouse Connections," relaxed sessions where they can meet other students with a disability and learn about how the University can support their success. The University of Toronto's Office of LGBTQ Resources and Programs provides orientation activities and events for lesbian, gay, bisexual, transgender, and queer students. Programs are also being designed to reach out to those who may be part of the student's support network, such as parents and other family members.

## Parent/Family Orientation Programs

Increasingly, parents and other family members are exerting influence on the lives of students and are expressing greater interest in the post-secondary institutions where they study. Acknowledging that parents and family members also experience transitions as the students in their families enter and progress through post-secondary study, family orientation programs are beginning to appear at many institutions. The University of Northern British Columbia, for example, offers a parent and family orientation day concurrent with student orientation activities. Mount Royal College and Sir Wilfred Grenfell College also offer parent orientation sessions. Other institutions have created websites to provide information to parents, a strategy employed more and more to capitalize on the accessibility new technologies offer.

## Internet Orientation

One of the most significant forces shaping best practices in orientation is the explosive growth of the Internet, particularly in combination with students' affinity for and reliance upon its use as a social and learning tool. The University of Guelph's ST@RT Online offers students the opportunity, over the summer months preceding their first academic term, to progressively explore time-sensitive issues using interactive Web tools such as video-streaming, surveys, moderated chat rooms, message boards, and pod casts. Once students begin their studies, they can access similar Web-based tools on topics that address typical first-year student concerns and challenges. The immediate success on campus of Web-based social network programs, such as Facebook, MySpace, and Friendster, further underscores the pervasive presence of these tools in students' lives and the potential they have for effecting the transition to college or university. Computer-mediated environments are here to stay in higher education and will continue to serve an important role in teaching and connecting to students.

## PROFESSIONALIZATION OF ORIENTATION

With the emergence of current models of orientation services at colleges and universities comes an expectation for professional personnel who are adept at planning large-scale activities, who understand the psychosocial and cognitive dynamics of students in transition, and who are capable of implementing strategies that support students' learning experiences. Advanced skills in marketing, communication, and human resources are needed to design and target information and experiences appropriately. The leadership to achieve this often requires advanced formal professional preparation such as that acquired in a master's degree in student affairs or a related field. Although few in Canadian colleges and universities have attained such credentials, there is a growing library of resources and materials that can support the training and preparation of orientation staff.

A pioneering and premier source for best practices to support first-year students is the National Resource Center for the Freshman Year Experience, established by John Gardner and associates at the University of South Carolina in 1982. Recently renamed the National Resource Center for the First-Year Experience and Students in Transition, its mission proposes "to support and advance efforts to improve student learning and transitions into and through higher education" (National Resource Center for the First-Year Experience and Students in Transition).

Despite these initiatives toward better information and services there remains a dearth of published research on the needs of entering students, or the experience of first-year students in Canadian post-secondary institutions. The single publication issued in the past decade on the topic of Canadian orientation services is *From Best Intentions to Best Practices: The First-Year Experience in Canadian Post-Secondary Education* (Gilbert, et al. 1997) Although an important resource, this monograph is already somewhat dated. Clearly, more current work is warranted.

Government agencies, such as the Canada Millennium Scholarship Foundation, have published the rare recent study that illuminates a specific aspect of the first-year student experience. Stakeholder groups, like the Association of Universities and Colleges of Canada (AUCC), or jurisdictional institutional collectives, such as The University Presidents' Council of British Columbia, have occasionally conducted further analyses of and shared publicly data on government demographics or institutional characteristics. The vast majority of this research has been undertaken to predict enrolment and funding needs.

To better understand the needs and experiences of diverse target groups of entering and first-year students, some institutions have conducted their own research to inform their orientation activities. Largely unpublished, this research is best accessed through participation in professional association activities, such as the Canadian Association of College and University Student Services (CACUSS) annual conference where information is freely shared.

Internationally there are other sources that can be helpful in the Canadian context, but it is important that cultural and institutional differences be considered in their application. For example, the *Journal of the First-Year Experience and Students in Transition* is published bi-annually by the National

Resource Center for the First-Year Experience and Students in Transition at the University of South Carolina. The Center also offers monographs on many topics related to orientation. The USA-based National Orientation Directors Association (NODA) publishes *The Journal of College Orientation and Transition* and provides excellent resources related to the field. NODA also maintains a data bank of its three-year survey of member institutions that compiles information on orientation structures, resources, and strategies at over 400 institutions.

There is great opportunity to conduct research that would benefit orientation services, and thus the lives of many college and university students in Canada. If only to make the transition easier, such research would be commendable. The fact that other outcomes would result from the findings makes the research valuable, as well.

## ISSUES AND CHALLENGES

A scan of the broader terrain in which orientation services are delivered suggests that there are several emerging and persistent issues that bear significant implications for policy and practice. The changing youth culture, shifting demographics, and issues of risk management will all continue to influence the provision of orientation to higher education in the future.

### Changing Youth Culture

The name *Millennials* (Howe and Strauss 2000), coined to describe the generation coming of age at the turn of the twenty-first century, has begun to creep into the Canadian lexicon, signalling recognition that the generation now filling our classrooms and residences is indeed different. Beloit College's annual "Class of" Mindset List® (Beloit College) offers a sometimes poignant reminder of the changing perspectives of first-year students. Regardless of the lens through which youth are viewed, there are clearly significant cultural shifts that will continue to have implications for their orientation to post-secondary education in Canada.

According to Howe and Strauss (2000), Millennials are co-operative team players, accept authority and follow rules, have some very specific health-related concerns, are technologically savvy, and have high expectations for their own achievements. Products of parents who scooped up baby monitors and enrolled their children in lessons and sports programs in record numbers, the authors suggest that this is the most watched-over generation in recent history and most have had very structured childhoods. Add to this that they have been made to feel special and their parents have expected a lot of them, the result is a dutiful but high maintenance lot of young people entering the academy. Although the characterization of the

Millennials resonates for many, it has been suggested that the assumption that Canadian culture is similar to the culture of the United States from which the Millennial Generation description has emerged is somewhat flawed, inasmuch as Canadian youth are products of a very different culture that emphasizes different social values.

Since 1983, pollster Environics Research has tracked the evolution of Canadian social values, interviewing more than 45,000 Canadians about their views of the world (Adams 1997). On the basis of the data collected over the years, Michael Adams, Environics founder and author, contends that there are six distinct "tribes" represented among the Generation X group of Canadians between the ages of fifteen and thirty-three, each characterized by the degree to which its members are inner-directed or other-directed, and prefer conformity and exclusion or ideals and individualism (Adams 1997, 2000). Adams and his colleagues have observed an increasing trend toward inner-directedness and individuality, noting that the fastest growing tribes of Generation X are the "New Aquarians," defined by values that embrace adaptability, hedonism, concern for the oppressed and the environment, and contempt for traditional authorities, and the "Autonomous Post-Materialists," who seek freedom and spontaneity. The other groups they describe include the "Aimless Dependents," who emphasize ostentatious consumption and desire for independence, "Security-Seeking Ascetics," who prefer security, simplicity, and deferred gratification; "Social Hedonists," who engage in risk taking, aesthetics, sexual permissiveness, and immediate gratification; and "Thrill Seeking Materialists," for whom money, possessions, recognition, and aesthetics are most important. Other Canadian researchers have also offered differing views of Canadian youth around the turn of the century (Bibby 1995, 2001).

Concomitant with these generational value shifts, students are now immersed in the world of ever-advancing technology. There is no question that the ubiquitous Internet, and technology generally, has also deeply influenced youth culture in recent years, and vice versa. Today students may be more inclined to ICQ ("I Seek You" – the largest multilingual community on the Web) someone in the next room to ask them to turn down their stereo than to get up to do so in person. Email has all but replaced "snail mail," and an email dialect is evolving: there is a good chance that, while most students understand the email short-form FOTFLMAO (falling on the floor laughing my ass off), many of their parents – along with university administrators and faculty – may not. Many courses are delivered entirely via the Internet, and even those with regular lectures are often accompanied by or partially delivered on an Internet-based platform. The Internet has become a legitimate research source, and literature in electronic format is increasingly available. With all of this, there is less and less motivation for students to leave their rooms to pursue academic tasks.

Cellphones and personal electronic devices abound, and with built-in cameras and text messaging, there is almost nowhere that students cannot be in touch with friends and family if they choose to be.

As always, characteristics of the student body continue to change. Involving students in program planning and delivery is one obvious and highly effective way to help assure that orientation is relevant and uses institutional resources wisely. All students, but perhaps most notably student leaders, residence life advisors, peer advisors, program volunteers, and the like, have a great deal of insight to offer to advisory and planning groups by serving as staff, co-op students, interns, and volunteers. Student surveys, whether in-house or with comparative benchmarks (such as the Canadian Undergraduate Survey Consortium, a group of approximately twenty universities across Canada that conducts an annual student survey), can also help paint the bigger picture of the student experience. Whether fueled by social forces, the influence of parents, or the rapid evolution of technology, it is crucial that programs and services keep pace with students in order to do the best job of orienting them to post-secondary life and study.

### Shifting Demographics

As the first decade of this century comes to a close, the effect of the so-called "echo baby boom" is reverberating through post-secondary institutions in Canada, though not in ways first predicted. Worry about elimination of the fifth year of high school in Ontario, Canada's most populous province and home to the greatest number of post-secondary institutions in the country, did not persist as anticipated, and there is currently a great deal of competition across the country to fill the seats created to accommodate students who did not materialize. Successful orientation programs will contribute to an institution's market position, especially as the cohort of eager students seeking post-secondary education diminishes.

One hopeful sign for long-term enrolment is an anticipated influx of new and older students seeking opportunities for "lifelong learning." The Association of Universities and Colleges of Canada predicts that population growth and increasing participation rates will produce as many as 200,000 more post-secondary students by 2011 (AUCC 2001). As the baby boomers march toward retirement and the workforce shrinks, employer training and education requirements and incentives are expected to send more adults back to school, supported by increased recognition of the value of education across the lifespan and improved accessibility. For example, Royal Roads University, created in the mid-1990s, focuses exclusively on applied and professional programs for people who want to advance in the workplace – the current average age of a Royal Roads University student is forty years. Orientation for these students will need to address the challenges of balancing work, family, and community commitments with learning pursuits. "Re-orientation" might better describe helping these adults with their transition to post-secondary studies, keeping in mind that it may have been a long time since they have read academic literature or submitted an assignment to be graded by another adult.

## Performance Indicators and Accountability

The call for public accountability has become more insistent across Canada; in response, performance indicators are increasingly being applied to post-secondary institutions. In most jurisdictions, institutional rankings can determine the share of the government pie that a college or university garners. Retention and employment after graduation are the most commonly applied indicators, but there is movement to expand to the use of satisfaction indicators, such as the National Survey of Student Engagement (NSSE) assessment now being applied in Ontario. Ongoing assessment strategies can not only improve the quality of orientation offerings but also make the link between student participation in orientation and the outcomes that the holders of government purse strings desire.

## Risk Management

Finally, exposure to risk – or more plainly put, "threat of a law suit" – is becoming a critical consideration in the planning and implementation of orientation services. Despite the moral obligation to account for the physical and psychological safety of participants in any institution-sponsored activity, there is real and present danger of costly legal action in today's increasingly litigious climate. Inclusive activities and communications that respect human rights and equality are fundamental requirements of all orientation activities, and all activities must clearly demonstrate that the institution upholds its duty-of-care responsibilities, especially if alcohol is involved.

## CONCLUSION

The range and variety of post-secondary education settings in Canada, coupled with an increasingly diverse student population, suggest that there can be no single uniform approach to orienting students on today's campuses. Student and institutional needs influence the goals and objectives of orientation at each institution. What is important in supporting a student entering a private or public college, university-college, or university may differ, depending upon the length of program, the institutional mandate, and other factors. In addition to traditional educational programs where students attend lectures and read texts, the contexts in which learning occurs is becoming increasingly complex as more and more post-secondary programs are offered entirely online or through blended models. Lastly, the residential character of an institution can also be important, as orienting and supporting first-year students at a highly residential institution is very different than at an institution with no on-campus housing. The key to designing and implementing effective orientation services that support student success lies in an informed understanding of the institutional mission and the students it serves.

# 6

# Housing and Residence Life

HEATHER LANE VETERE

Most colleges and universities in Canada have some form of residence housing available for students coming to study on their campuses. Housing on campus provides students with an introduction to, and a path to find, their place within the campus community. It is also, obviously, a convenient option for students outside the immediate vicinity of the campus who require accommodation during their studies. There are over 75 universities and 140 colleges in Canada, and at the universities alone, over 100,000 students live on campus each academic year.

Institutions have always needed to provide housing for students travelling some distance from their permanent homes to study full-time. Since 1990, more and more institutions, recognizing the recruitment value and the importance of a residence experience for students, have established enough residence space to house every student for at least one year regardless of the location of their permanent residence.

Canadian residence halls range in age and style from traditional ivy-covered architecture of the 1800s with wide double-loaded corridors, original wood mouldings, high ceilings, and stately common rooms to new modern townhouse- and apartment-style buildings with clean modern lines and functional materials. Most of the residence buildings in Canada are owned and operated by the institutions themselves, but some are run by private housing companies or community agencies, such as religious or cultural organizations that have a connection to the specific institution for the purpose of housing its students.

Residence operations that are owned and operated by a college or university can follow one of three general administrative reporting structures. In some institutions, such as the University of British Columbia and the University of Guelph, the housing function reports through the vice-president or associate vice-president(student affairs or student services) at the institution. At some institutions, such as the University of Saskatchewan and the

University of Western Ontario, the housing operations report through the vice-president (finance, administration or operations) along with other ancillary operations such as food services, retail operations, and parking. A third possible model has housing reporting jointly with all but the residence life components through the vice-president (administration) and the residence life staff and programs reporting to the vice-president (student affairs). Such a structure is in place at Victoria University (in the University of Toronto).

One organizational structure might be preferable to another, but in addressing the merits of each, Upcraft (1994, 201) stated:

> Is there an 'ideal' way to organize and administer residence halls? The answer to that question is a resounding 'no' because of the contextual choices and organizational choices that are unique to each institution. The bottom line, however, is that institutions that are committed to quality must develop residence halls that are efficiently managed, affordable, safe, and well-maintained, and most important, that contribute to the personal and academic development of all residents.

This chapter offers an overview of housing and residence life in Canada's post-secondary education system, with specific attention to the contributions of the housing experience to student success. Following a summary review of the basic functions of housing and residence life, the chapter addresses the professionalization of the field, hallmarks a few resources for understanding the purposes and practices of housing and residence life, and concludes with observations on continuing and future challenges.

## ESSENTIAL FUNCTIONS IN STUDENT HOUSING

The portfolio of a student housing and residence director includes components related to the facilities of the system, as well as the various personnel who function within them in service of the residents. Each component is framed within the context of its own unique challenges and issues that must be accommodated and integrated at the department level for overall mission success.

### Facility Operations

Unlike many other areas within student services, housing is a very capital-intensive operation, due to the extensive financial commitment implied in the operation and maintenance of buildings. Costs associated with mortgages and other debt servicing; ongoing building operations, in the form of utilities; custodial services; and preventative maintenance can make up the largest percentage of operating expenses of a typical housing budget. Given the age of many residence buildings on Canadian campuses and the hard wear they endure, many campuses have faced and continue to face an increasing deferred maintenance problem that requires significant investment into capital renovations and replacement projects.

Ensuring that buildings remain functional, aesthetically pleasing, in tune with new students' needs and expectations, safe and secure, and able to support expanding technological infrastructure, along with the costs outlined above, makes clear the capital-intensive nature of housing operations and the financial challenges inherent in running a housing operation. Implications of this part of its mission are underscored in Winston, Anchors, and Associates (1993, 45):

> Adequate personnel and resources must be available and utilized to ensure that the physical facilities are safe, comfortable, clean, reasonably esthetically agreeable, and adequately maintained. Until the basic needs are satisfied neither the staff nor the students can be expected to address 'higher-order' concerns seriously.

The facilities must be attended to adequately in order to ensure that the focus can be placed on other aspects of the student experience.

## Residence Life

When offering housing to students, the residence life component of a college or university operation is what makes the institution more than just a landlord. Other than convenience, the residence life program provides a value-added benefit for students living on campus versus those living in a rented room or apartment off campus. Residence life programs should be designed to build community in the residence halls and provide and/or support learning opportunities that promote student development.

Through the work of residence life staff, both professional (residence life managers and coordinators) and paraprofessional (resident and community assistants, and dons), as well as residence hall student councils, a well-structured residence life program strives to create a sense of community where residents feel at home and in turn feel a sense of connection to the institution and to the larger campus community. Much of this effort to build community is focused on programming that includes both social and educational activities. The social programming that takes place in residence halls helps students meet other students, make friends, and develop a sense of belonging and pride in their residence floor, house, hall, or school.

There is also a great deal of educational programming conducted every year in Canadian residence halls. These programs are intended to raise awareness, challenge thinking, promote development, address problems, or deepen students' exposure to or understanding of an endless array of topics, such as diversity, the environment, hate crimes, eating disorders, healthy sexuality, career planning, or study skills. Residence life is home as well to any number of "enriched" or "specialized" programs, such as learning communities, living/learning centres, and theme houses, offered as options in support of academic learning and overall development. Examples of such programs include the University of Guelph's Residence Learning Communities, the University of Alberta's International House, and the Focused Interest Floors at the University of Western Ontario.

Another substantial component of the residence life program at most Canadian colleges and universities is the development and enforcement of student behaviour codes. While often complex and requiring a great deal of staff time and energy, this function is, quite simply: determining the rules and policies, communicating expectations and consequences to students clearly, and applying the consequences when violations occur (See chapter 8). Residence life staff address a whole range of behaviours in the course of their work, from simple noise complaints to drug and alcohol violations, vandalism, harassment, and violence.

The residence life program also provides exceptional opportunities for students to develop leadership skills. Through the training, advice, and support provided by professional staff in housing, there is a myriad of leadership opportunities for students in Canadian residence halls, as residence assistants or dons, programmers, desk and security staff, elected residence hall executive and council members, as well as in more informal roles.

Another important function of residence life is crisis response. Staff are expected not only to respond to a great variety of crises when they occur but also to support students or communities in crisis and to make referrals to other campus and community services. In the course of an academic year, crises can include physical or sexual assault, self-harming behaviour, suicidal threats and attempts, broken relationships, family tragedies, medical emergencies, eating disorders, hate crimes, and even the death of a community member. Since housing is a 24-hour operation, residence life staff are often the first to see signs of problems, to respond to immediate crises, or to help a student through a particularly rough patch.

Community building, activity programming, policy development and education, and student leadership development are all proactive initiatives at the core of what residence life entails. A great deal of staff time and energy are also spent on more reactive activities such as policy enforcement and crisis response.

## Other Functional Areas

In addition to facilities and residence life, there are a number of other important areas that are essential to most housing operations. While the following may not be an exhaustive list, it touches on the most common additional areas found in Canadian college and university housing departments.

## RESIDENCE ADMISSIONS AND ROOM ASSIGNMENTS

Depending on the size of the housing operation, residence admissions and room assignments can be a very complex set of services. Staff, processes, specialized databases, and connections with the institution's admissions office, liaison and recruitment activities, services for students with disabilities, international student services, and other campus offices are all necessary for the efficient and effective functioning of this important service. This area of the housing operation might be responsible for all or some of a number of activities such as producing marketing and recruitment information about housing, processing residence applications and deposits, matching roommates, doing room assignments, maintaining an accurate database and lists of resident information, providing occupancy statistics, managing room transfers, handling contract cancellations, minimizing vacancies through careful projections and planning, and developing and maintaining waitlists during times of higher demand for residence space.

## TELECOMMUNICATIONS AND INFORMATION TECHNOLOGY

Residence students expect access to telephones, television, and high-speed and/or wireless Internet connections in their rooms. While some housing operations leave it to students to make arrangements with outside vendors within the community for telephone and television service, most at least include basic telephone service in the room fees. Most institutions also provide high-speed Internet access and/or wireless capabilities in all residence rooms and other areas of the building, either as part of the room fees or as an additional charge. Of course, providing increased telecommunications and information technology within residence rooms requires infrastructure, support staff, billing procedures, and acceptable use policies, all of which have become standard components of most housing operations across Canada.

## FOOD SERVICES

As long as students are living in residence halls that do not include extensive cooking facilities, food outlets and cafeterias will be needed. At many institutions, the food services department is part of the housing operation; at others, it is separate. Some institutions (such as the University of Guelph) run their own food service, while many others (such as Queen's University and Simon Fraser University) outsource the operation to an external institutional food service provider. Either way, when students are required to purchase a meal plan, the quality and flexibility of the food service can have a significant impact on the student experience in residence.

CONFERENCE AND HOSTEL HOUSING

Most institutions are able to make use of vacant residence halls in the summer to provide short-term housing to visitors to campus, and conference groups. Some also maintain a number of spaces throughout the year for rental as hotel rooms to campus visitors. These operations are usually only viable if they can provide additional income for the operation.

FAMILY HOUSING AND GRADUATE HOUSING

Many institutions, universities in particular, manage housing facilities dedicated to meeting the housing needs of student families (e.g., couples, couples with children, and single-parent families) and of single graduate students. These are usually self-contained apartment or townhouse units leased for a twelve-month term. While there are extensive community support programs in place at some institutions, the family housing and graduate housing arrangement between the student and the housing department often more closely resembles a landlord-tenant relationship rather than that found in a traditional residence hall. For the purposes of this chapter, the following section on student success focuses on more traditional single student undergraduate residence operations.

## HOUSING, RESIDENCE LIFE, AND STUDENT SUCCESS

Much has been written in the USA student affairs literature about the impact of residence living on students and their development and success. In a review of the empirical research in this area, Pascarella and Terenzini (1991, 611) described the positive links that come from living in residence: "increases in aesthetic, cultural and intellectual values; a liberalizing of social, political, and religious values and attitudes; increases in self-concept, intellectual orientation, autonomy, and independence; gains in tolerance, empathy, and ability to relate to others; persistence in college; and bachelor's degree attainment." Such outcomes are certainly measures of a successful higher education experience.

The specific influence of housing and residence life on student success can be understood in terms of four aspects of the post-secondary experience: convenience and access, retention, educational programming, and leadership and life skills. These are addressed here with a focus on how residence services and housing contributes to each of them.

### Convenience and Access

Living in residence gives many students their introduction to the college or university community and surrounds them with peers sharing the same experience, while senior students, serving as residence life staff or orientation volunteers who can answer questions, give directions and make referrals.

The residence hall provides a convenient home base, with built-in peer support, and close proximity to classes and recreation, making it easier for students to access all that is available on their campus. Convenience and access to support services associated with on-campus living can also assist residents by removing some of the common stressors that might distract them from their academic responsibilities.

## Retention

Research over the years has shown that retention after first year is higher for students who live on campus compared to their off-campus peers. "Students who live in residence halls consistently persist and graduate at significantly higher rates than students who have not had this experience" (Pascarella, Terenzini, and Blimling 1994, 27). The social support network, access to services, and exposure to involvement and leadership opportunities all influence this outcome. Furthermore, Winston, Anchors, and Associates (1993, 48) stated that, "the more involved students are in the collegiate experience, the more likely they are to be satisfied with the collegiate experience and the more likely they are to persist to graduation." Living in residence clearly advantages students in their adjustment and matriculation to the post-secondary experience.

## Educational Programming

A number of areas are the usual foci of programming activities in residence. While residence living lends itself well to community building and social and recreational activities for students, there is also great potential for extensive educational experiences to enhance their learning environment. "Powerful learning occurs in situations where people come to know each other as friends ... college [university]-operated residence halls provide ready-made communities that can have major impact on students" (Chickering and Reisser 1993, 399). Through films, workshops, activities, games, guest speakers, contests, field trips, and poster campaigns, the educational experience of residence students at the institution can be enhanced significantly.

Programming is also done in residence halls to raise awareness about more immediate issues affecting students, such as alcohol and substance abuse, sexual assault, STDs, eating disorders, depression, and suicide. Awareness programming also includes issues and societal concerns such as sexual diversity and homophobia, racism and hate crimes, poverty and homelessness, environmental responsibility and sustainability, and other current world challenges.

Furthermore, residence life staff can have a direct impact on student success through sponsored workshops on time management, study skills, overcoming procrastination, and managing exam stress. Efforts are also made, for example, to connect students with others in the same academic programs to form study groups. In addition, some Canadian universities have created more formal academic support communities in residence. These may take the form of living learning centres, based around a specific theme such as creative arts, international issues, or the environment, or learning communities where all the residents of a certain area share courses in common and have a senior student and/or faculty mentor. According to Schroeder (1994, 178), "Research conducted by the Washington Center on a variety of outcomes of model learning community programs indicates that retention, persistence, degree completion and achievement have been substantially enhanced [by them]." Much of the success of such programs can be attributed to the synergy of their purposes and resources.

The most recent trend on Canadian campuses, another feature of the residence life program offering, is the increased focus on good citizenship and service learning. Programs promoting civic responsibility, the political process, fundraising activities, community service projects, and commitment to influencing one's own community in a positive way have all added significantly to educational opportunities for students. Schroeder (1994, 180) suggested that institutions should form learning communities, "on the basis of supporting ongoing service projects that reflect the collective commitment of residents to altruism, social justice and community service." Again, such opportunities align well with the goals of post-secondary learning.

### Leadership and Life Skills

The very nature of residence living, with many students from diverse backgrounds expressing different ideas, lifestyles, and expectations living together, provides a ready-made laboratory for the learning of important life skills that have the potential to significantly impact students' future interpersonal relationships and career successes. Students are forced – by the situations they encounter, the activities of those with whom they share space, the issues they confront, or the intervention of the residence life staff – to face their abilities to function interpersonally on many levels. Interacting in a close community of peers, with the appropriate support from staff, provides the opportunity for students to learn and teach communication skills, mediation, conflict resolution, negotiation, personal responsibility, independence, and other important life skills. There are also opportunities for students to learn compassion, respect for others, tolerance, acceptance of diversity, and the impact they can have on a community.

Beyond life skills, leadership opportunities also help promote student success through involvement and co-curricular learning. Residence life staff and elected residence executive and council members have the opportunity to develop leadership skills and experience in the course of their day-to-day responsibilities, during extensive pre- and in-service training programs, and through the advice and mentoring of professional housing services staff. Komives (1994, 238) suggested that residence life should aim to teach all students about leadership through civic responsibility: "The civic learning experience should enable each resident to say, 'I know I can make a difference in my community and I have an obligation to be involved and active in our shared vision for the greater good.'"

In summary, the residence experience contributes greatly to the success of students, particularly in the areas of retention, educational programming, life skills and leadership opportunities. Such contributions to student success are possible despite the ongoing challenges and complexity inherent in the operation of student housing programs.

## PROFESSIONALIZING HOUSING AND RESIDENCE LIFE

Student housing and residence life is a very diverse and complex function. It requires professional managers with varying skills and knowledge bases, including experts in finance, facilities, student development, crisis intervention, and marketing. Finding individuals who are experts in all of these areas is unlikely, but leaders (e.g., senior managers or directors) of such organizations should have knowledge and experience in human resources, business and finance, and student development and services. Residence life professionals in particular are generally expected to have some graduate-level education in counselling or student development.

Professional development for those who work in housing and residence life is normally offered through organizations such as the mainly USA-based Association of College and University Housing Officers – International (ACUHO-I). This association publishes a magazine called *Talking Stick* as well as *The Journal of College and University Student Housing*. It also holds a large integrated annual conference and smaller annual conferences and workshops focusing on topics such as information technology, apartments, conferences, and marketing. ACUHO-I also offers joint programs with the Association of Physical Plant Administrators (APPA) to serve the professional development needs of facilities managers who have responsibility for residence buildings.

There are a number of regional housing-oriented organizations affiliated with ACUHO-I that include Canadian provinces in their membership mandate, but there is no wholly Canadian housing professional organization. The Ontario Association of College and University Housing Officers (OACUHO) sponsors an annual conference in May and draws attendees and members from across Canada.

Student housing and residence life can be considered a microcosm of all student services, given its 24/7 nature and the fact that students live their lives in residence, where all their academic, health, recreational, psychological, social, and leadership issues become part of their experience and that of their community. Many of the hallmark publications and resources in student services can be found on the bookshelves of housing professionals. There are, however, three books that are principal compilations of housing and residence life information and research: *Student Housing and Residence Life: A Handbook for Professionals Committed to Student Development Goals* (Winston, Anchors, and Associates 1993), *Realizing the Educational Potential of Residence Halls* (Schroeder, Mable, and Associates 1994), and *Residence Life and the New Student Experience* (3rd edition)(Zeller 2008). Each is a very useful resource for those beginning a career in student housing and residence life; together, they are essential references for professionals in this field.

## ISSUES AND CHALLENGES

As colleges and universities in Canada move forward, two general areas of the housing operations will continue to compete for resources and administrative attention and energy: (a) residence life, including educational and developmental programs, and (b) facilities management, with all of its challenging expenses. The key to success has been and will continue to be finding an appropriate operational and financial balance between the two – in particular, ensuring that the educational role is not overshadowed in light of some of the following facility-related issues.

First, an aging infrastructure and significant demands and expenses of deferred maintenance problems plague many Canadian campuses. Many of the major components of buildings constructed thirty or more years ago, such as roofing, heating and ventilation, plumbing, and electrical systems are reaching the end of their lifecycle. Repair and replacement costs are substantial. Related to this is the tendency for deficiencies in facilities, rather than programs, to be more immediately noticeable to students and their parents, especially in their role as consumers. This raises serious concerns about potentially negative impressions we might be creating among them.

Second is the challenge of increasing numbers of students, unaccustomed to sharing rooms, who come with expectations of more personal space and privacy than many of our facilities allow. Many institutions house students in traditional-style residence buildings that have mainly double rooms and large shared washrooms. A lot of our students have never had the experience of sharing a room and struggle with the issues that result from communal living; that can be a challenge for the staff in the community.

Third, many new students express a preference for apartment- or townhouse-style accommodations when residence life staff believe that traditional-style halls are more conducive to community building and the promotion of learning and development. This potential disconnection between student-consumer desires and the purposes and promises of residence life bodes a difficult balance in the future for campus housing. Efforts both to market to students the benefit of traditional-style residence halls and to build community and reach students in suite-style accommodation will become increasingly important.

Housing professionals need to address these challenges as they plan for buildings sufficient to meet the needs and expectations of students ten and twenty years from now. They will always be expected to first provide safe, well-maintained, and comfortable facilities so that they and their students can focus energy on student learning and student success.

Many of the most pressing issues housing and residence life professionals encounter in their work have been challenges for many years – and will continue to be so as each new generation of students moves into residence halls with the same excitement, anxiety, promise, motivation, and defiance as the preceding group. Staff will need to keep looking for effective ways to address alcohol abuse and its resulting behaviours. Issues of sexuality, that is maintaining health, setting personal limits, exploring values, respecting partners, and accepting diversity, will remain persistent topics for future awareness campaigns and educational programming. Professionals will continue to respond to eating disorders, suicidal crises, self-harming, and mental health issues. They will continue to find ways to meet increasingly complex accommodation requests due to disabilities, health issues, and special needs, and to house students struggling with identity concerns, who may not be prepared to manage their new independence, may lack coping skills, and may behave in ways that reflect a seemingly growing incivility in the larger society. In responding to these issues, residence life professionals will require close and effective partnerships with other departments on campus, such as health services, counselling units, services for students with disabilities, and security services or campus police.

Ultimately, student services personnel who attend to these functions will need to ask whether housing and residence programs fit well within the educational mission of their college or university. In Schroeder, Mable, and Associates (1994, 14) the authors offered four objectives as a framework for "residence halls committed to student learning":

- Promoting growth and development of students as whole persons with coherent views of knowledge, life, integrity, and intellectual and social perspectives.
- Constructing a residence hall curriculum that teaches students responsibility, altruism, aspiration, persistence, empathy, ethics, and leadership – along with fluency in answering the questions, "Who am I?" and "What will I be?"

- Emphasizing skills that challenge a student's ability to use knowledge in work and leisure; critical thinking and interpersonal skills, as well as technical skills; teamwork abilities; flexibility; and creative, cognitive and caring attitudes.
- Creating environments that celebrate diversity by bringing students together in a community where differences are respected, but where there is a common goal to create learning.

Such guiding principles are essential the work of housing and residence life professionals since, along with addressing facilities challenges, the focus of this work should be the promotion and support of student learning and student success.

## CONCLUSION

Housing and residence life is a highly complex area within student services. It includes stewardship and management of finances and facilities, assisting with recruitment, and serving the educational mandate of the institution. It is a 24-hour operation that requires attention to a variety of crises and behavioural issues. The role that housing and residence life can play in helping students to connect with one another, the institution, and its services is undisputed. If housing professionals are to be successful in managing a residence operation, they must not lose sight of the potential of the residence experience to contribute to student success. Finances, facilities, all aspects of the operation should ultimately be in service of the residence life program that is focused on the student experience, student leadership, and education and community development, which significantly influence student retention and enrich a student's college or university experience.

# 7

# Student Leadership, Involvement, and Service Learning

## NONA ROBINSON

Canadian institutions are fortunate to have many passionate, involved, and effective student leaders who take an active role in institutional governance, service delivery, and advocacy. Many are also involved in community service work and social change. This legacy has evolved in Canadian higher education in ways that are very different from other systems (e.g., United States), although the genesis for its current state is rooted in the 1960s era of student activism. It was during this movement that student leaders in Canada pressed for greater representation in university governance (Knopf 1960; McGrath 1970; Morison 1970) and were able to obtain seats on boards of governors and academic senates. Over time this led to collaborative arrangements with their college and university administrations, achieving significant partnership in the development and implementation of institutional policies and practices, especially in student services.

Today, student leaders are likely to be included at all levels of institutional governance – they comprise 9 per cent of the members of university boards of governors (Jones and Skolnik 1997) and 17 per cent of academic senates (Jones 2002) – and are routinely included on other university decision-making bodies such as search committees and strategic planning groups. Depending upon agreements with the administration, they also often play oversight roles in institutional activities, the management of non-academic fees, and the assignment of campus space and facilities. In all, student leaders in Canadian colleges and universities hold a prominent position in the affairs of post-secondary education, exerting their influence primarily through campus-based student associations, national student organizations, and various community leadership and service opportunities. This chapter offers an overview of these domains of student leadership, involvement, and service learning in Canadian higher education, including a review of these principal mechanisms of student engagement and some of the initiatives that are emerging out of the recent increasing involvement of student services professionals.

## STUDENT ASSOCIATIONS AND GOVERNANCE

One of the notable facets of student life in Canadian colleges and universities is the high degree of responsibility held by central student associations for service provision, student life programming, and advocacy. All public universities have central student associations/unions, both undergraduate and graduate, that collect fees from students in order to provide services. The scope varies from institution to institution, with some focusing on service delivery and some on advocacy. Often, student associations are responsible for the management of other student groups, such as clubs or academic student associations, and may also transfer fees or dedicate funding to them. In a Canadian survey of one hundred university and community college student associations, Jones (1995) found that membership fees generate average annual revenues of near $400,000 (adjusting for inflation). Student associations typically employ full- and part-time staff (averaging seven full-time and thirty-nine part-time), such as general managers, student advisors, health plan administrators, social programmers, and so on. Although they fulfill a variety of roles, student politicians regard their monitoring and influencing of institutional policies as highest priorities, closely followed by helping students through institutional bureaucracies, monitoring provincial policies, and providing students with information about the work of the organization. They also organize social activities, fund student groups and clubs, provide information about institutional policies, and offer academic and non-academic services.

Activities and services provided by student associations are numerous (Robinson 2003a) and, in many cases, could be considered similar to the purview of student affairs. These activities can be loosely divided into three categories: (a) student life services, (b) retail service operations, and (c) advocacy/equity services. *Student life services* are those that support the day-to-day activities of students beyond the classroom, such as orientation, student handbooks, club recognition and funding, peer support programs, events programming, spirit teams, and student union building management. *Retail service operations* attend to students' sundry and personal needs through bookstores, variety stores, copy centres, food services, and campus pubs. A number of campuses in Canada also have active student co-ops, primarily organized around housing, but also in some cases around bookstores and food or retail operations. Finally, *advocacy/equity services* range from those targeting groups of students, like centres for women, Aboriginal students, those with disabilities, international students, mature students, and lesbian, gay, bisexual, or transgender students, to those addressing the needs of individual students, such as information centres or call lines, health and dental plans, legal aid, walk-home foot patrols, financial aid or bursaries, day care, exam databases, transit passes, human rights, and academic and judicial advocacy.

The total impact of these activities and services is considerable in Canadian colleges and universities, and students who serve in such roles assume major responsibilities for the overall quality of student life in their institutions. However, given the scope of these activities and services, full-time elected student leaders who fill the executive positions of student associations have a daunting task. The usual term of office for student association leaders is one year, running from spring to spring. During the summer they must plan the fall and winter student association activities, as well as rapidly assimilate substantial quantities of information for the committees and issues on which they are expected to represent their constituents. They must also make financial and human resource decisions and assume significant fiduciary responsibility. Furthermore, they must quickly adapt to working in a politicized environment that can easily lead to internal conflict (Robinson 2004).

Student associations are generally legally incorporated and are overseen by elected boards of directors who usually serve one-year terms. Consequently, sufficient training and knowledge relating to their responsibilities is of utmost importance, as repercussions of bad board or executive decisions can reverberate for years. For example, a case involving a fired staff member suing for improper dismissal would likely be heard at a time when the original directors are no longer in office. Thus, creation of clear bylaws, policies, and manuals is paramount in guiding effective and appropriate board decisions (Robinson 2003b).

While the focus of most student associations tends to be local, in their mandate to manage and deliver various activities and services, the importance of their involvement extends beyond the immediate locale of their institutions. In addition to very active local campus-based organizations, students in Canadian higher education are also usually affiliated with various provincial and national groups.

The Canadian Federation of Students (CFS) and its regional chapters lobby federal and provincial politicians in support of educational issues, provide educational resources and issue-oriented campaigns (e.g., date rape prevention) to member schools, and also provide services such as a national health plan and the International Student Identity Card. CFS has a membership of over 500,000 students across Canada, with over eighty student association members (college, undergraduate, and graduate) and several prospective members (Canadian Federation of Students 2008). Each institution collects a per-student membership fee and remits it to the federation; these fees are used to cover services, staff, research, and programs, both nationally and in the provincial/regional offices (CFS 2006). Another national but smaller student association, the Canadian Alliance of Student Associations (CASA), also works to bring post-secondary issues to the attention of the federal government. CASA, founded in 1994, has twenty-three student association members (Canadian Alliance of Student Associations).

In spite of their active presence in Canadian higher education, the role and influence of these local, provincial, and federal student associations has been all but ignored in the literature and certainly merits further attention. At institutions across Canada, students are involved in many different aspects of campus life: student governance, clubs, athletics, and institutional administration, to name a few. The development of student activities and their role in the creation and maintenance of campus community has to a large extent been driven by student groups. While institutional administrators have supported such campus involvement as a means of enhancing the student experience, administrators have generally not, until relatively recently, made it an intentional programming priority.

## STUDENT SERVICES AND LEADERSHIP DEVELOPMENT

Student affairs staff work extensively with elected student leaders and, in some cases, are involved in their transition and training. Thus, student life staff at a growing number of Canadian post-secondary institutions have begun to recognize the importance of leadership training, not only for elected student leaders but to address the expectation that, in addition to achieving important academic outcomes, university graduates will have developed useful leadership skills. Institutional leadership and involvement programs now focus on skills development, leadership theory, and community involvement. This approach has linked leadership to the promotion of civic responsibility, incorporating a focus on equity, consensus-based decision-making, transparency, and accountability. Increasingly, leadership development is being directed toward the general student population, fuelled by an emerging understanding of its value as a co-curricular educational goal.

In general, training programs for both students in leadership positions and students interested in leadership development are becoming more and more common on Canadian post-secondary campuses. Student leaders tend to receive mentorship and training from within their association or group, although there is an increasing desire in many Canadian institutions to deliver student leadership training and to provide students with active learning opportunities in the community. This provides an excellent opportunity to harness and harmonize existing student leadership with institutional mandates related to service. Learning opportunities for elected student leaders are often delivered by central student associations, student affairs staff, and provincial/federal student groups, and typically include many of the following components:

- Organizational skills development:
  financial management
  human resources

    planning and goal setting
    meeting procedures
    team building
    membership development
    public relations
    bylaw/policy development
    service planning and delivery
- Personal skills development:
    time management
    stress reduction
    conflict resolution
    anti-oppression training
    ethical decision-making
    communication skills
- Issues-based training:
    institutional policies and procedures
    institutional governance and committees
    student organization history
    post-secondary student issues
    campaigns and lobbying
    position-based issues and history

Student associations will often manage their own transition training, usually with the assistance of full-time staff. Former student leaders have identified that, while specific position-based training is useful, group "soft skills," such as conflict resolution, consensus-based decision-making, and early goal setting can all be of great assistance in reducing stress throughout the year. There is also the strong perception that for political student leaders, training is best delivered by outgoing leaders, student association staff, or provincial/federal student groups. Given that student issues are the most prominent focus of such programs, it is generally assumed that institutional staff should not deliver the respective training around those issues (Robinson 2004).

An important context for gauging the challenge of working with elected student leadership is the local campus culture. If there has been a history of mistrust and confrontation between the administration and student leaders, then development of collaborative programs, such as leadership training or service delivery, is likely to be difficult. However, cultivating an atmosphere of "controversy with civility" (Astin and Astin 2001) can be of great assistance in mitigating such circumstances. If administrators and student leaders recognize that there are issues on which they can work together, in spite of areas of inevitable disagreement, they can develop a more productive relationship. Student association staff, with their greater longevity, can also be usefully involved in such discussions, although it is important to recognize that they are not the elected representatives of the students.

In light of these needs and challenges, it is important that those responsible for the training of student leaders be informed by the best theories and models of current practices in the field. Serving that end has been an emerging and distinct literature on student leadership programming in higher education. Komives, Lucas, and McMahon (1998) called for a new focus on relational or transformational leadership that emphasizes collaboration and encourages individuals to inspire each other to make change. Accordingly, leaders must be inclusive, ethical, purposeful, and empowering. They can be developed through servant leadership, wherein an individual transforms himself or herself into a leader by focusing on the needs of others. In addition, this approach stresses the importance of this being done within an organization having a common vision and core values. Astin and Astin (2001) suggested that the development of transformational leadership is dependent on both individual and group traits. Individual qualities include self-knowledge, authenticity, empathy, commitment, and competence. Group traits include collaboration, shared purpose, disagreement with respect, and the presence of a learning environment. This approach believes that students can make meaningful change within and outside of their institutions, particularly when they collaborate with other student groups, faculty, and administrative staff; they can also build coalitions, share governance responsibilities, and become major institutional stakeholders.

Increasing numbers of Canadian post-secondary institutions have student affairs staff dedicated to leadership development. For example, at the University of Guelph, the Citizenship and Leadership Education program provides training for emerging leaders with a focus on exploring opportunities, time management, women in leadership, multicultural awareness, leadership for social change, mentoring others, and lifelong leadership. Students also have the opportunity to take a multidisciplinary series of undergraduate courses leading to a Certificate in Leadership, with a focus on social justice issues (University of Guelph 2005). Another example of such efforts is the University of British Columbia's Leadership and Involvement Program, which provides leadership training and conferences for emerging and existing student leaders, peer support programs, and community service projects (University of British Columbia 2005).

Focusing on student leadership development requires the commitment of institutional resources, a goal that may prove especially challenging for smaller institutions with limited student affairs budgets. However, student leadership training could potentially be incorporated into a service-learning model, where academic courses deliver leadership theory in conjunction with students' co-curricular involvement. Universities with faculties of education, social work, political science, Canadian studies, or management that deal with public policy or higher education would be particularly well positioned to deliver this type of academic course. Providing links between involvement and academics can also help alleviate a growing concern related to co-curricular leadership: in a time of increasing costs, students from lower-income backgrounds may not have the time to undertake voluntary unpaid co-curricular activities. Similarly, working or commuting students may have time restrictions. Further inquiry is needed into the factors and influences that contribute to student participation in leadership opportunities in order to guide future programming in this area and shape the development of better policies and practices.

Promotion of student leadership requires not only that institutions understand the barriers to such opportunities but that they also commit resources to the recognition and rewarding of this form of engagement. Institutional recognition of student leadership and involvement helps demonstrate administrative understanding of the rigours and significant learning experiences involved in co-curricular activity. Such recognition is usually in the form of administrative receptions and awards ceremonies, though emerging recognition strategies include co-curricular transcripts, academic credit for leadership training, and student association awards. Perhaps most crucial is an explicit mission statement or senior-level administrative endorsement of the student co-curricular experience.

While involvement and leadership training opportunities have formed the foundation for student services' support of student engagement in Canadian colleges and universities, new venues of participation have begun to appear in co-operation with the academic side of the institution. More specifically, these include opportunities for service learning, experiential education, and civic engagement. Important features of such initiatives have been the collaboration with faculties and a common focus on student learning outcomes. Thus, learning traditionally confined to classrooms and libraries is now being acquired and tested in field-based situations that also lend themselves to the achievement of important community goals.

## SERVICE LEARNING AND STUDENT LEADERSHIP

Service learning is growing rapidly in popularity in other systems (e.g., the USA) and is beginning to appear in Canadian higher education as well. The fundamental concept of this approach is to link academic learning with service to the community. Differing from co-op programs in that the work of student volunteers at non-profit agencies both benefits the organization and relates to academic content (Prentice and Garcia 2000), service learning has been found to improve academic performance and enhance students' values, self-efficacy, leadership, choice of a service career, and plans to participate in service following graduation (Astin et al. 2000). Such involvement is enriched by the opportunity to discuss and reflect on the service experience with other students and faculty and to consider the extent to which the academic material is linked to the service.

Unlike volunteerism, which in its own right can be a positive involvement experience, service learning is linked specifically to an intentional learning opportunity for students. A good service-learning program not only encourages student contribution to the community but it does so in a meaningful and mutually beneficial way that includes an academic learning component and encourages students to think critically about the underlying issues related to community needs. Ideally, service learning leads to an understanding of social justice issues and promotes among students the desire to enact social change.

One of the challenges Canadian institutions face in implementing service learning is acquiring institutional resources and faculty involvement. Bringle and Hatcher (1996) described the growth of service-learning programs as beginning with a core group of individuals – administrators, faculty, students, staff, and community leaders – who perform an initial assessment. Next, awareness of service learning in the institution is expanded beyond the core, a prototype is developed, and resources are assigned. Expanding the program requires further monitoring, evaluation, and recognition. The final stage institutionalizes service learning by including it as part of the university mission and academic programs.

A number of service-learning programs have emerged since 2000 at Canadian post-secondary institutions, generating an informal service-learning network. The Canadian Association of Community Service-Learning (CACSL) received a grant from the J.W. McConnell Family Foundation in 2004 to promote curricular service-learning programs on Canadian campuses. In 2007, the association changed its name to Canadian Alliance for Community Service-Learning (CACSL). This alliance has also launched a website, with a variety of useful resources, where it emphasizes that service learning should be experiential, involve community partners as co-educators, and include a strong reflective component (Canadian Alliance for Community Service-Learning). A shared benefit in such an arrangement is the understanding gained through the hands-on research often generated in these service-learning opportunities.

One advantage to Canada in its early stage of developing campus-based service-learning/civic-engagement programs is the number of best practices examples, publications, websites, and conferences available from other systems that have been active longer in this domain (e.g., the USA). Albeit there are differences in social policy and student leadership practices that need to be taken into account, Canadian institutions would do well to build on these models. For example, most Canadian campuses already have a number of equity-related centres, such as women's centres and ethnic-based groups or service organization clubs with natural ties to the community. Working with these groups provides a natural linkage between interested students, the institution, and the community.

## PROFESSIONALIZATION OF THE FIELD

From observation, many of the student affairs professionals in Canada working in student leadership are themselves former student leaders. Others have worked closely with student associations and student groups. There is little current formal professional preparation in Canada for this work, and as with many student affairs positions, staff members are often self-directed in their learning. Student affairs staff may consider enrolling in graduate degree programs in Canada to enhance their understanding of leadership issues. York University, for example, offers an MBA program in non-profit management, which would be applicable. A number of Canadian universities have programs in higher education studies. There is also the option of studying in the USA; a caveat is that student leadership there is generally quite different from Canada. Considerably more research needs to be done regarding student leadership in this country, and increased participation by student leadership staff in graduate education is one way to enable this.

There are numerous books and web resources addressing aspects of student leadership; it is important to distinguish between personal leadership trait development (e.g., Kouzes and Posner 2005), which focuses on individual students, and transformative leadership development (e.g., Astin and Astin 2001; Komives, Lucas, and McMahon 1998), which promotes the idea of students and student groups actively engaging in social change and social transformation. The former is helpful in personal and career-related student learning; the latter is more appropriate for citizenship and civic development purposes.

Student affairs staff working with student leaders may benefit from other non-student affairs resources, such as management tools, meeting facilitation models, equity awareness, political studies, and so on. There is an extensive literature on non-profit management that meshes well with the organization of many student groups.

Conferences are another source of professional development, both in terms of formal presentations, and for networking with colleagues, who can be of great assistance with professional development ideas. An increased number of sessions on student leadership have been part of the annual meeting of the Canadian Association of College and University Student Services

(CACUSS). Student affairs staff may also wish to attend or present at student-driven conferences or meetings, both provincial and national. As well, there are several American conferences each year related to student leadership.

The CACUSS *Communiqué* is always a good publication to contribute to and to read for reports and ideas on current issues and student services program developments in Canada. Publishing in refereed journals is an option for anyone pursuing academic studies, with numerous suitable publications in the United States (e.g., *Journal of College Student Development*). In Canada, there is the *Canadian Journal of Higher Education*, as well as several smaller journals, such as Ontario Institute for Studies in Education's (OISE) *Higher Education Perspectives*. Given the specialized nature of student leadership development in Canada, student affairs staff will likely need to be creative and self-directed in pursuing professional development.

## ISSUES AND CHALLENGES

The Canadian legacy of student leadership in higher education is a system that serves students well, and that contributes significantly to the quality of the their post-secondary experience. Zuo and Ratsoy (1999), studying student participation in governance at the University of Alberta, found that students' impact was related to their philosophical approach, educational level, maturity, attitudes, and leadership style. The administration's perception of student leaders was also a factor, as was the level of confrontation and the student body's apathy or enthusiasm related to university governance. Student leaders were also affected by details such as meeting schedules and governing body rules. An ongoing question among student associations is whether elected student leaders should assume a middle-of-the-road position, while representing the political opinions of their constituents, or advocate on behalf of the student body from a more activist posture. The latter position has been fuelled in many Canadian institutions by cutbacks to educational funding over the last fifteen years, along with anti-globalization and anti-war sentiments – with varied outcomes. In 1997, for example, students at nine Ontario, one Quebec, and two British Columbia universities occupied administrative offices to protest increases in tuition fees (Hudson et al. 1997). While these actions focused attention on the issue, they did not cause a freeze or decrease in tuition.

Beyond issues relating to approach and perspective, there are other questions that arise from this level of student association service activity. Student associations are funded through student fees, often determined through referendum. Having them provide extensive services reduces the institutional financial obligation for student service provision, placing a larger financial burden for such services on students. In addition, services operated by student associations are vulnerable to concerns of accountability, assessment, and professional delivery. While the climate at Canadian institutions is generally one of tolerance for error as students learn the management process, some services may be deemed by institutional administrations essential to the student experience. It is clear that in service delivery there are advantages to the administration and students working more collaboratively on achieving goals of common interest.

Student affairs staff members are often seen as the bridge between institutions and student associations, including negotiation of civil exchanges around a variety of issues. While elected student leaders have access to senior administrative staff, it is helpful for student affairs staff to establish a solid working relationship with each year's executive. This can involve early meetings to identify areas of common concern and mutual goals, assistance in navigating institutional decision-making, and provision of continuity regarding past decisions and activities.

## CONCLUSION

Student engagement in the workings of Canadian colleges and universities has evolved from a singular focus on select issues and concerns to a full enterprise of service and advocacy that makes significant contributions to the quality of students' experiences, and ultimately, to their degree of success. Through multiple organizations and programs managed by student leaders, student associations in Canadian higher education today provide conduits for much-needed services, as well as opportunities for student achievement within a rubric of potential learning outcomes. It is this involvement that warrants the full attention of student services professionals who are in a position not only to implement student leadership initiatives but also to inform them with the knowledge of best practices and understandings.

# 8

# Student Judicial Affairs and Academic Integrity

DEBORAH EERKES

Student discipline is a system of crime and punishment – at least according to conventional student wisdom: a violation of a rule is inevitably followed by a penalty. Given this assumption, students might have difficulty believing that the system is designed to protect their interests, or that our processes are part of student services. This perception, however, is worth examining more closely both in terms of the students who are sanctioned under the disciplinary processes and the rest who are protected by the policies and procedures.

Whether students misbehave on campus or engage in conduct designed to gain unearned academic advantage, members of the campus community are harmed by those actions. While the consequences are varied, any kind of behaviour that interferes with activities related to teaching, learning, and/or research hinders the institution's ability to fulfill its mandates both to members of its community and to society in general.

In reality, student success is of paramount importance to student judicial affairs professionals, whether dealing with academic or non-academic misconduct. By ensuring that our response is measured, fair, and appropriate, we help equip students who have committed offences to take responsibility for their actions and become productive members of the academic community and Canadian society. At the same time, we strive to create a level playing field for those students who conduct themselves with integrity and respect for the community. In this manner of promoting success both for students who violate codes and for those who abide by them, student judicial affairs provides a student service.

With student success as a focal point, we must ensure that our purposes are clear when addressing student misconduct. For example, disciplinary sanctions under our codes of conduct can serve various – sometimes complementary, sometimes competing – purposes. Sanctions can be used to educate or rehabilitate the offender. They may also have a restorative function for the institution or other injured party. In cases where behaviour has been deemed destructive to the academic mission or general safety of the institution, sanctions may be used to punish or deter. These purposes may be codified to varying degrees in policy, and should be identified to ensure that disciplinary decisions are consistent with the academic mission and conducive to student success. Identifying our purposes in imposing sanctions helps students to better understand both the process and the consequences of their actions.

## ESSENTIAL FUNCTIONS AND SERVICES

The primary goals of student judicial affairs (in terms of both academic and non-academic conduct) are to preserve and maintain the safety of our campuses and the integrity of our scholarship so that the activities of the college or university can unfold as intended. Despite this common purpose, Canadian institutions have developed distinct structures and take a wide variety of approaches. Moreover, views about academic integrity and student judicial affairs can vary as much within as between institutions. In all cases, however, practice should be guided by institutional policies.

While the relationship between the student and the institution was once based on the concept of *in loco parentis*, or the institution standing in for the parents, student protests and ensuing court decisions in the 1960s and 1970s brought an end to the quasi-parental role of post-secondary institutions. Some claim that no clearly defined relationship has emerged in its wake, leaving the role of the college or university loosely defined relative to its students (Hoekema 1994; Dannells 1997). What remains, however, is a complex relationship based on something similar to a contract, in which institutional policy manuals, calendars, handbooks, and other documents lay out the terms and students indicate their agreement by registering in their programs. Under these circumstances, it is important to acknowledge an institution's duty, in addition to legal and contractual obligations, to treat students fairly as well as the role of statutory and administrative law in its student judicial processes (Hannah 1998; Smith 1998).

At one time, non-academic student discipline was the purview of the dean of students (or equivalent) and academic misconduct was handled by professors at the classroom level, but most institutions now have a consistent system for all students. What has been termed "preoccupation with proceduralism" (Dannells 1997, 22) and the increasing involvement of lawyers and courts in college and university processes has likely contributed to this shift in approach. The formalization of processes may also be attributed to issues of risk management, inconsistency of response to student misconduct, and the need to track repeat offenders.

In his collection of case law related to post-secondary students and their institutions, Hannah (1998, 137) noted that the courts have given colleges and universities the authority to regulate student conduct when enforcing their own internal policies. Responsibility for Canadian students lies ultimately with provincial governments that, through legislation, delegate authority for student conduct to the governing body of the institution. Despite provincial variation, a common emphasis on fairness has resulted in many similarities in post-secondary student judicial systems across the country.

Canadian student judicial systems are based on the concept of natural justice. At its core, natural justice comprises the right to be heard and the right to an unbiased decision-maker (Martin 1997). Most institutions have recognized that fundamental fairness includes a series of corollary rights. For example, the right to be heard necessarily requires reasonable notice, reasonable disclosure of the case against the student, and the right for the accused student to be present at a hearing, respond to the charges, and provide evidence. Other rights might include entitlement to an advisor, written reasons for disciplinary decisions, and a timely process.

The majority of Canadian institutions use balance of probabilities in making disciplinary decisions, the same standard of evidence as is used in the civil courts. Balance of probabilities allows a decision-maker to find a student responsible for committing an offence if the available evidence demonstrates that the student is more likely than not to have done so. If the evidence does not tip the balance one way or the other, the charges against the student must be dismissed.

Without exception, Canadian institutions offer processes for appealing disciplinary decisions. Any mistakes or misapplications of procedure at earlier stages of decision-making can be remedied at the appeal level, affording a student one last opportunity to be heard and to respond to the allegations. Only when institutional avenues for appeal are exhausted may a student turn to the courts for judicial review.

The courts have shown deference to institutions' decisions in most cases of judicial review. Because Canadian educational institutions are expected to provide clear policies, along with fair and unbiased procedures (Hannah 1998), the courts are able to simply review the process to ensure that the institution has followed its own policies. Where a college or university is found to be lacking in fair process or where bias against the student was demonstrated, the courts have typically sent the issue back to the institution to be reheard. Only in the very few cases where the courts were convinced that a fair hearing would be impossible within the institution did they impose a decision on the substance of the matter in question (Devine 2006).

While Canadian student judicial systems share many common features, there is remarkable variety in the administrative structures and practices of student judicial affairs. The day-to-day responsibility for addressing academic and non-academic student misconduct depends on the type of offence and the policies of the institution. For example, professors at the University of Lethbridge may impose sanctions for academic dishonesty, but the University of Alberta requires instructors to forward all suspected cases of academic misconduct to the dean of the faculty. The University of Northern British Columbia allows for possible resolution at the instructor level, but has a process in place for deans or directors to address more serious charges. Queen's University refers academic offences to a senate committee for adjudication. Faculty adjudicators at McMaster University make decisions in cases of academic misconduct; Grant MacEwan College follows a similar model, with a tribunal in place for more serious offences. The academic integrity policies at the University of Toronto and Concordia University apply to the entire university community, although violations are adjudicated under different procedures for students, faculty, and staff.

Non-academic conduct procedures likewise vary from institution to institution. For example, York University addresses complaints through local adjudicators, followed by a hearing before a tribunal. The University of Alberta funnels complaints from campus security services to the office of student judicial affairs to be decided by a discipline officer. Queen's University features a unique student-administered system for non-academic offences, while Ryerson University delegates authority under the Code of Non-Academic Conduct to the director of student services. Many residences also feature independent, student-run judicial systems to uphold their community standards.

Whereas American institutions have a long history of addressing academic integrity (for example, with "honour codes"), it has only been since the late 1990s that academic integrity education has been identified as an issue requiring serious attention in Canada. An academic integrity survey published by Christensen-Hughes and McCabe (2006, no. 1 and no. 2) surprised many with the finding that Canadian students reported cheating just as often as their USA counterparts, with only some subtle differences in the types of cheating to which they admitted. Their study found, for example, that 53 per cent of Canadian undergraduate students reported having engaged in at least one instance of "serious cheating on written work" during their post-secondary careers (Christensen-Hughes and McCabe 2006, 2:10). The popular media picked up the story (Birchard 2006; Foxman 2006; Gulli et al. 2007) and many administrators were taken aback by the statistics.

The eleven Canadian institutions that participated in the original survey in 2003, and many others who did so soon thereafter, were already alert to the problem of academic dishonesty in Canada. Christensen-Hughes and McCabe's study, however, provided much-needed evidence that the issue required attention; even before the findings were published, the academic integrity movement in Canada had begun. Some institutions across Canada, including the University of Windsor, McMaster University, Brock University, and the University of Alberta have created positions or offices dedicated to the promotion of academic integrity. Many others have added responsibility for academic integrity to existing positions or offices.

Changing the student culture to one that embraces academic integrity on college and university campuses is no small task; students' choice to engage in academic misconduct involves internal, organizational, institutional, and societal dimensions (Bertram Gallant 2008, 47). Given the enormity of the undertaking, there seems to be no standard job description for academic integrity officers in Canada; duties might include coordinating hearings, advising decision-makers, and/or managing educational programs. Whatever the organizational structure, however, student judicial affairs and academic integrity personnel are perfectly positioned to be a part of the solution to the problem by engaging in prevention, creating academic integrity programs, and imposing educational sanctions designed to address the behaviour at its source.

## PROFESSIONALIZATION OF THE FIELD

The wide variety of activities carried out by student judicial affairs and academic integrity professionals requires a corresponding variety of skills. At a minimum, they must be familiar with academic culture and processes, and skilled in the area of policy interpretation, application, and development. Additionally, a familiarity with the principles of natural justice and fundamental fairness, as well as a basic understanding of administrative law, is crucial. Canadian student judicial affairs professionals draw on backgrounds in counselling, law, psychology, conflict resolution, human rights, social work, or various academic careers, among others.

Professionalization of student judicial affairs is in its infancy in Canada. If, as claimed earlier, student judicial affairs constitute a student service, then specialized, qualified personnel are central to ensuring that students are served in the best way possible. Student judicial affairs personnel may face the additional challenge of less than enthusiastic support from faculty members who, in some cases, see the professionalization of the field as yet another symptom of the slow and steady devolution of our colleges and universities from educational institutions to administrative behemoths. The academic–administrator divide is an ongoing challenge for those working within judicial affairs and academic integrity – even if they move between academic and administrative roles – and, to some extent, a problem faced by all student affairs professionals (Shea and Patterson 2007).

While graduate degrees in student personnel administration and similar programs proliferate in the United States, only a few Canadian institutions offer them. Most Canadians who work in student judicial affairs or academic integrity have learned *in situ,* requiring them to draw on skills and abilities gained in other contexts. The nature of the work requires Canadian student judicial affairs personnel to undertake professional development from a variety of sources.

The Centre for Higher Education Research and Development (CHERD) at the University of Manitoba offers a range of training opportunities for student affairs professionals, including sessions on the basic principles of administrative law as it relates to higher education. Courses on administrative law offered through various law schools may also be beneficial in order to understand the context in which we work.

Conflict resolution involves a series of skills helpful to student judicial affairs professionals. Besides offering an invaluable framework for dealing with students in a heightened state of anxiety or frustration, conflict resolution training teaches how to listen for students' interests and values, and how to use those to help students understand their own behaviour and express themselves in more constructive ways. Additionally, some institutions are incorporating mediation into their disciplinary processes. Most provinces have organizations that provide training in conflict resolution.

Understanding and abiding by provincial privacy law is another requirement for those involved in student judicial affairs. It is difficult at times to find the balance between an accused student's right to privacy on one hand and, on the other, defining a legitimate need to know in order to protect the safety of the institution and integrity of the degree. Privacy law might also conflict with students' right to know the case against them. While it is crucial to safeguard confidentiality, it is equally important to build in the flexibility to inform those who have a legitimate need to know as well as the opportunity to learn from one's mistakes and successes through debriefing once a case is concluded. Being overly cautious with privacy law may be as problematic as being reckless with confidential information. The only way to ensure judicious application of privacy law is through proper training, available through provincial governments or internally from one's own privacy offices.

While discipline-specific training opportunities in Canada are limited, some Canadians have taken advantage of applicable training in the United States. For example, the Gehring Academy for Student Conduct Administration, an annual summer institute offered by the Association for Student Judicial Affairs (ASJA), offers training for various professional levels, as well as mediation and conflict resolution programs. Organizations like the National Center for Higher Education Risk Management (NCHERM) provide webinars and other applicable educational programming.

Some of the best professional development opportunities come in the form of conferences. The ASJA holds an annual conference in which all of the sessions relate to student judicial issues; however, beneficial as it is, the focus on American law does not provide a Canadian context for the practice of student judicial affairs. Consequently, while attending the 1998 ASJA conference, Ellen Schoeck (University of Alberta), Lynn Smith (University of Manitoba), and Kathleen Kwan (University of Guelph) decided that there was a real need to connect Canadian student judicial affairs practitioners with each other, in order to approach issues arising from a Canadian legal and cultural perspective (Smith 2007; personal communication, 13 June).

The first Canadian Conference on Student Judicial Affairs (CCSJA) was held in Banff in 1998, hosted by the University of Alberta (Utgoff 2005; personal communication, August). Since then, despite having no formal structure or resources, conferences have occurred nearly annually. In 2007, at the CCSJA in Windsor, Ontario, the conference participants voted to formalize their association. It was decided that any initiative should include both student judicial affairs and academic integrity, partly because the practices are so closely linked and also because the number of people in either category is very small.

Given this group's dedication to student success, a student services organization seemed to be the best fit. As of December 2007, the group became a division of the Canadian Association of College and University Student Services (CACUSS), an umbrella organization for student services and student affairs professionals across Canada. The division, named Canadian Academic Integrity and Student Judicial Affairs (CAISJA), is now fully integrated within CACUSS. The annual CACUSS conference provides a venue for ongoing professional development in both academic integrity and student judicial affairs, set in the wider context of Canadian student services.

The Center for Academic Integrity (CAI) annual conference provides yet another opportunity for professional development, with a focus on promoting positive academic behaviour. Despite what can seem to Canadians as an over-emphasis on honour codes – discussed later in this chapter – there are many valuable resources available at the conference. In recent years, it has become more internationalized, featuring presenters, for example, from Canada, Australia, Egypt, and Lebanon.

Due to limited professional development and training opportunities, literature and ongoing research have become indispensable resources. Smith's *Procedural Fairness for University and College Students* (1998) provides an overview of the basic requirements for treating students fairly throughout the judicial process. The CACUSS journal, *Communiqué*, produced a special issue on student judicial affairs and academic integrity in Spring 2008. Peer-reviewed journals on higher education and related topics can also provide information on current research in student judicial affairs.

Various professional student affairs organizations offer a range of written resources in addition to their annual conferences. Gary Pavela writes a weekly column, the "Law and Policy Report," which is distributed to ASJA members. It identifies legal issues related to higher education and analyzes their implications for institutional policy and practice. Although the reports often stem from American court decisions, Pavela's analyses speak to issues in the Canadian context as well. For a perspective specific to Canada, the *Post-Secondary Law Reporter* offers case law from Canadian court decisions.

With the exception of Hannah's 1998 work, there is very little research on student judicial affairs in general, and almost none in Canada. Several books published in the United States are applicable to the practice in Canada. Dannells (1997) provides a comprehensive overview of student judicial affairs and reviews various models, including a discussion on student development in the disciplinary context. The College Administration Publications *Higher Education Administration Series* offers several volumes directly related to the kinds of issues faced by student judicial affairs professionals, including titles such as *Exercising Power with Wisdom* (Lancaster 2006) and *Academic Integrity and Student Development* (Kibler et al. 1988).

### ISSUES AND CHALLENGES

Many of the issues and challenges faced by Canadian post-secondary institutions are similar to those encountered south of the border. For example, Canadian institutions, like their American counterparts, struggle with questions of jurisdiction: is the college or university responsible for student conduct off campus? If so, when and to what extent? Some policies explicitly state that off-campus conduct is only regulated when a clear and tangible link to the institution can be demonstrated; however, campuses integrated into surrounding communities may find jurisdiction to be a more ambiguous concern.

### *Technology*

The fast-paced advance of technologies and electronic communications poses another common challenge. Examples are ubiquitous: a student copying and pasting information from the Internet into an essay, or using Facebook as a tool to intimidate, threaten, or harass another; a group of students text-messaging answers to each other during an exam; an institution subscribing to text-matching software in order to detect plagiarism. Student judicial affairs and academic integrity professionals often find themselves having to apply policies that do not neatly fit the issue before them. Technology progresses much more quickly than the glacial pace of policy development on campuses. Consequently, the use of technologies like Facebook, MySpace, Second Life, and other Web 2.0 applications poses unprecedented challenges in the post-secondary environment, including considerations of jurisdiction over misconduct in the virtual world. We can only assume that the rate of change will continue to increase and ensure that our policies are flexible enough to address new technological issues that arise (Bohun et al. 2007).

## Personal and Public Safety

All student judicial affairs professionals must necessarily be concerned with balancing the needs of the community – including public and personal safety and integrity of the degree – with the needs of the accused students. The disciplinary process lends itself exceptionally well to student development initiatives, offering the institution the opportunity for a one-on-one teachable moment specific to the individual student, whether through educational sanctions or an investigation process that helps students move toward taking responsibility for their actions. A singular focus on student development, however, may not always serve the needs of the community or the increasing demand for legalistic processes. The balance lies in a measured response to violations: imposing sanctions for unacceptable conduct that, as much as possible, work toward student development while aligning with other institutional goals.

## Legalistic Approaches

The progressively more legalistic approach has itself proven to be a challenge in student judicial affairs. Students who hire lawyers in response to charges increase the demand for legalistic language and processes. Furthermore, this stance positions students only as potential defendants in the process, rather than members of an academic community. Using the disciplinary processes to reinforce students' role in the academic community – for example, by imposing educational sanctions specific to the offence – is one way student judicial affairs can work toward the goals and missions of an institution.

## Psychological and Psychiatric Disorders

A topic receiving significant attention at recent conferences is misconduct resulting from psychological and psychiatric disorders. The changing student demographic may also be signalling a shift in the types of behaviours confronting student judicial affairs personnel. While much of the misconduct encountered in the past may have resulted from a seemingly natural adolescent penchant for mischief, it seems that behaviour stemming from a wide range of mental disabilities is increasing (Dannells 1997, 73-74). Pharmaceutical developments have allowed students with psychiatric disabilities to attend universities and colleges – an opportunity they would not have had a decade ago. Considerations of human rights law naturally arise in cases where a documented illness causes unacceptable behaviour. Almost all Canadian institutions make reference to and abide by provincial human rights legislation in their policies. Consequently, student judicial affairs officers may be forced to grapple with the limits of reasonable accommodation and undue hardship when addressing student misconduct.

## Risk Management

Risk management also forms a part of the responsibility placed on student judicial affairs professionals. Risks to the institution can range from torts to educational malpractice, but students are also vulnerable to risk since the value of their degree relies on the institution's reputation for fairness and good scholarship. While managing risk is important, there is danger in allowing the possibility of risk to dominate disciplinary decisions. Student judicial affairs officers can be a part of the solution here, too, by creating educational and preventative programs and using the disciplinary process as a developmental, rather than purely punitive, tool.

While Canadian and USA student judicial affairs professionals have much in common, some issues set us apart. For example, American institutions encounter a wide range of conduct issues stemming from their athletics programs; Canadian institutions do not seem to face nearly the same level of difficulty in this regard. The difference may be in part because college sports are not as central to campus culture in Canada, or because funding levels are lower in Canada (with much less reliance on college sports as a source of revenue). However, this may change in the future if Canadian university teams join the National Collegiate Athletic Association (NCAA), as has been discussed on some campuses.

## Alcohol

Alcohol-related misconduct is problematic both north and south of the border. Unlike the United States, though, no Canadian province has a legal drinking age higher than 19 years old so the majority of students in Canadian post-secondary institutions are of legal drinking age (Canadian Centre on Substance Abuse). This allows us to shift our focus from illegal conduct to the social and health concerns around alcohol abuse and binge drinking, and to use preventative programs and disciplinary sanctions to address the underlying problems.

## Honour Codes

The use of honour codes seems to be another point of departure between the USA and Canada. Traditional honour codes consist of five elements: a pledge signed by all students on each exam and assignment, unsupervised exams, a student-run disciplinary system, zero tolerance (for example, a single sanction approach), and a requirement that students report others' cheating activities (Pavela 2000). Many honour code schools have moderated their approach and now use modified codes (Kibler et al. 1988, 21). Honour codes, whether traditional or modified, are used to promote academic integrity in some American institutions but there are no true honour code institutions in Canada.

This has been the subject of much discussion, debate, and head-scratching among Canadian academic integrity officers and administrators. Why is it that the honour code has not taken hold in Canada? There has been no clear answer to date. Many honour code schools are smaller, private, residential institutions with long traditions of honour codes and more cohesive student and alumni cultures. It might be, as Adams (2003) suggests, a difference in societal values between the Canadian tendency to value communitarian ideals and civic engagement versus American individualism and competitiveness. It is also possible that honour codes do not resonate with Canadian students precisely because they are so strongly associated with American colleges and universities.

*Academic Integrity*

A review of academic integrity websites from across Canada reveals that, in addition to addressing the cheating behaviours, there is a second focal point: addressing the systemic causes of academic misconduct. Many institutions, for example, offer guidance to the instructional staff to help them prevent academic integrity violations. Christensen-Hughes and McCabe (2006, 2:3-4) discuss the role of authentic assessment and other institutional factors in students' decision to cheat. They suggest that institutions bear a level of responsibility for creating an environment in which academic integrity is encouraged and cheating is discouraged.

There seems to be a strong emphasis in Canadian colleges and universities on shared responsibility, whereas the traditional honour code emphasizes individual responsibility and leaves little room to acknowledge the institutional contribution to the problem of cheating. It is understandable, therefore, that a primary focus on community approaches to academic integrity – efforts to acknowledge shared responsibility both in creating the problems and finding solutions – makes honour codes seem unproductive. However, not wishing to overstate the differences, most Canadian and American institutions have similar approaches to academic integrity. It seems the honour code is the one element that does not translate across our cultures.

Student judicial affairs and academic integrity in Canada are new and developing fields. In establishing their roles on campus, personnel in this area have been developing systems that serve the interests of the student who violates policies, the student who abides by the rules, and the wider university or college community. By maintaining student success as a central goal, student judicial affairs and academic integrity professionals play a small but crucial role in post-secondary institutions.

# 9

# Counselling Services

JACK RUSSEL

Counselling services in Canadian higher education have existed for more than fifty years and perform a critical and supporting institutional role in helping students maximize their opportunities for academic and personal success. Counselling services on a university and college campus cover a wide spectrum of programs and interventions, all aimed at addressing student needs. This chapter focuses on: (a) the essential role that counselling plays in the personal, social, emotional, and career development needs of students; (b) models of service delivery and organization; (c) professionalization of the counselling field; and (d) various issues and challenges that shape such services on the college and university campus today.

## FOUNDATIONS OF COUNSELLING IN CANADA

Counselling services in Canadian higher education began in 1946, when the federal government provided funds for universities to assist returning Second World War veterans with career development needs, and the University Advisory Services (UAS) was formed to represent these counsellors. By 1949, the UAS expanded to include other student services personnel who were working in university settings. In 1952, the UAS formally changed its name to the University Counselling and Placement Association (UCPA), to more accurately reflect the functions of its members, and in 1963 the University Counselling Association (UCA) was established. The UCA evolved once again in 1961: renamed the Canadian University Counselling Association (CUCA), it became one of four divisions comprising what was then referred to as the Council of Associations of University Student Personnel Services (CAUSPS-2). With the growth of counselling at the college level, CUCA went through one more change to become the Canadian University and College Counselling Association (CUCCA) under the umbrella of the Canadian Association of College and University Student Services (CACUSS). With only minor subsequent changes to organizational structure, CUCCA remains a vibrant professional organization representing practitioners across the country (Canadian University and College Counselling Association).

The original purpose of providing counselling assistance to university students for their career and financial needs has evolved dramatically over the past fifty years. Counselling at the post-secondary level now includes services for: learning and study skills, career development and management, personal issues, students with disabilities, transition and adjustment issues for entering and departing students, international students, and Aboriginal students. Counselling services play a fundamental psycho-educational role in making the university experience for students successful and personally meaningful.

As early as 1929, Alfred North Whitehead suggested that education's role is to stimulate and guide students' self-development. Practitioners in the student services field are guided by ethical guidelines and mission statements that build upon a rich history emphasizing student development, self-direction, experiential learning, and the integration of the whole student, both personal and intellectual. Holistic learning, integration, and self-development are crucial elements emphasized in counselling practices. Counsellors themselves are bound by ethical practice and may be responsible to different professional organizations and licensing bodies/colleges depending on the province in which they practice. The work of counsellors, though sometimes remedial and requiring intensive psychotherapy, is ultimately aimed at providing students an enriched university experience so that they are able to maximize their strengths, overcome obstacles, and effectively manage life's difficulties and challenges.

## ESSENTIAL FUNCTIONS AND SERVICES

Counselling services in Canadian higher education vary from institution to institution in terms of both function and form. How the service is delivered and what is delivered reflect the practices and policies inherent in the post-secondary context of which it is a part. Administrative structures vary across Canada, as do funding models. Crozier and Willihnganz (2005), in their comprehensive study of counselling services at the post-secondary level, reported that the typical structure consists of a director, manager, coordinator, or chair who reports to a vice-president (academic or administration). Additional administrative operations revolve around function, such as support, training, and outreach. The average number of permanent counsellors in counselling services is 4.9 with a range of 1 to 18, complemented by contract staff and graduate interns. Funding for services comes from a variety of sources: the university's operating budget, ancillary student fees, direct charges to students, research grants or special contracts, or combinations thereof. In some instances, students may be charged for career assessments and workshop materials, a practice followed by many counselling services. Students being assessed for learning disabilities will either finance this independently or can access special bursaries to cover costs.

Coniglio, McLean, and Mueser (2005), in describing Canadian post-secondary counselling services, noted three distinct organizational types or forms of counselling services delivery: the Integrated (macro) model, the Traditional model, and the Minimal (store-front) model. The *Integrated model* includes a range of counselling services, from personal development, learning skills development, and writing skills and development to career development and placement, and health and wellness. These centres may also include specialized services for students with disabilities, international student services, health and medical services, and services for First Nations students (Stone and Archer 1990). The Integrated model has emerged on some campuses by design as well as by an accumulation of services from other offices.

Counselling services following the *Traditional model* typically offer personal counselling, with limited career counselling options (Stone and Archer 1990). The emphasis of this approach is clinical, primarily providing psychotherapy. Given the trend toward integration of services, the need for holistic approaches, and an increased emphasis on student success, this model has become less prevalent in Canada since 2000. On some campuses the counselling centre provides career counselling (e.g., career interest assessment and interpretation) while the campus employment centre assists with job preparation and placement (See chapter 11).

A third approach found at some institutions is the *Minimal model*. Although most offer some on-site counselling services (Stone and Archer 1990) and provide crisis intervention, distribute information, and make referrals within the university and community, the breadth of student issues addressed is much more limited due to the level of staffing and resources. Even in responding minimally to students' needs, this model falls short because of its tendency to outsource counselling functions to independent providers in the community rather than rely on college and university counselors who may have a more specific understanding of students' concerns and needs (Coniglio et al. 2005).

Counselling services in universities and colleges across Canada offer help for personal psychological needs, learning skill development, and career development, including the identification and achievement of a career goal. In recent years, significant effort has been devoted to assisting students with disabilities, helping international students deal with special circumstances, and providing culturally relevant assistance to Aboriginal students. On many campuses, counselling for psychological and personal issues is also available through student health services with campus physicians.

Depending on the theoretical orientation and working alliances, the student services professionals, counselling practitioners, and physicians in such settings work collaboratively on case management. Additionally, one finds faculties and departments engaged in providing academic counselling, to help students with course and program planning, and career-related assistance.

Since the late 1980s, Canadian counselling services have benefited from an increase of undergraduate and graduate students as paraprofessionals in the delivery of counselling services. Undergraduate students frequently connect with other students about personal, academic, social, and career-related questions prior to speaking with a professional. Across Canada, students are assisting more and more in many counselling service areas, such as career, learning, personal/psychological, international student services, First Nations student services, reception, and research.

Many counselling services provide internship opportunities for students in professional graduate and undergraduate programs such as PhD students in clinical psychology, MEd students in a counselling psychology program, and BSW or MSW students as well as, in some cases, students enrolled at independent professional training centres. In contributing to this direct service, such students receive extensive training and supervision as part of their internship experience.

Intervention and treatment models vary from institution to institution and often include individual counselling, group counselling/psychotherapy, crisis counselling, consultation with faculty and other student services practitioners concerning student crises, psycho-educational programs, and outreach programs and activities. A variety of factors, including environmental demands and resources, institutional and counselling service goals, student pressures, and the theoretical orientations of the counselling staff influence adherence to one model or another; the aim is to choose the one that works best in a particular situation and with a particular population. In working with clients, clinicians monitor effectiveness and outcomes, not only for their own professional practice but also for institutional accountability. Maximizing therapeutic and counselling effectiveness, evaluating program outcomes, assessing change in student behaviour, and the impact of psycho-educational workshops are requisites for day-to-day work with students. Given student demand and decreasing institutional resources, university and college counselling services are endorsing time-limited counselling and are more inclined to provide brief and solution-focused counselling interventions.

Psycho-educational programs and workshops are typically short term (two to twelve hours), topic-focused, and a blend of instruction and processing for better personal integration of the information. Workshops can be offered whether the concern is learning-, personal/psychological-, or career-related. Topic examples include self-esteem, stress management, procrastination, mindfulness, time management, writing multiple choice exams, critical writing, career interest and assessment, personality assessment and careers, resumé writing, and job interviewing, to name a few.

According to Lambeth and Haslett (2002), outreach activities are becoming central to the mandate of counselling services. For example, training residence or orientation staff how to intervene in crisis situations prepares them to be better helpers and may prevent the development of serious mental health problems among the students they are advising and assisting. Providing these student leaders with information about their own learning styles and career development needs alerts them to recognizing these issues in the students they encounter. All students can benefit from classroom outreach visits that underscore the relationship of transferable skills acquired from academic studies to their personal and career development decisions.

## PROFESSIONALIZATION OF THE FIELD

Practitioners in Canadian university and college counselling services have different training backgrounds and levels of education, and may possess board registration as psychologists (specific to each province), counsellor certification as provided by the Canadian Counselling Association (CCA), or registration as social workers. Generally, services are staffed by professionals with PhDs or EdDs in psychology or counselling-related disciplines, master's level counsellors in either psychology or counselling psychology, and counsellors with a background in social work. Crozier and Willihnganz (2005) report that 60 per cent of the permanent counselling staff have faculty status. Others may hold adjunct faculty positions and teach in related graduate programs, such as clinical psychology, social work, medicine, and counselling psychology. Registered and certified counsellors sign and adhere to a strict code of ethics that directs their professional conduct and behaviour. To ensure that registration or certification is kept current, practitioners are required to attend a minimum number of professional development workshops within a set period of time. In many instances, counselling professionals also carry additional professional liability insurance. Many counsellors are members of CUCCA; while not a licensing organization, it does provide professional development opportunities at both regional and national levels and offers financial support for research. Counsellors may also hold memberships in relevant American and Canadian professional organizations affiliated with their specific discipline.

## ISSUES AND CHALLENGES

Four significant challenges currently shape counselling services and practices on Canadian university and college campuses: (a) the needs of a diverse student population, (b) the increase in the severity of students' presenting problems, (c) the importance of mental health to student success and retention, and (d) the provision of additional and alternative service delivery through emerging technologies. These are challenges will require a concerted focus among professionals in order to maximize the use of their resources for effecting the best outcomes.

## Diverse Student Needs

*Diverse* is an excellent descriptor of students at Canadian colleges and universities (Coniglio et al. 2005). Students today vary in terms of their race, ethnicity, culture, gender, age, sexual orientation, religion, socioeconomic status, and disability (Comprehensive Student Survey 2002; Heslop 2004; Western Facts 2004). The number of international students is increasing dramatically across Canada; the University of Western Ontario reported, for example, significant increases in both the undergraduate and graduate student levels (Aquino 2006; personal communication, 19 February). The diversity of the student population adds immensely to the richness of the college and university experience for all, but also brings particular special challenges. Counsellors need to become more culturally competent in respecting and recognizing the unique issues of these diverse students as they relate to post-secondary studies. For instance, Khanna and Qadeer (2005) and Sue, Arredondo, and McDavis (1992) identify essential multicultural counselling competencies that include: the importance of being aware of one's own cultural values and biases, understanding the world views of the client, and developing culturally appropriate intervention strategies. Counsellors are challenged to assess their biases and assumptions about individualism and Western-based practices. For instance, in studying cultural and group differences, counsellors must understand the dynamics of how each unique individual relates to his or her culture (Axelson 1993).

## Severity of Student Problems

Students seek out counselling services for a variety of reasons, including help with relationship issues, stress and anxiety, family issues, situational crises, depression, educational and vocational concerns, and developmental issues faced by adolescents and young adults (Coniglio et al. 2005). Since 2000, university and college counselling services across North America and England have reported a distinctive shift from students presenting with developmental and informational needs to more severe psychological problems (Benton et al. 2003; Coniglio et al. 2005; Crozier and Willihnganz 2005; Kitzrow 2003; Pledge et al. 1998; Stone and Archer 1990; Surtees, Wainwright, and Pharoah 2000).

To illustrate this trend, the first nine clients seen by one graduate student interning at Psychological Services in the Student Development Centre of the University of Western Ontario (UWO) in 2004 presented with the following issues: (a) an active eating disorder with a history of child abuse; (b) suicide ideation; (c) feelings of isolation due to a relationship breakup (out-of-province graduate student); (d) an abusive relationship, requiring anger management, and also waiting for an assessment of possible attention deficit disorder; (e) grief issues; (f) cognitive and emotional regulation difficulties following a brain injury; (g) severe anorexia and depression; (h) a history of child abuse (female student); and (i) a relationship breakup with no emotional support available (international student). Furthermore, Personality Assessment Inventory test scores of 67 per cent of students assessed for counselling within UWO's Student Development Centre's Psychological Services unit indicated the presence of diagnostic levels of depression, anxiety, or post-traumatic stress disorder. Additionally, about 16 per cent were assessed with more chronic and complex problems such as anti-social or borderline disorders (Hutchinson, 2005; personal communication, 26 January).

Pledge et al. (1998, 387) reported that increasing numbers of clients presented with severe and distressing concerns, including "suicidality, substance abuse, a history of psychiatric treatment or hospitalization, [and] depression and anxiety." According to a survey by the American College Health Association (Duenwald 2004), nearly half of all students have problems functioning because they are feeling depressed; 15 per cent of students meet the criteria for clinical depression. Furthermore, the author noted that the number of students accessing counselling services who are taking medication for a psychiatric disturbance rose from 17 per cent in 2000 to 24.5 per cent in 2003-04. Not only has there been an increase in the severity of issues being presented but also a record number of students are using campus counselling services for longer periods of time than ever before (Levine and Cureton 1998).

Similarly, students expressing career-related dilemmas are facing an increasingly difficult time. Niles and Harris-Bowlsbey (2002, 1) suggested that:

> translating experiences into career choices requires people to acquire a high level of self-awareness. People often need help clarifying their values, life-role salience, interests, and motivation as they attempt to make career choices – many clients present with low self-esteem, weak self-efficacy, and little hope that the future can be more satisfying than the past. Such clients often require more assistance in resolving their career dilemmas than a test battery can provide.

Morgan and Ness (2003), in a study at the University of Manitoba, further substantiated that effective career decision-making is related to self-efficacy;

the higher the self-efficacy, the better the student is at making career-related decisions.

Not only are university and college counselling services finding themselves stretched to capacity, community agencies are similarly over-subscribed and unable to respond when a referral is requested (Miner 2003). Having increased the range of issues and concerns they address, college and university counselling centres find themselves more and more beyond the limits of their resources in handling the duration and severity of the problems they are being asked to accommodate.

### Student Success and Retention

A third emerging issue relates to concerns of student success and retention as universities focus energy and resources to ensure that students benefit from their experiences, both classroom-based and beyond. From a holistic perspective, students are engaging in life planning, overcoming personal problems, and developing strong foundations for the future. Effective counselling services help students in their journey and play a crucial role in enhancing the quality of the experience. Student success can be equated to the functioning of a mentally healthy young person, one who is engaged in productive activities, experiences fulfilling personal and social relationships, is able to adapt to change and cope with adversity, acquires effective critical thinking and communication skills, and is able to identify and achieve a meaningful life and career goal. Mental health serves as a foundation for cognitive, emotional, and spiritual growth and equips an individual to grow in self-esteem and confidence. All are the hallmarks of an educated person.

Regardless of the motivation behind the support of student success on campuses (i.e., philosophical or economical), there is substantial literature supporting the role of counselling as it relates to student retention (Astin 1975; Chiste and Rathgeber 1998; Duenwald 2004; Gordon 1998; Hoyt and Winn 2004; Sharkin 2004; Wyckoff 1999). Persistence and commitment to education and career goals is a significant factor associated with students attaining their degree (Wyckoff 1999). Effective educational and career decision-making, as it relates to retention, is also highlighted by Astin (1975), who suggests that prolonged indecision about academic and career goals is correlated with attrition. Gordon's work (1998) and that of Hoyt and Winn (2004) further emphasize the need to understand career indecision among the university-age population. In reviewing initial choices of students, Titley and Titley (1980) raised the question as to whether only the undecided students are truly the undecided. Students change direction and refine their initial choices in seeking their identity, allowing them to pursue self-determined paths and career goals.

Chiste and Rathgeber's (1998) comparison of three distinct groups of students (voluntary withdrawal, required withdrawal, and completers) subsequent to their first year of studies at the University of Saskatchewan underscores the value of counselling in strengthening student retention and success. Significant differences were noted between the three groups in academic integration, social integration, goal commitment, skills and motivation, student expectations, utilization of university resources, and social and interpersonal distractions. In particular, Chiste and Rathgeber concluded that external factors such as family, personal, or medical problems had a profound impact on academic performance and consequently retention. Polansky, Horan, and Hanish (1993), in a study of at-risk students, noted that those receiving learning and study skills and career counselling, or both, reported increased persistence in their studies and a higher grade point average.

As noted, personal, relational, family, and emotional factors can interfere with the successful completion of college and university studies. In some instances, social and emotional factors may exceed general academic factors in determining whether a student persists (Gerdes and Mallinckrodt 1994). Turner and Berry (2000) completed a longitudinal study over a six-year period comparing retention rates of students who received counselling for personal issues with those of the general student population. The results confirmed the value of psychological/personal counselling in supporting students with regard to their academic performance and remaining in school. According to the data, an average of 70 per cent of the students replied that personal problems were interfering with their academic studies and approximately 20 per cent reported that they had thought about dropping out of school because of their personal problems. The authors also reported that, on average, students who sought out counselling had a retention rate of 85 per cent over a five-year period, in comparison to 74 per cent for the general student population. Overall, these data suggest that counselling services can play a critical role in the success and degree completion of post-secondary students, if such services are offered at the appropriate time and in the appropriate manner.

## Emerging Technology and Service Delivery

The Internet and other emerging technologies provide viable alternatives and endless possibilities to assist students with a variety of issues and concerns. The application of Web-based information will only increase, requiring scrutiny to ensure relevancy and addressing of ethical considerations. To benefit both the student and the counsellor, some university career services and learning skill services offer an early self-assessment online. Further and more complex assessment is provided through computerized career assessments, such as the Strong Interest Inventory and the Myers-Briggs Type Indicator, and learning skills assessments, such as the Learning and Study Skills Inventory (LASSI). The University of Waterloo Career Services provides a computerized and interactive Career Development eManual that includes self-assessment and a series of job interview questions and responses. An excellent and general website for career-related information is the Job Hunters Bible site (www.jobhuntersbible.com). This website, a spinoff from the book *What Color Is Your Parachute?* (Bolles 2002), is well researched with cautions about using online assessments.

Psychological and personal counselling services provide students online information and self-assessment tools concerning both their mental and physical health. Students are either referred to outside resources, such as the Canadian Mental Health website or the unabridged student counselling virtual pamphlet collection available at http://ccvillage.buffalo.edu/vpc.html, or students can respond directly to information provided online by the university counselling service, such as at Simon Fraser University. In order to track change and encourage positive movement in psychotherapy, Western Ontario University's Psychological Services uses an online interactive assessment tool available at a cost from Scott Miller's website (*The Heart and Soul of Change: What Works in Therapy*, www.talkingcure.com). The use of technology like Facebook and My Space is common among students and may provide additional ways for counselling professionals to help students connect with each other in supportive ways. Confidential chat rooms are another form of connecting students with common concerns and could be created to address issues and questions related to stress management, procrastination, career-related matters, and some learning-related topics. And finally, electronic therapy or E-therapy – delivering counselling services through online means – is an emerging trend that may be useful in a variety of settings (Coniglio et al. 2005).

### CONCLUSION

Counselling services in Canadian higher education hold a central, fundamental, and functional position. With a holistic view of students, counselling practitioners endorse and support the primary functions of universities and colleges. In performing this crucial role, counsellors face both societal and institutional pressures. As they juggle the demands of student expectations, professional responsibilities, increased demand for services, increased severity of student issues and concerns, and tightened budget allocations, counsellors are increasingly expected to show evidence of and account for the impact of their practices. Guided by professional criteria, counsellors strive to understand what treatment works best with what student population and in what situation. Research related to the value of counselling services and its relevance to learning and institutional objectives, on both local and national levels, is increasing.

Counsellors will continue to be challenged as the student population increases in diversity. Sensitivity and respect for cultural, ethnic, racial, and sexual orientation differences is an absolute as counsellors ensure that they are engaging competently and professionally with students individually and in groups. Diverse student groups experience considerable pressure encompassing academics, finances, and cultural transitions and adjustments. Counsellors will be required to understand the issues that face all university and college students as they strive for purposeful independence and meaning.

With the marked increase in severity of presented problems, a swell in demand and use of services, the appearance of a more diverse student mix, and the emergence of new technologies, counsellors will be challenged to develop innovative methods of service delivery that will fit within their professional obligations and ethical responsibilities. The inclusion of undergraduate paraprofessionals in the delivery of certain counselling services will become more commonplace as practitioners are pressed to meet the expanding needs of students. Furthermore, counselling services will benefit from providing supervised internship opportunities for graduate students.

As students experience developmental concerns in their journey of self-identity, and some struggle with serious and potentially debilitating problems, counsellors will be continually challenged. As our society and world become more complex, questions about life purpose and meaning will prevail and counsellors will be required to help students weave the strands of their post-scondary life into a complete tapestry that will benefit both the individual and society.

# 10

# Health and Wellness Services

### PATRICIA MIRWALDT

Almost all post-secondary educational institutions in Canada offer their students health and wellness services, although scope and programming varies widely because of differences in provincial health system organization, size of the institution, and proximity to other health resources. In addition, because of universal health care in Canada, many institutions rely on the accessibility of medical resources in the surrounding community for basic medical services to their students. At the very least, most schools offer wellness programming and immunization for students in the health sciences, while some offer primary medical care. This chapter gives an overview of the basic functions and practices in the areas of wellness and health care in Canadian post-secondary institutions; included are those that address students' physical as well as mental well-being. The chapter then looks at the professionalization of campus health and wellness services and considers the range of issues that form a context for implementation those services in the college or university setting.

## ESSENTIAL FUNCTIONS AND SERVICES

Generally speaking, most campus-based health services are engaged in the delivery of some primary care, proactive wellness programming, immunization and certification services, and a range of educational initiatives responsive to the particular needs of a diverse student population. By virtue of their status and life circumstances, students often bring to the campus a profile of health concerns that both parallel and diverge from a typical youth population. It is important for institutional health and wellness professionals to recognize these similarities as well as to take into consideration those features that distinguish the college or university community. The American College Health Association (ACHA) has created guidelines for both health promotion (ACHA 2004) and health services (ACHA 1999); similar guidelines are yet to be developed in Canada.

## Primary Care

Primary care, when offered, is delivered by a cadre of professional staff: family physicians, with an interest in young adult health; registered nurses; and nurse practitioners. Many campuses also boast dental practitioners, pharmacists, nutritionists, physiotherapists, acupuncturists, and athletic and massage therapists. Caring for students who are well read and insightful and who have good research skills challenges health care professionals to provide evidence-based investigations and treatment and to communicate effectively. Excellent linkages to specialists in psychiatry, orthopedics, dermatology, and gynecology are essential in providing timely and appropriate care.

## Wellness Programming

Recognizing that the majority of Canadian students are emerging adults (eighteen to twenty-five years old), most wellness programming emphasizes issues of transition from childhood to adulthood. Many use the World Health Organization definition of health: "a state of complete physical, mental and social well-being and not merely the absence of disease or infirmity" (World Health Organization). Increasingly, stress management and skills to maintain and improve emotional resilience and a healthy mental state have been added to the more traditional areas of wellness programming: relationship and sex education, safer sex and contraception, substance use and misuse, weight preoccupation and nutrition (Kezar 2007). Wellness programming must first and foremost contribute to student success by influencing students to strive for and maintain optimal brain health (American College Health Association 2004). However, the environment heavily influences health: the health and well-being of students is strongly correlated with the extent to which the entire college or university community embraces it (ACHA 2002). Each member of the institution – academics, students, and staff alike – must consider student well-being in crafting every academic and non-academic policy, program, and service.

## Immunization

Immunization services for education programs are designed to serve students in disciplines that may expose them to unusual dangers or to human and animal blood and body fluids (Fairservice, Komonoski, Mirwaldt, and Tan 2007). Specific areas of study require specialized vaccines: for example, those exposed to animals or rural areas in which rabies may exist may require rabies vaccine; health sciences students, in the course of their learning, must not expose the public to illness and certainly must be protected from infection through their interactions with patients with a preventable illness. Teaching universal precautions and ensuring that students are appropriately immunized are obligations often shared with faculties and mandated by professional and provincial bodies. Periodic review of emerging epidemiology, new testing, and vaccine availability is also required to ensure optimal protection for students.

Immunization recommendations for the general student body are best created in consultation with local public health officials, taking into account the origin of the student populace and their living conditions on campus. For example, meningococcal meningitis is much more likely to occur in crowded conditions, such as residence halls, whereas classroom exposure does not seem to increase incidence of this particular disease. Recommendations are also influenced by the epidemiology of infection in the local community. In addition, national guidelines, cost considerations, extent of supplemental health insurance coverage, and supply must also be figured into any recommendations. Recently, Canadian guidelines from the National Advisory Committee on Immunization (NACI) recommended influenza vaccine for healthy adults (National Advisory Committee on Immunization). Recognizing that in 2008, for example, 33 per cent of University of British Columbia undergraduate students reported suffering academic consequences as a result of the flu or a cold, institutional health care providers offered immunization clinics in co-operation with local public health authorities (Mirwaldt and Trew 2008). This responded to a specific UBC concern and extended the reach of the institution's health personnel to reduce the incidence of absenteeism and the academic consequences of illness. Just immunizing individuals is not enough. Health promotion campaigns that target influenza and colds as one of the top impediments to academic performance must include a handwashing campaign, to reduce the spread of respiratory and gastrointestinal illnesses (Hildebrand 2006). Effective campaigns can include Web and newsletter articles and placards in washrooms.

Infection control on campuses is increasingly becoming a responsibility of health services as well. Academics and students travel abroad frequently and educational instruction brings together a large number of students from around the province, the country, and the world. The spread of Sudden Acute Respiratory Syndrome (SARS) in 2003 is a stark example of the kind of problem that can suddenly necessitate quick decisive measures. More routinely, tuberculosis, rubella, and hepatitis cases require contact tracing and exclusion from educational activities until the period of infectiousness has passed. Depending on the physical layout and extent to which washrooms and cooking facilities are shared, quarantining in a residence hall can be very problematic. It may not be possible to allow an infectious student to remain in residence without putting other residents at risk. In such cases, students are advised to recuperate away from campus, with family or friends. Prompt consultation with provincial or health authority infection control experts for advice, education, vaccines, and sometimes personnel, is recommended.

## Disability Certification

Certification of illness and disability, whether chronic or episodic, has always been a challenging service for campus health care professionals. Knowing and influencing the institution's academic accommodation policies is the most effective means for helping students. Each province has a different set of regulations and requirements for educational accommodation that play out differently in each institution and in each classroom. Problems arise when health services is asked to come between professors and students who can reasonably manage most absence and illness issues together. Unfortunately, institutions often do not treat their students with the same respect and confidence that faculty and staff are accorded when suffering from minor time-limited illness. Awarding marks just for attendance perpetuates the problem. In most circumstances, the academic concession should be negotiated between the professor and the student. Certain situations, such as a student's demonstrated pattern of repeatedly asking for deferrals or late withdrawals, should trigger an academic review that can include a request for certification of both the illness/disability and, more importantly, the student's readiness to proceed with academic responsibilities (University of British Columbia). Judicious use of requests for supporting medical documentation should lead the student to re-evaluate whether their academic plans are realistic, in light of their current health conditions and life situation. Acknowledging that time off for recovery or stabilization of a chronic condition is reasonable and that it carries no academic penalities can be very reassuring and supportive to an affected student. However, occasionally students may not recognize the severity or risk of their condition. In such cases the institution should require students to take a leave of absence until the health condition stabilizes and they are no longer a threat to themselves or others. Many Canadian universities are currently creating policies to support involuntary leaves, and a few are already in place (Fitzgerald, Pouyat, and Wood 2008). Student health services supports students most by being part of a multidisciplinary case conference to determine the best course of action. Too often, medical personnel consider that the confidentiality of their interactions with the student unduly limits their effectiveness in working with deans and advisors, as well as other institutional staff, to resolve attendance and performance issues. Health services personnel can often, in general terms, act as consultants with faculty and other service units to help resolve such issues. With the student's informed consent, health care professionals can be much more specific in offering documentation and appropriate recommendations for concessions and support.

## Education for Use of Health Services

Finally, health and wellness functions include educating students about health issues in general, and the management of their own health issues specifically. Generally, students are first-time users of health care, with limited parental support and little previous experience. Young people are often naive in how the health care system works, and are uncertain about appropriate use of self-management techniques or when to seek professional assistance. Helping first-time users navigate the health care system and learn strategies for maintaining optimal health requires health care professionals to spend more time with students and ultimately reduces the viability of a fee-for-service model that depends heavily on provincial health insurance coverage. However, this well-spent, extra time to initiate students into appropriate use of the health care system results in their becoming more informed and interactive managers of their own health and more savvy consumers of health care now and in the future. One innovative solution to this dilemma features nurse clinicians who review health concerns with students (meeting either in the health services office or in their residence halls) and help them work through independent decision-making: how to appropriately respond with self-care practices, when to seek professional help, and when to look to family and friends for support (Burrage 2001). An informative and responsive health care partnership builds expectations and behaviours for when these future decision-makers are in their own communities.

## HEALTH AND STUDENT SUCCESS

A wide variety of health care may be required to allow a student to successfully study and/or live on campus. Timing and convenience of care is essential to reduce absence from academic responsibilities. Health services may be called upon to offer urinary catheterization to quadriplegic students, weekly allergy desensitization injections and monitoring, and daily dressing changes for those with pilonidal abscess repairs. While off-campus versions of these services may be available, their time requirements and location may preclude meaningful attendance at school. Liaison with off-campus resources on behalf of the student to arrange the most effective combination of on- and off-campus services may allow a student to remain in school.

Historically, directors of health services have had to justify the existence of their unit at an institution by explaining what makes student health services distinct and valuable (Caulfield 2007). As an integral part of the student development team, health personnel can influence institutional polices and practices to favour students' well-being. Timely access to health care can minimize disruption of studies for illness and contribute to student retention. By combining a patient-centred approach with a thorough understanding of the demands and requirements of the institution's educational programs, student health personnel can support good academic, career, and life decisions. Ultimately, well-being is the cornerstone of student success: resilience, energy, and healthy lifestyles promote intellectual functioning and achievement of personal potential.

## FUNDING AND ORGANIZATION OF HEALTH SERVICES

The success of campus-based health services requires sufficient funding and a strong organizational commitment from the institution. This in turn requires that health care professionals become familiar with and connected to other units of the institution that collectively support the success of students (e.g., faculty associate deans and advisors, counselling, international student advising).

Funding arrangements for health and wellness services vary from province to province and among institutions. Operations may be totally dependent on internal funding, fully or partly supported by student health fees, or actually generate net revenues for the institution. Some institutions receive grants from the provincial health ministry to provide alternate payments for physicians and operating funds for a clinic. Health services that include a medical clinic are extremely costly to operate, given that competitive salaries for health care professionals are expensive and that student health is not a very profitable specialty. Many student visits are for mental health issues, for first-time contraceptive counselling, and physical concerns that can have a psychological component. Illnesses like dyspepsia, fatigue, and neck and shoulder pain can often be managed with a lifestyle treatment that will improve health without necessarily using medication.

Wellness programming is not sufficiently funded in most Canadian institutions. Often provincial grants and fee-for-service funding do not include non-physician personnel and health promotion programming. Health educators are often paid through general operating funds or a specific health fee levied on students. Because of very small budgets, wellness programming is usually aimed at specific high-profile issues and funded by time-limited project grants. Programs are mostly provided by student volunteers (peers) under the guidance of a health educator. If agendas are similar, working with internal and external partners can bring resources and expertise to wellness education. Opportunities sometimes arise from external priorities, for example, smoking prevention and cessation. While it is a high priority in this general age group, the select population of a particular institution's students, who are highly educated and of higher socioeconomic status, may be the least likely to smoke. Funding opportunities may not match the specific needs of the student population. A more effective approach combines student development theory with a holistic view of wellness, and addresses development of resilience, skills, and healthy habits that are prerequisites of well-being.

Integration with the institutional service network is critical to the effective support of student health care needs. For example, campus counselling services have long been traditional allies of student health services in recognizing and treating student distress and mental illness (See chapter 9). A very good working relationship with such a centre allows complementary programming to extend mental health resources on campus (Sedgwick et al. 2008). Joint services such as stress management workshops, mood management psycho-educational group therapy, and suicide prevention programs can reduce the burden of illness as well as extend the reach of services into the student community. Streamlined and expedited referrals between the two services can reduce waiting periods and time away from academic duties for affected students. Understanding the perspective and tools that each can offer is vital to a team approach. Using informed consent to allow communication between the counsellor and the student health professional can also reduce duplication of services and the "pinball effect," where a distressed student bounces from office to office seeking help. An essential responsibility for both services is to assess the student population's mental health status, to work with disability services to report on medical and psychological disability, and to make recommendations for accommodation by all community members of the institution. Working together, counselling services, disability services and student health can be leaders in systemic changes that will improve student well-being and safety.

## PROFESSIONALIZATION
## OF STUDENT HEALTH SERVICES

Student health services are most valuable on a campus when there is an opportunity to fully integrate with a rich cadre of student services professionals. Effective health care professionals are highly trained in their respective fields and understand the developmental concepts of young adulthood. Their contributions can enhance a holistic understanding of the student that will improve programming and services offered to support student success. Conversely, and just as important, health care professionals can gain knowledge about student development theory, learning theory and practices, and evaluation techniques from their student services colleagues. Meeting and working with other on-campus professionals in the student services field can too often be overlooked because of time and work constraints. However, release time from clinical duties to do so is vital to ensure that student health personnel are able to contribute meaningfully. The annual Canadian Institute on Student Affairs and Services is an excellent resource for new student health care professionals. Ongoing professional activities and opportunities to learn from colleagues from around the country occur as well at annual conferences of the Canadian Association of College and University Student Services. In addition there are chapters and national conferences of the American College Health Association that are highly relevant to the clinical and policy aspects of student health and well-being.

## ISSUES AND CHALLENGES

The transitory nature of students and many of the features particular to the student lifestyle suggest a range of issues and challenges that must be considered carefully in the design and implementation of campus health services. Among these are the changing demographics of college and university campuses and the needs of emerging student subgroups. Also in this mix are numerous health considerations embedded in the young adult life cycle, such as sexual activity, alcohol use, addictive behaviours (e.g., gambling and video gaming), sleep patterns, body image preoccupation, and increasingly, mental health. All of these warrant the attention of campus health care providers in order to shape policies and practices supportive of students' concerns.

### Health Issues

Developing well-targeted health care and wellness programming requires a clear understanding of an institution's student population. Surveys such as the National Survey of Student Engagement (NSSE), the Centre for Addiction and Mental Health (CAMH) Monitor (Adlaf and Ialomiteanu 2002) and the National College Health Assessment (ACHA 2008) can detail the health characteristics and concerns of the student body. However, caution must be observed in interpreting perceptions of "typical student" behaviours that often can be incorrect or exaggerated. While national data trends offer an important context, the profile of any particular institution's student population is at least as important, since it reflects the institution's educational programs, the communities from which it draws, and the demographics of its recruitment base. The specific composition of students enroled should dictate the kinds of programming most responsive to their needs, increasing the possibility of making a positive difference in students' health status.

A case in point is the experience of the University of British Columbia (UBC), where health care providers rely on several assessments to understand student needs. In addition to available national health trend reports, UBC has regularly administered to students (most recently in March of 2004, 2006, and 2008) an electronic version of the *National College Health Assessment*, designed by the American College Health Association (Hoban and Leino 2006). This survey generates a report on national trends as well as local institutional characteristics. Such data have become important indicators of health issues and trends among students in general, as well as how local demographics shape the campus profile. Survey results, for example, have established that UBC students generally rate their health as good to excellent. Interestingly, significantly more self-identified Chinese students rate their health as "fair" or "poor." However, these differences are not explained by varying rates of illness or serious health conditions, or by student visa status. Nonetheless, the differences in the data between self-identified Chinese and Caucasians persist in the areas of alcohol use, non-academic use of the Internet, sexual activity, and exercise and weight preoccupation. Thus, such findings highlight the need for campus health services to understand and respond appropriately to UBC's student population rather than rely on available national or international data. Further illustrations of national trends and the UBC context are found in the data generated by such surveys on a range of health-related issues, including mental health, alcohol and substance use, sexual activity, sleep patterns, exercise habits, and body image.

MENTAL HEALTH

Across Canada, health and counselling services report that mental health is a serious concern (Crozier and Willihnganz 2005). Nationally, forty per cent of Canadian undergraduates have reported receiving a lower grade on an exam, receiving an incomplete course grade, or dropping an entire course because of stress. Ninety-five per cent reported feeling overwhelmed by what they had to do; 68 per cent felt hopeless; and 48 per cent were so depressed that they had difficulty functioning at least once in the previous school year (Mirwaldt et al. 2007). At UBC, in 2006, more than 90 per cent of students reported knowing when they were starting to experience stress, but 29 per cent of females and 20 per cent of males indicated that they did not know how to cope with stress when it occurred. More than 18 per cent of undergraduate females and 21 per cent of males reported that they had experienced depression; of those diagnosed, fewer than 35 per cent were taking medication or had participated in therapy to manage their depression. Ten per cent of females and 6 per cent of males indicated that they had experienced an anxiety disorder. Even more disturbing, 10 per cent of students had seriously considered suicide within the previous year, and 1 to 2 per cent reported making an attempt. Tragically, a few do kill themselves each year, although accurate numbers are not available. Clearly there is a significant burden of stress and mental illness on Canadian campuses that interferes with academic functioning and is under-treated. A carefully considered systematic approach, using an ecological framework involving the entire university community (administrators, service providers, faculty, staff, and students) (Banning and Kaiser 1974), has been recommended by various groups (Jed Foundation).

ALCOHOL AND SUBSTANCE USE

In the 2008 American College Health Association (ACHA) survey, Canadian undergraduates reported a significant amount of binge drinking, as defined by the consumption of five or more drinks on the last occasion of "partying": 41 per cent reported having a binge at least once in the previous two weeks (the timing of the survey covered a very busy part of the academic year and deliberately avoided traditional high periods of socialization, such as during orientation). More than three episodes of binge drinking in the previous two weeks were reported by: 8 per cent of females and 18 per cent of males. Perceptions of use by other students on campus are also significantly at odds with self-reports of their peers. Although 11 per cent of undergraduates reported never using alcohol and only 0.4 per cent admitted to using it daily, students perceived that only 2 per cent of their peers did not use alcohol and 34 per cent used it daily. Unfortunately, 39 per cent of students have experienced at least one negative consequence as a result of their alcohol use. Cigarette smoking in the previous thirty days was reported by only 15 per cent of Canadian undergraduates, yet classmates thought that 85 per cent of their fellow-students were smokers. Fifteen per cent of undergraduates reported having used marijuana at least once in the previous month, although peers estimated that 87 per cent of their classmates used marijuana at least once in the same time period. (Interestingly, despite some well-publicized speculation that Canadians are much more likely than Americans to accept and use marijuana, Canadian students reported almost identical rates to the comparison group from American colleges and universities.) The divergence between actual and perceived uses brought to light by this survey suggests that application of a social norm marketing strategy is an appropriate tool for reducing alcohol, tobacco, and other substance use among these post-secondary students. Further research and application of best practices, especially about substance use, may help to reduce alcohol and substance use and other negative consequences on Canadian campuses.

SEXUAL ACTIVITY

In the 2008 UBC survey, significant proportions of undergraduate students reported no sexual intercourse (oral, vaginal, and/or anal) in the previous year: 36 per cent of females and 43 per cent of males. Of those who had experienced sexual intercourse in the previous year, the vast majority reported doing so with only one partner. This finding contrasted with perceptions that peers were much more experienced. Even though only 7 per cent of undergraduates reported three or more partners, their perceptions were that 47 per cent of females and 35 per cent of males had more than three partners in the previous year. Only 53 per cent of those having vaginal and 30 per cent of those having anal intercourse reported using a condom, suggesting that, despite a multitude of promotion messages, safer sex with condom use is not consistently practiced. Clearly, basic sexual health programming must remain a high priority for health services.

For heterosexually active students, contraception is an important consideration, as the vast majority reported that they were not planning a pregnancy in the coming year. Although it can be costly, student supplemental health plans were among the first in Canada to include prescriptions for contraceptives. Access to low-cost contraception is an important aspect of health services on any campus. Often, campus clinics are a resource for local students who do not wish to utilize their usual health care providers as they become sexually active and explore contraception, sexual practices, and other aspects of sexual health. Of those UBC students who reported having had vaginal intercourse, only 31 per cent relied on oral contraceptives and 35 per cent said they had used condoms to prevent pregnancy. National data from the same survey indicated that 50 per cent reported use of the pill and 39 per cent use of a condom to prevent pregnancy. Other reliable methods were reported very seldom; however, unreliable methods such as withdrawal were reported by more than 15 per cent of women who had engaged in vaginal intercourse. Emergency contraception – using medication within seventy-two hours of intercourse – is not uniformly available on Canadian campuses. In some provinces, though, it can be purchased in pharmacies without a prescription; in others, a doctor visit and prescription are required. According to its 2008 NCHA data, at UBC, in a province with very liberal access to emergency contraception, 14 per cent of sexually active students said that they or their partners had used emergency contraception within the previous year, and only 1 per cent reported an unplanned pregnancy, either their own or their partner's. Across Canada, 11 per cent reported using emergency contraception and 2 per cent reported unintentional pregnancy. Knowing the individual institution's experience helps to guide which health issues to emphasize in programming. Helping students to manage conception by offering information and ready access to contraceptives on campus has traditionally been a part of student health programming and will continue as an important service.

## SLEEP PATTERNS

While concerns of substance use and sexual practices might demand significant staff resources in most campus health services, more ordinary issues warrant no less attention. For example, one of the most pervasive student health issues is lack of sleep. The pressures on students to master their subjects and to complete timely academic work, combined with commitments to part-time jobs, volunteer activities supportive of career choices, and recurring family obligations, have created a sleep-deprived student body. In many faculties there is a certain bravado and expectation to "pull all-nighters," while faculty in professional programs model normative excessive workloads. Just 16 per cent of Canadian students report getting enough sleep to feel rested on six or more of the previous seven days (National College Health Assessment 2008). Optimal cognitive functioning depends on adequate sleep, for adolescents as much as eleven hours per night and not less than seven hours for most adults. The vast majority of Canadian students appear to be working with reduced cognitive functioning simply because of a lack of sleep.

## EXERCISE HABITS

Exercise is under-practiced by post-secondary students, despite the fact that it contributes to improved cognitive functioning, stress reduction, and a sense of well-being. While 42 per cent of Canadian undergraduates reported getting the minimally acceptable amount of thirty minutes of moderate exercise three days per week, the 2008 UBC study discovered that 46 per cent of Chinese female undergraduates never exercised, with only 20 per cent reporting minimally adequate levels. Men fared somewhat better: 54 per cent of Caucasian undergraduates and 30 per cent of Chinese undergraduates reported exercising regularly. Many health authorities now recommend sixty minutes per day of exercise, but less than 8 per cent of UBC students reported even half that amount.

## BODY IMAGE

Body image, eating disorders, and weight preoccupation are common factors that can have a significant impact on students. At UBC, more than 30 per cent of females reported being overweight, and yet it is estimated that 80–90 per cent of females are at or below a healthy body mass index (BMI), a calculation incorporating their reported weight and height. Of those who are at a healthy BMI, about half are trying to lose weight. Even more disconcerting, of those who are below their healthy BMIs, at least

31 per cent are trying to lose yet more weight. Among those who wished to lose weight, the following methods were used: exercise (49 per cent), dieting (34 per cent), laxatives or vomiting (3 per cent), and diet pills (2 per cent). Males at UBC also struggled with weight issues, with 27 per cent reporting being overweight. Of those at a healthy weight, 32 per cent were trying to gain additional weight. Males more often used exercise for weight control: 40 per cent exercised, 16 per cent dieted, and less than 1 per cent used laxatives or diet pills. Without adequate sleep, exercise, and nutrition, students are ill-prepared to manage academic challenges or life in general.

### Chronic Medical Conditions

Advances in human rights legislation, health status, and care and practices for those with chronic medical conditions have improved access to post-secondary education and have increased the number of students who require both academic accommodations and health care support to complete their post-secondary studies. Of particular note are chronic mental health conditions like schizophrenia, bipolar disorder, and severe personality disorders. Earlier recognition and better treatments for such diseases can control their symptoms to the point that success in post-secondary education is possible. With many mental health conditions, the first signs develop in young adulthood or are sometimes brought on by the stress of academic demands, such that initial symptoms and diagnosis may occur on campus. A disturbing trend to discontinue successful medication regimes prior to starting university is called a "fresh start" on campus. That, in combination with the usual stresses of first-year academics, such as living alone for the first time, away from family and usual health care providers, often precipitates a relapse. Reluctance to disclose a mental illness because of concerns of discrimination in admissions or evaluation can hamper a smooth transition to campus.

Good transition planning for those who experience chronic health issues often involves creating a contract between the student, the present caregivers, parents, and campus health services providers. To support these students, the latter must become knowledgeable in medication management and help arrange the special services a student may require. Often students with specific mental health issues must be linked with off-campus specialists, and it falls to campus health personnel to educate those specialists about the demands and stresses of the campus experience and the nature and limitations of residence life. Sometimes psychiatrists view residence halls as therapeutic communities that can serve as step-down units following a hospital admission for a serious mental health problem. Working closely with hospital and residence life staff (See chapter 6) can set limits on inappropriate discharge immediately back to residence and classes until personal safety and community issues are addressed. Being well enough to leave hospital is often not synonymous with being well enough to return to academic responsibilities. Encouraging students to include access and diversity staff to develop appropriate academic accommodation is essential to a successful outcome.

It is not enough though to be interested in young adult health; knowledge of the institution's policies and decision-makers equips health care professionals with specific information and contacts to effectively advocate for the specific student-patient and for all students in general. The health services staff must have a working relationship with policy-makers and student advisors, and must understand life on their campus and how it affects student well-being.

### Student Subgroups

Subgroups exist on each campus with specific service requirements and health issues that differ from the "typical student." Campus health services providers can develop a relationship and communication with diverse student groups in order to be as responsive as possible to their needs. Although there are numerous other groups on campus, the following are illustrative of how the conditions and circumstances some students face may shape the context of their personal health.

#### GLBTQ STUDENTS

Students who are heterosexual, gay, lesbian, bisexual, or transgender will often first acknowledge and explore their sexuality as young adults. Campus health providers may be the first health care personnel the student talks with about sexual identity and emotional health concerns. Health personnel who actively display a high level of interest and acceptance encourage both heterosexual and GLBTQ students to feel more confidence in the health personnel and to comfortably seek appropriate care. Health personnel should receive awareness and sensitivity training in order to strengthen their understanding of issues related to homophobia, heterosexism, transphobia, queer culture, and local resources (See chapter 12). Other specific strategies include partnering with campus diversity programmers; helping to initiate support groups on campus, and supporting those already established such as PRIDE (a peer group supportive of GLBTQ students); extending the reach of wellness programming to those who feel discounted or ignored in health and wellness programming or who are targeted only by sexual health messages.

#### FIRST-GENERATION STUDENTS

Many Canadian post-secondary students are the first in their families to attend a college or university, bringing with them a mix of health beliefs,

lifestyles, and health behaviours that blend current young Canadian practices and values with the cultural and family expectations of their parents
and their parents' country of origin. Cultural competency training prepares
health providers with attitudes and approaches that offer respectful, responsive, and appropriate care to each student. Often the student is experiencing
a combination of normal transition issues and cultural dissonance that leads
to significant distress. The campus health provider, if viewed as different
from the family doctor, can provide anonymity and lessen students' concerns
about the local cultural or ethnic community hearing about or disapproving
of their lifestyle. Equally, campus providers can dispel misconceptions these
students may have about what is typical student behaviour.

INTERNATIONAL STUDENTS

International students do not often bring family members with them, and
may therefore experience more severe adjustment issues. The stress of
becoming a student in a new country, which may differ in every conceiv-
able way from their home, can have a significant impact on health. Lack
of knowledge about how to navigate health care in Canada, lack of usual
self-care aids, and change in diet and environment can all conspire to make
them feel illness or distress more keenly. Some international students arrive
with health concerns that have not been acknowledged or treated because
of a lack of resources or acceptance in their country of origin, concern
that their illness is not acceptable at the new institution, or apprehension
that disclosure will lead to dismissal, interruption in academic progress, or
student visa problems. This is especially true for mental health issues and
blood-borne illnesses, such as hepatitis B, that are viewed very differently
in Canada than in many other parts of the world. Illness and its attendant
impact on intellectual and physical functioning significantly threatens the
international student's self-perception as being strong and capable in the
face of already significant pressure to succeed. For campus health services,
the challenge is to communicate effectively, to provide culturally sensitive
care, and to learn from these students an expanded view of health, self,
and family responsibilities. Campus health services can improve acceptance
of Canadian health care and attitudes by communicating with international
student services and campus social and ethnic groups, addressing the specific
concerns of the institution's particular international student population.

In many provinces, international students are barred from provincial health
insurance plans and, thus, most off-campus care, unless they can afford to
pay privately. Even when students do have private health insurance, many
off-campus providers in Canada – hospitals, labs, and physicians – charge
cash first for services, as collecting from insurance companies is time con-
suming and uncertain. Many students gamble that they will not need care
or they do not understand that their travel insurance or home system of

medical care may not apply once they are living in Canada. Institutions that have made medical insurance mandatory for international students (and collect it as part of student fees) avoid most of these problems. The best type of insurance is "expatriate insurance" that treats the students as if they were Canadian and covers complete health care, including prevention services, contraception, and maternity services. Recently, medical malpractice insurance carriers have advised their member Canadian medical doctors, who treat non-Canadians for non-emergency conditions, to have each patient sign a waiver. The waiver, called a Governing Law and Jurisdiction Agreement, stipulates that any legal action arising from the interaction between doctor and patient be brought and settled in Canada. This impacts the campus health service that must institute and explain the waiver; even worse, this causes many off-campus doctors to reject non-Canadian patients altogether. Each year limitations in medical insurance have been cited in cases where diagnostic or treatment services are delayed until the student returns home or until the condition worsens, sometimes with tragic results.

## Privacy of Care

Each institution is bound by its provincial freedom of information and protection of privacy legislation. These laws and long-established professional obligations of confidentiality can come into conflict with the changing roles of students, who are becoming independent, and parents, who often assume that the educational institution will both preserve parental privileges and responsibilities and act *in loco parentis*. Increasingly, as students from all over the world attend Canadian institutions, there are very different expectations and demands for parental involvement. The age of majority differs between provinces and countries, and the view of students as emancipated minors or full adults is not universal. Students have differing expectations for privacy and parental involvement depending on their own development and experience and the situation they are facing. Nowhere is this more apparent and angst-ridden than when a student becomes ill. In the event a student opposes family involvement, medical personnel often grapple with deciding when a condition dictates that one must break confidentiality and notify parents or other family members. Current student trends indicate that many gladly involve their parents in health care decisions, often even prior to doctors being consulted. As well, most parents understand confidentiality guidelines and appreciate the opportunity to express their concerns about their child with health staff, without receiving specific information. Welcoming parent phone calls to allow them to express their concerns, while maintaining confidentiality of the student's medical information, can smooth the transition from family care to self-care for all concerned. Given the normal transition tasks of an emerging adult, this can take place very rapidly or in degrees over a period of years.

## CONCLUSION

Students' well-being must be supported by all aspects of the college or university community: academic policies and practices, physical and social environments, access to healthy food and recreational facilities, and various work and volunteer opportunities, to name a few. Although these are not in the traditional portfolio of campus health services, acknowledgment that health care professionals deal with only a limited aspect of students' health and well-being in the clinical setting will lead to the development of partnerships that will maximize their influence on students' well-being.

# 11

# Career and Employment Services

ROBERT SHEA

The development of career and employment services in Canadian higher education evolved over the decades in the spirit of helping students succeed. The genesis of specific departments addressing such needs dates to the post-Second World War era, when campuses responded to a national need to assist returning veterans make a successful transition to civilian life. In many instances, this included opportunities for further education and in others, a transition to employment. Thus, the focus on student success in the delivery of these services has been a persistent theme for at least the past six decades.

Typical Canadian campus career centres focus on multiple aspects of career development, including employment counselling, resumé preparation, interview skills, career counselling, career planning, and navigating the world of work. Most often added to these basic services is an enhanced process of advising students, from their entry into to their completion of programs of study, and beyond. Career centres of today are also challenged as never before to embrace new technologies, with the Internet revolutionizing the delivery of many services through Web-based resources designed to ensure greater utilization by greater numbers of students. Web cams, podcasts, and video conferencing as well as synchronous and asynchronous mediums of delivery are all gaining in popularity among users. Finally, as the career and employment services field has advanced, so too has its need for quality outcomes research to engage academic colleagues and senior administrators in the planning and implementation of programs and practices.

This chapter offers a synopsis of the historical trends and developments of Canadian college and university career centres, with a focus on their functions and services, typical programs and creative practices, their administrative portfolio and structures, and the professional knowledge and skills required to work in them. The chapter concludes with a review of anticipated issues and challenges, as well as connections to student success.

## ESSENTIAL FUNCTIONS AND SERVICES

The traditional model of career development and employment services in Canadian post-secondary institutions includes a number of interrelated functions. Each function is designed to meet the needs of individuals, groups of students, the faculties who prepare students for their chosen fields, and the employers who hope to capitalize on graduates' talents. In addition, career and employment services execute a range of administrative tasks related to remaining current in the world of work and documenting the impact of their programs and practices for the institutions that sponsor them.

### Student Needs

Among common career centre services addressing the needs of incoming and in-course students are workshops on navigating the world of work; advising on curriculum vitae and resumé writing; marketing of students to employers; individual advising; group work, such as job-finding clubs and workshops; and focused workshops and programs meeting the needs of specific student populations (such groups might include, for example, Aboriginal students, single parents, women in engineering, graduate students, and undergraduates).

One example of a specialized student-focused initiative can be found in the Student Work and Service Program (SWASP), first implemented at Memorial University of Newfoundland in 1995. SWASP is dedicated to the career development needs of single parents, and resulted from a partnership between the federal and provincial governments, the campus career and employment services centre, and two student societies dedicated to single parents and students older than average. The program provided mature students career-related employment and much-needed tuition support, in addition to funding of other costs associated with the post-secondary experience. In return, students worked on campus for varying numbers of hours throughout the academic year. Through learning contracts and reflective learning agreements, program participants capitalized on a range of experiential opportunities to develop much-needed competencies for their successful transition to the labour market or further education.

Another example, for graduating students, is illustrated in the Applied Career Transitions (ACT) Program at the University of Victoria. This initiative guides recent graduates through a systematic and applied approach to managing their career transition, from the classroom to the world of work or additional education. Students are ushered through three modules: (a) building career foundations, (b) developing career opportunities, and (c) getting career experience through an internship (University of Victoria).

Initiatives for students from immigrant families are also evolving, such as those at Ryerson University, where the Tri-Mentoring Program strives to assist culturally diverse students in their pursuit of personal goals, academic achievements, and career success. Through meaningful relationships with students, employers, and the community-at-large, Ryerson's culturally diverse students are encouraged to experience the benefits of guidance, communication, leadership, and a supportive community as they grow academically and personally (http://www.ryerson.ca/trimentoring).

McGill University's career centre has pursued a career planning strategy titled Program for the Advancement of Career Exploration (PACE), a collaborative effort between the University Counselling Service and the McGill Career and Placement Service (CAPS). PACE is a two-hour workshop series designed to help students make successful decisions related to their personal field of study, assisting them in discovering whether their chosen undergraduate degree is the best choice for their individual talents and interests. The four workshops that constitute PACE are spaced one week apart to allow time for vocational testing and occupational research (http://caps.mcgill.ca/programs/pace/).

### Faculty Needs

Career and employment services also functions as a link between programs of study and employment opportunities for which these programs might prepare students. Connections between interests and applications may range from the indirect and general, as is most often the case with Arts and Science majors, to the applied and specific, as is typically the case with many professional programs. The role of faculty is paramount in orienting students to the fields they have chosen. Thus, effective career and employment services entails developing and maintaining close relationships with faculties so they are aware of the applications and choices students encounter in translating interests into viable employment or other workplace activities. Such liaison, at the very least, might include the posting and coordination of employment opportunities.

There are currently three main models of service delivery among faculties and schools in Canadian post-secondary education: (a) centralized services, (b) decentralized services, and (c) hybrid services. The foundation of the *centralized* model is a campus-wide central repository of programs and services designed for the entire institution. This model provides support to all students regardless of faculty or school.

In the *decentralized* approach, faculties and schools provide their own career services. Offices focus on the career needs of individual students enrolled in their specific faculties. While such dedication has benefits, this model can potentially isolate some faculties – especially those that are smaller or not profession-based. Decentralized career and employment centres are most often found among university faculties of business, engineering, law, and medicine. The final model is the *hybrid*, which features some centralized career services, such as graduate recruitment, but with faculties maintaining their own career centres.

A centralized system offers numerous benefits, including ease of administration, one-stop shopping, and a capacity for responding to students' needs without duplication. This approach might maximize an institution's ability to assist students make a successful transition to the labour market or find their way in a confusing array of career possibilities. Although the decentralized model might allow faculties with significant resources to tailor their services to a specific cohort, its potential for program duplication and other inefficiencies is high. The hybrid approach perhaps capitalizes on the benefits of both, without the drawbacks of either. Whichever the model, its fit for any particular campus is predicated on that institution's culture, environment, and politics.

### Employer Needs

The ultimate goal of career and employment services is to connect prepared candidates with work opportunities that are both satisfying and appropriate to their interests and skills. To achieve this, institutions must cultivate and maintain strong relationships with current and potential employers. This entails recruitment of employers, coordination of career and job fairs, and administration of on- and off-campus employment programs. While earlier approaches tended to focus almost exclusively on the job placement of graduates, in more recent decades, centres have moved toward accommodating, and efficiently delivering and administrating, a broader range of career development services.

### Administrative Functions

In addition to the above, an active career and employment services office must look after a range of program management tasks, maintain academic research on career issues, and track various performance indicators and outcomes. The administrative functions of a career centre designed to enhance student success include leadership, program planning, staff evaluation, budgeting, program evaluation, labour relations, research, grant writing, and outcomes assessment. The organizational structures of most career centres in Canadian higher education must support a complement of career counsellors, career development advisors, recruiting coordinators, and assistant directors, who ultimately report to a director of career services.

The director would, in turn, report to a senior student affairs officer in an academic or administrative portfolio.

## PROFESSIONALIZATION OF THE FIELD

The field of career development has undergone a metamorphosis since 2000. The need for professional preparation in the area of career and employment services has challenged a growing number of institutions to ensure that staff at all levels have appropriate graduate credentials, such as a master's degree or related professional certificate. The general move in North America in the 1990s toward credentialing spawned numerous discussions regarding preparation for the field of career development. Research in 2005–06 by the Canadian Education and Research Institute for Counselling (CERIC) established that current credentialing for the career planning and development field tends to be interdisciplinary in nature, a feature that undoubtedly results in a rich resource for college and university students. Yet, this same feature will challenge existing post-secondary institutions to review carefully how career services practitioners are trained.

Competencies required for career and employment services professionals depend much on the specific role of the position within the respective institution. Practitioners completing career counselling certification requirements, maintained by provincial psychological and social work associations, are subject to the varying standards of provincial registration bodies. For example, provincial career counselling certification in Quebec includes a macro understanding of career theory, models of career development, group presentation skills, and workshop development. More specific administrative and leadership competencies, offered through various graduate-level programs, include a focus on leadership styles, labour relations, budgeting, proposal writing, and assessment and research.

In addition to pursuing basic credentials, career and employment personnel also have many opportunities to maintain currency in the field through involvement in professional organizations. To date, there are five primary organizations that support the needs of college and university career and employment professionals in Canada: (a) the Canadian Association of Career Educators and Employers (CACEE); (b) the Student Affairs and Services Association (SASA) and (c) the Canadian University and College Counselling Association (CUCCA), both affiliates of the Canadian Association of College and University Student Services (CACUSS); (d) the Canadian Education and Research Institute for Counselling (CERIC); and (e) the Canadian Association For Co-operative Education (CAFCE).

The origins of the Canadian Association of Career Educators and Employers (CACEE) lie in the wake of the Second World War, when campus career advisors were appointed to assist veterans starting or returning to post-secondary education. In 1946, CACEE was inaugurated under the name of University Advisory Services. Its first conference, attended by thirty-nine veterans' advisors, was held in Vancouver, British Columbia. This gathering eventually led to the formation of the Canadian University and College Counselling Association (CUCCA).

With the growth of other services devoted to supporting the needs of college and university students, the University Advisory Services (UAS) invited other campus student services personnel to join their effort. In 1952 it evolved into yet another, more broadly based, organization: the University Counselling and Placement Association (UCPA). In 1963, reflecting both the extent and specialization of services represented, UCPA enacted several internal constitutional changes to further recognize and accommodate the emergence of several focused divisions, including the University Career Planning Association (UCPA), the University Counselling Association (UCA), and the Canadian Student Affairs Association (CSAA).

In 1965, UCPA was renamed the Council of Associations of University Student Personnel Services. In 1971, the umbrella organization was reconstituted as the Canadian Association of College and University Student Services (CACUSS), and the career planning and placement sector became a stand-alone entity, incorporating both employers and career services providers. (The UCPA title persisted for another twenty years as an organization comprised of federal government employees and national employers affiliated with colleges and universities.) At that time, the University of Toronto was among the first to feature an institutionally supported career and employment service in a post-secondary setting. The University of Toronto Career Centre rose to a place of prominence in modelling the possibilities of an institution that effectively supports the career development of its students.

By the early 1990s the organization's name was changed once again, to ACCIS – The Graduate Workforce professionals. During this period, the federal government began its transition away from campus-based career and placement services, and institutions were consequently challenged to fill the resulting void. Transition agreements were reached with many institutions and funding was provided for some, compelling colleges and universities to assume greater responsibilities in this area. Most accepted the challenge and began to develop their own models of service. During this same period ACCIS - The Graduate Workforce Professionals grew to almost 800 members, representing most colleges and universities in Canada, as well as over 300 employers. In 1995, after cross-Canada consultation and much discussion, the association was renamed the Canadian Association of Career Educators and Employers (CACEE). For the first time the employer partnership was validated and confirmed in the organization's title. Today CACEE is a national non-profit partnership of employer recruiters and career services professionals, whose stated mission is to provide information, advice, professional development opportunities, and other services to employers, career services professionals, and students (Canadian Association of Career Educators and Employers).

Another closely aligned national organization is the Canadian Association for Internship Programs (CAFIP), founded in 1992 to promote the growth and development of internship programs among educational institutions and employers in Canada. Among its purposes is to assist new members in establishing a foundation for nurturing the development of successful programs and interns. In December 2003, CAFIP entered into a formal partnership with CACEE.

Under the auspices of the Canadian Association of College and University Student Services (CACUSS) are two additional specialized divisions supporting the needs of career professionals working on college and university campuses: the Canadian University and College Counselling Association (CUCCA) and the Student Affairs and Services Association (SASA). CUCCA represents the interests and professional development concerns of career and personal counsellors, while SASA serves those who work within the field of career and employment services. These two distinct affiliations for career counsellors and career and employment practitioners mirror the service framework found on most campuses today. A third organization and interwoven in the field of career and employment services, is the Canadian Association For Co-operative Education (CAFCE). CAFCE represents the needs of professionals working in the field of co-operative education. While not traditionally viewed as a student service, CAFCE is included here as its initiatives are often listed among the mandates and administrative responsibilities of senior student affairs officers.

Many hybrid service models exist on current campuses, with career and co-operative education services led by a senior student affairs officer who reports to a vice-president (academic) or the university/college president. The development of CAFCE in the early 1970s encouraged co-operative education professionals across faculties to affiliate with a national association. The ultimate existence of the national association itself validated the importance of this dynamic form of experiential learning. The growth of co-operative education in Canada can be linked to the national presence of CAFCE and its continuing role in the promotion of standards and professionalism in the field.

### ISSUES AND CHALLENGES

The importance of preparing students for the world of work has fluctuated throughout the history of Canadian post-secondary education, but this goal appears to be on the rise in today's colleges and universities. The tying of government performance indicators to graduate placement rates increasingly places emphasis on this outcome. In addition, parents' concerns for their sons' and daughters' transition to viable careers following convocation and students' expectations of themselves for gainful employment and capacity to pay off debts are ongoing motivators for rejuvenating career and employment services on many Canadian campuses. An interesting advancement in that regard is York University Career Centre's statement of Career Centre Identity, aptly titled, *The Role of the Career Centre at York University* (York University). This document is a testimony to the need for career centres to establish their own unique identities based on the four pillars of a post-secondary institution – culture, politics, environment, and power. Accordingly, York University's statement addresses the following key components:

- Making a difference in students' careers
- The interdisciplinary university
- The structure of career support services at York
- The unique role of the central career centre
- Eligibility for services
- The career centre's role with employers
- Outside of the scope of the career centre

This statement is significant in that it defines and enhances the roles and responsibilities of career centres in the implementation of student success services.

The future of career and employment services in Canadian higher education is solid, but not without its challenges. New applications of experiential learning, for example, are causing some to question the value and structural effectiveness of traditional department domains. The advent of new technologies is also changing the nature and mode of communications on campus, while new student bodies, more diverse and complex, are challenging the ways in which career and employment services are delivered. Finally, higher expectations for accountability are spotlighting an apparent dearth of data on either the impact of such services or their contribution to the retention and success of students.

### Experiential Learning

Concepts of experiential learning, work-integrated learning, alternative education, practice-oriented education, co-operative education, and internships have made significant gains among the practices of career and employment centres in Canada. Collectively, these approaches to learning have brought a renewed focus to the career and employment role in the post-secondary scene. As such concepts are embraced, the environmental, cultural, political, and structural dimensions of our work promise to undergo further change.

With the continued focus on co-curricular learning, there will likely come a merging of some campus units that have long separated the academic side from the support side. This evolution will present greater opportunities to meld the strengths of career services, experiential learning, co-operative education, and learning that occurs in the classroom. Such new approaches will, in turn, place a greater emphasis on credit courses that focus on the career needs of students as they take responsibility for their own development. As career and employment services professionals anticipate what may lie ahead, they would do well to embrace this new holistic learning agenda, reclaiming the development of human capital as their raison d'être and strengthening their connection to the world of work through practices that are both applied and reflective.

A recent development of this integrated strategy has been the growth of service-learning opportunities on Canadian campuses. While sharing a common focus with experiential learning on the importance of application and reflection, service learning also incorporates a commitment to serving community purposes and ends. Interest in experiential learning has grown exponentially in the past five years, as evidenced by the creation in 2005 of the Canadian Association for Community Service-Learning (CACSL), perhaps signalling a more formal coordination and professionalization of this area. With the recent investment by the Montreal-based J.W. McConnell Family Foundation in a number of service-learning pilot projects, the momentum has continued. Certainly, with their commitment to educating students for the world of work and their desire to produce graduates who have an understanding of and dedication to community service, post-secondary institutions are once again responding to the world's call for "citizen leaders" in a global economy. All of this suggests that career and employment services of the future must become more conversant in alternative pedagogies and capable of connecting disparate interests and resources both within the academy, as well as between the campus and the community beyond.

## New Technologies

The advent of new technologies in the 1990s created a major shift on college and university campuses that led to widespread development of career centre websites and the increased use of computer-mediated communication techniques. This trend quickly upended the traditional "pin and post" approach to job notifications and listings and replaced it with a new vision of technology-driven access and service. During that same period, the Canadian government promoted the use of Job Banks kiosks placed in high traffic areas, such as shopping centres, federal government offices, and numerous post-secondary campuses.

With the availability and increased use of job banks came a more computer-literate student, challenging post-secondary institutions to capitalize further on the capacity of these technologies to provide more and better career information. The creation of the National Graduate Register, an innovation of the University of Moncton in partnership with Industry Canada, signalled a shift in placement centres, away from the traditional task of posting job orders and toward the new possibilities of career development technologies. Online job databases served to increase both the functionality and efficiency of career and employment services, and heralded the opportunity for colleges and universities to become signatories to a system that would also increase their accessibility and performance. The evolution of this service, known today as Workopolis™, found support among members of the Canadian Association of Career Educators and Employers and continues as a vibrant and lucrative service that most institutions in Canada subscribe to on behalf of their students. Such developments signal the need for viable career and employment services of the future to be proficient in the use of new technologies. It is also clear that the delivery of future services, such as digital portfolios, sophisticated searches, and distance interviewing, will depend greatly on the state of these new technologies. As an example, York University Career Centre's Career Cyber Guide features fifteen online workshops that contain video presentations, PowerPoint slides, and downloadable handouts and templates. Through the Career Cyber Guide, students access career information when they need it and proceed at their own pace. Current workshop topics include job search, networking, resumé writing, cover letter writing, interview skills, summer employment, and career stories.

### Changing Student Populations

The profile of the college and university campus has changed dramatically in recent decades and continues to evolve at a frantic pace. In addition to students considered "traditional," there are increasing numbers of older-than-average students, single parents, students of color, international students, Aboriginal and First Nations students, part-time students who are full-time workers, distance students, and students with physical and emotional disabilities and so on. Each cohort will present new opportunities as well as significant challenges for Canadian post-secondary career development and employment centres. Leading up to 2020, in particular, open immigration policies and the continued assertive recruitment of international students to Canada's colleges and universities will further shape the texture of these new enrolments, challenging career and employment centres like never before. An increase of Aboriginal and First Nations students especially will present an opportunity to understand a distinct way of life and to approach the world of work through a different lens. The challenge to career centres will be to understand the cultural and work issues of students who differ from those they are accustomed to serving. The recent inclusion within CACUSS of the National Aboriginal Student Services Association (NASSA), and the work on Aboriginal career counselling being done at the University of British Columbia indicate the kind of developments career and employment services must support in order to respond to this changing profile.

Potential cultural issues related to preparation for the labour market, variance in oral and written English skills, and differences of personal comfort in approaching employers promise to challenge how professionals deliver workshops, advise individuals and groups, and offer support to these new students. The lessons of more diverse institutions will need to be studied carefully, and modelled, if we are to succeed in providing career and employment services for the students of tomorrow.

### Research and Accountability

Finally, the future of campus career and employment services calls for greater accountability in what is delivered and how it affects students. There is a void in the Canadian literature on career development on college and university campuses. Little data exist on the impact and outcomes of career centre interventions or the effect of work-related factors on student retention. The data are equally limited on the connection between various forms of experiential learning and debt load and whether some interventions more than others assist students to make a successful transition to the world of work. Answers to such questions can offer compelling evidence for the efficacy of what career and employment services have to offer on campus.

Literature on the administration and leadership of career centres is also quite limited. The field can benefit further from a greater understanding of the competencies and skills required for career and employment centre leadership (e.g., proposal writing, human resources, and management styles). In addition, more information about national trends and service-level benchmarks will become increasingly important for justifying resource allocations, generating revenues, developing personnel, and establishing appropriate staff-to-student ratios and caseloads. Such concerns bear import for all professionals in the field and warrant a more systematic focus from those involved.

CONCLUSION

Career and employment services have evolved in important ways since the late 1980s in Canadian higher education. Beginning with a modest invest-ment in job postings and employment connections, most campuses now feature a full range of interventions to orient students in the world of careers and to develop their decision-making skills so that upon graduation they can transition into meaningful employment or further education. Campus career and employment professionals have also embraced a broader understanding of their work as an integral aspect of the student learning process, with potential for blending classroom concepts and real-world experiences. Given the result – students who move forward with a sense of purpose and direction that capitalizes on the full range of their under-graduate experiences – the importance of career services to the development and success of students on Canadian university and college campuses has never been more imperative.

# 12

# Services for Diverse Students

CHRIS McGRATH

From the first meeting of the University of Toronto Homophile Association in 1969 to the unique opportunity today for indigenous Black Nova Scotia students to meet with Dalhousie University's Black Student Advisor, the ways that post-secondary institutions promote and provide support services for diverse and often under-represented student populations indicate Canada's social commitment to the value of higher learning for its citizens, regardless of age, race, ability, size, gender, ethnic background, religious experience, sexual orientation, or gender identity. Much has transpired since those early stirrings of student voices caused post-secondary educators to reconsider the manner in which those under-represented, and sometimes invisible, students on campus were being served in their pursuit of success. This chapter examines more closely how educational issues and social attitudes have naturally pushed Canadian colleges and universities to become more actively and often broadly engaged in equity issues, and to establish innovative ways to overcome challenges and barriers to providing support for students and their diverse range of experiences.

Since 2000, numerous forces of change have influenced Canadian post-secondary education, not the least of which has been a growing, more dynamic, and more diverse student population. As well, colleges and universities face increasing pressure to expand a broadly accessible education to as many qualified students as possible. The complexity of student needs in combination with other pressures, including increased accountability and shifting perspectives on the institution's role in the student experience, has shed light on identifiable gaps in institutional support for diverse students. Consequently, many colleges and universities have begun to carve out programs and mechanisms that provide direct service to students from under-represented backgrounds and diverse experiences. While the human diversity of the student community is often a hallmark and source of institutional pride, the existence of human diversity alone on campuses is not enough to ensure that students from a range of under-represented populations have equal and inclusive access to all facets of post-secondary life. Designed to help facilitate access and inclusion for students from under-represented groups, the range of services available is as diverse as students themselves. However, the existence of the services is not intended to functionally reinforce the problematic binary of under-represented students being "diverse" and students from dominant cultures or minority groups being "not diverse." The exploration of this topic articulates how, in spite of often being one of the first functional areas to bear the pressures of political, financial, and resource constraints, these services have helped to ensure that the Canadian post-secondary environment has always been a place for students, staff, and faculty to explore and understand the diverse dimensions of their own personal identity and sense of otherness.

## CANADIANS AND DIVERSITY

Anderssen and Valpy (2003, A8) concluded that,

> although the 3.9 million Canadians today in their 20s defy a label ... There is one label they do carry: they are the most deeply tolerant generation of adults produced in a nation known for tolerance. They were babies when the Charter of Rights and Freedoms was signed ... and now, as adults, they rank that piece of paper higher than their parents do as a source of pride in their country. They are a reflection of the Canada their parents began constructing half a century ago.

Canadian college and university campuses are home to a "millennial generation" (Howe and Strauss 2000) of youth for whom diversity, in all of its forms, is seemingly a more common and broadly accepted dimension of everyday life. A survey by the Centre for Research and Information on Canada (Parkin and Mendelsohn 2003) painted a vivid portrait in its observation that "acceptance of diversity is the norm in the new Canada." Highlights of the Centre's findings that illustrate very low levels of opposition to the diverse character of Canadian society include:

- Only 10 per cent of Canadians agree that "It is a bad idea for people of different races to marry one another."
- Eighty-three per cent of Canadians report that they feel comfortable hearing languages other than English and French spoken on the street.
- Fifty-seven per cent of Canadians in major centres report that multiculturalism is a source of pride in their nation.

- Only 18 per cent say that immigrants have a "bad influence" on the nation, as compared to 43 per cent of Americans and 50 per cent of those in the United Kingdom.

Students on college and university campuses are the children of baby boomer parents who voted for governments that established critical policies related to diversity and immigration in the 1960s, 70s, and 80s. Significant legislation and policies were crafted in support of immigration, in an attempt to diversify the Canadian social landscape. For example, the 1982 Canadian Charter of Rights and Freedoms ensures "the equal protection and equal benefit of the law without discrimination and in particular, without discrimination based on race, national or ethnic origin, colour, religion, sex, age or mental or physical disability." Furthermore, in a nation that does not have as lengthy a history of oppression as some of its neighbours and trading partners, it is not surprising that there seem to be fewer barriers to equity nationwide. This is not to say that oppression does not exist in Canada and that barriers to ensure free access to social institutions, like education, are not prevalent. One need look no further, for example, than the legacies of residential schools on Aboriginal people and of Chinese head taxes, and of Japanese internment during the Second World War on people of Asian descent to understand the socio-political history and context for racial, ethnic, and cultural exploitation and oppression in Canada. However, while some under-represented populations, particularly Aboriginal people and those who identify as gay, lesbian, bisexual, transgender, and queer, still struggle to feel welcomed and included on college and university campuses, the recent emergence of specialized access programs and services has occurred with relatively minimal controversy and discord, indicating that post-secondary education is moving in a positive direction.

## DIVERSITY ON CAMPUS

Since Canadian colleges and universities do not formally collect data relative to race, ethnicity, sexual orientation, or religion, limited public data on the enrolment, attrition, engagement, and graduation rates of students from traditionally under-represented populations makes it challenging to assess the state of diversity at Canadian colleges and universities. However, Statistics Canada does track the post-secondary participation and attainment of men and women and, in some cases, individuals of Aboriginal descent. The *Report of the Pan-Canadian Education Indicators Program* (Statistics Canada 2005) highlights that:

- Diversity among the [Canadian] school-age population generally increased between 1991 and 2001.

- In Toronto and Vancouver, over 25 per cent of the school-age population in 2001 came from immigrant families, and approximately 20 per cent had a home language other than English or French.
- The proportion of the school-age population with Aboriginal identity is significant and growing in metropolitan centres and in areas outside major centres in certain provinces and territories.

Furthermore, a paper by Looker and Lowe (2001, 6) explored the gaps in access to post-secondary education, particularly those that stem from limitations in financial aid. Their findings illustrated that:

- Women have made considerable progress in their participation in and completion of post-secondary studies, now representing nearly 60 per cent of undergraduate degrees conferred.
- Concern about achievement among young men is growing because of lower literacy and high school completion rates.
- Speaking a first language other than English is less likely to be a barrier to attainment, yet young adults for whom French is the first language were less likely to participate in post-secondary education.
- Aboriginal persons have generally lower post-secondary completion rates than do people from non-Aboriginal backgrounds.

The lack of available specific data limits any comprehensive statement on diversity or the engagement of students from under-represented communities in Canadian colleges and universities. However, in a keynote address to faculty at the University of Toronto, Mary Gentile (2005), a consultant and former senior research fellow at the Harvard Business School, noted that,

> by defining diversity as a problem we predetermine and constrain the structure our response [to diversity] can take. But when we can frame diversity as a resource and process for growth and new learning, we begin to see why the educational environment can be a particularly fruitful context for attending to diversity.

No doubt, in the current context of Canadian post-secondary education, this statement makes logical sense. However, colleges and universities have not always viewed the diversity of its community members as either a valued resource or an asset for enhancing the climate of the campus. Only within the past few decades have Canadian institutions demonstrated a growing commitment to understanding diversity and working toward equity and inclusion on campus, although it has not always been an easy or smooth journey. This commitment is illustrated in the range of offices and programs that comprise diversity services on many campuses today.

## CAMPUS DIVERSITY FUNCTIONS AND SERVICES

Many of today's campus diversity initiatives find their origins in the work of student activists during the 1960s. During that era, college and university student governments first gave birth to the movement toward greater equity in Canadian post-secondary education. Students on many campuses organized themselves as smaller communities in order to establish a stronger presence of historically under-represented groups. In 1969, for example, fifteen men and one woman gathered to form the University of Toronto Homophile Association, now recognized as one of the nation's oldest organizations focused on advancing the interests of lesbian, gay, bisexual, transgender, and queer students. Since then, the organization has evolved to openly embrace all dimensions of sexual orientation and gender identity and has become a driving force behind the creation of the nation's first university office supporting the needs of queer students, staff, and faculty. Additionally, the organization, now known as LGBTOUT (Lesbians, Gays, Bisexuals, and Trans People of the University of Toronto), helped establish the nation's largest campus-based safe space ally program in 1996. The group also helped energize the formation of the university's undergraduate major program in sexual diversity studies in 2004 and the Centre for Sexual Diversity Studies. With membership in the hundreds and a history that has been celebrated across the country, this association evolved from its activist roots to embrace opportunities to partner with administrative advocates and positively effect social change at the University of Toronto.

The preceding example is not unlike the experiences of other post-secondary campuses, where issues of diversity and equity were rooted in the activism of organizations that, over time, found an administrative home and support in various institutional departments. Campus responses to these issues have come in the form of institutional policies, educational initiatives, and programmatic interventions focused on assuring basic rights, educating various constituents, providing service to specific populations, and sometimes most significantly, ensuring institutional compliance with statutes and directives established by municipal, provincial, and federal governments.

### Institutional Policy and Equity

A number of institution-specific policies have emerged over the years in support of broader national mandates to ensure equity for all Canadian citizens. For example, McGill University's *Handbook on Student Rights and Responsibilities* (McGill University 2003) clearly outlines a range of student fundamental rights and freedoms, the foremost of which is:

> a right to equal treatment by the University; this right must not be impaired by discrimination based on race, colour, ethnic or national origin, civil status, religion, creed, political convictions, language, sex, sexual orientation, social condition, age, personal handicap or the use of any means to palliate such a handicap.

Approved by McGill's Senate in 1984 and amended in 1988 and 2001, this statement of human rights and freedoms came into existence only two short years following Canada's adoption of the Constitution Act, 1982, which includes the Charter of Rights and Freedoms. Such a policy statement is common at Canadian institutions, as they, along with most other social structures, were quick to embrace the fundamental principles of the Charter and explore ways to ensure its application in all facets of student learning and student life. However, meaningful implementation of such policies does not always occur as swiftly. Statements like these are beneficial in articulating an institutional position on issues associated with diversity and equity, a position that is often prompted by changes to legislation and governmental policy. Translating statements into practice (e.g., curriculum development, pedagogy, or administrative procedure) can be a more tenuous and difficult exercise. While some institutions are less public about the ways in which they address the challenges presented by inequities on campus, others are far more forthright in identifying inherent institutional barriers and the ways their commitment to the principles of the Charter help to overcome these challenges.

The existence of human rights policies alone, however, cannot fully accomplish the change necessitated by the goals of diversity and equity on Canadian campuses. Policies serve administrative roles functionally, in that they state the rules and articulate the expected outcomes of policy implementation and infractions. As a framework for understanding and measuring institutional legal obligations to address issues of diversity and equity, statements of policy are sufficient: they ensure that colleges and universities fulfill their obligations under provincial and federal statutes. However, most institutional policies fall short, in that they neglect to address the ways in which an institution holds a goodwill obligation to educate the community on issues of diversity and strategically overcome attitudinal barriers that are most often the source of tension and discord. Furthermore, policies rarely hold institutions to a higher standard than that prescribed by the law, and shy away from moving beyond the limitations of statutes to articulate a leadership position on societal diversity, equity, and inclusion such as one would hope to see coming from a post-secondary institution.

As a result, policy alone is destined to fail in the same ways as do provincial and federal laws – subsequently doing very little to advance the access and inclusion of students from under-represented groups in the academy.

Astin and Astin (2000, 88) proposed that many institutions believe that availing themselves of greater financial resources alone would help to overcome the challenges of creating a diverse and equitable campus community. They suggested further that,

> resources ... most vital for transformative change are readily available both within and around us [including] our individual personal 'resources' of academic freedom, autonomy, critical thinking and a willingness to challenge, and our institutional 'resources' of new starts, celebrations and mission.

By identifying the importance of personal resources, and exploring the role of institutional resources beyond the traditional concepts of time, money, and human resources, Astin and Astin (2000) encouraged leaders in higher education – students, staff, faculty, and administrators – to explore ways in which they can exercise transformative leadership toward creating an inclusive campus community. Their research on transformative leadership and engaging institutions in social change addresses the personal dimension of leadership that is often the source of attitudinal hurdles in moving toward an inclusive and equitable campus. By recognizing human rights legislation as a foundation for and building up of the personal resources of academic inquiry, autonomy, critical thinking, and an ability to challenge individual ideas and practices, campus communities can more readily break down inherent attitudinal barriers to diversity that often appear to be the most insurmountable of roadblocks along the road to equity and access for all.

### Putting Policy into Practice

Numerous campuses have negotiated attitudinal roadblocks and successfully activated their policy commitment to diversity by establishing various program initiatives, ranging from community centres focusing on the identification and support of specific student groups (e.g., Aboriginal and First Nations) to comprehensive offices committed to monitoring and intervening across a wide scope of campus inequalities related to many different identifiers (e.g., ethnicity, gender, and disability). Current exemplars of such initiatives include:

- The Access and Diversity Office at the University of British Columbia, whose mandate is to provide "leadership in identifying and eliminating

systemic barriers to full participation in university life, that students experience, arising from race, ethnicity, disability, gender and sexual diversity, and intersecting inequalities" (University of British Columbia).
- The Aboriginal Student Centre at the University of Manitoba, which promotes an "educational environment that include[s] the affirmation of Aboriginal cultures, values, languages, history, and way of life by virtue of increasing the knowledge foundation offered at the University of Manitoba" (University of Manitoba).
- The Black Student Advising Centre at Dalhousie University, which "provides programs, individual and/or group assistance, mediation and advocacy services, relevant resource materials and a referral service which may benefit [the] personal and social development on and off campus, [of students of the African Diaspora]" (Dalhousie University).

In order to effect social change and ensure the establishment of equity among students from all backgrounds and experiences, it is critical to work within the existing systems and structures of post-secondary education. Characterists common to the internal services of successful institutions are: (a) a commitment to promoting the various aspects of any given group's identity, (b) efforts to minimize institutional and attitudinal barriers for students from their respective diverse populations, and (c) programs to provide ongoing support and intervention for students as they work toward achieving their academic goals. Furthermore, services with legacies and reputations of resiliency and impact share a common commitment to working in partnership *with* students to address issues associated with equity and diversity, as opposed to solving problems *for* them and alienating the students who are central to the issues the institution's services are endeavouring to advance. Many students who work from an activist perspective to effect community change struggle to navigate the internal channels of the institution, while also experiencing inconsistency in leadership due to student transition, burnout, and resource limitations. In contrast, a shift from student organization–based *activism* to institution-based *advocacy* can facilitate greater access to institutional resources and support, stable and often broad-based leadership on equity, and an advocacy function that becomes integrated within the institution's mission, systems, structures, and organizational policies.

As a case in point, offices that support students with disabilities have quickly emerged as leaders in their commitment and ability to address issues of diversity and equity in its many dimensions. For example, a partnership between the Equity Office and the Office of Access and Diversity at the University of British Columbia (UBC) has effectively implemented an Equity Ambassador program whereby student leaders from across campus engage members of the community in activities and programs to heighten students' awareness of issues of diversity and to broadly address attitudinal barriers to equity. This team of volunteer ambassadors, through outreach workshops, a campus-wide newsletter called *Think Equity*, and other initiatives, seeks ways to develop partnerships with faculty, staff, and peers who want to expand their capacity to effect social change at UBC.

The administrative reporting structures of these centres and offices are varied. However, the most common administrative accountability for offices that provide direct service to diverse students rests with the senior student affairs officer. Such reporting relationships give the diversity office or program a direct connection to the network of other support services and programs focused on supporting student learning and development. When the diversity office has responsibility for overseeing policy development and implementation, it may report to a senior vice-president, in some cases, with a connection to human resources and employment equity; in other arrangements, it may report directly to a vice-president whose portfolio team is completely equity-based. In a limited number of other instances, an equity officer might also serve as a special advisor with direct accountability to the college or university president. This could ensure greater visibility and access to resources that focus on core institutional functions and mission.

Staffing and resource support for diversity services areas vary tremendously from one campus to the next. Institutions that have a broad-reaching commitment to diversity and equity are often characterized not only by the existence of a senior administrative position focused on these issues but also by the appropriate financial and human resources necessary to enact this broad commitment. As colleges and universities face increasing financial pressures and are subject to changes in government leadership, the funding equation for diversity services is not always stable. In situations where a college or university is subject to legislative accountability for equity (e.g., in dealing with persons with disabilities), external funding can be available, yet unreliable, since changes in government priorities are common. In a few best-case scenarios, colleges and universities commit institutional funding to ensure that diversity and equity issues are addressed broadly and consistently across campus. It is in these situations that students are likely to experience their greatest opportunities for success and achievement during their post-secondary years.

## DIVERSITY SERVICES AND STUDENT SUCCESS

Diversity services is an important means to enhancing student learning and success. Chickering and Reisser (1993) proposed that helping students to develop an overall personal identity, integrity, and purpose is essential to supporting overall student growth and development. Central to the development of a strong sense of personal identity – the foundation for establishing subsequent levels of integrity and purpose in their model – is ensuring that students have the opportunity to explore and reconcile the many dimensions of their identity (e.g., comfort with body and appearance; gender and sexual orientation; ethnicity; sense of self in social, historical, and cultural contexts; lifestyle; and self esteem). At the same time, Jones and McEwen (2000) proposed that such exploration and identification involves not only an understanding of the many dimensions of identity (e.g., gender, sexuality, ethnicity, socio-economic status, ability, religion, and race), but also how these dimensions conflict with and complement one another. For example, Jones and McEwen's research illustrates this dynamic in the case of a young lesbian woman of colour, who needs to explore how individual dimensions of her identity (i.e., sexual orientation, gender, and race) intersect in order to achieve a greater understanding of self and the world around her.

Additional research on the various dimensions of identity (e.g., Cass 1979; Cross 1971; Josselson 1973) (See chapter 2) underpins our knowledge of student development and reinforces the importance of how developing an understanding of one's own diversity and its many facets positively enhances overall personal development and success. This is certainly the case for students and may well apply to institutions as a whole. Pascarella and Terenzini (2005, 130) challenged the assumption that diversity is "good" for a college or university campus by critically examining research that measured the influence diversity had on the student experience. Their findings illustrated consistently that,

> diversity experiences such as attending a racial-cultural awareness workshop, discussing racial or ethnic issues, and socializing with someone from another racial-ethnic group had modest, but statistically significant, positive effects on specific self-reported gains in knowledge and skill acquisition.

Diversity, then, is essentially "good" for the well-being of the campus community at large. However, extant research on the achievement and retention of minority students at post-secondary institutions (Allen 1992; Bennett 1995; Feagin, Vera, and Imani 1996) demonstrates that students who come from traditionally under-represented populations encounter barriers to success and educational attainment, and are often less likely to persist and graduate from college or university altogether. These barriers often manifest as social isolation and alienation; racial, sexual or other discrimination; and active or passive curricular limitations. This alone underscores the need for institutional responses to inequity and for colleges and universities to more broadly embrace diversity and difference on campus.

## ISSUES AND CHALLENGES

The creation of specific offices and services oriented toward the support and retention of under-represented students indicates a significant shift in the role institutions play in forming inclusive communities. While originally conceptualized as a mechanism to comply with legislation and implement equity policies, such offices have the potential to become clearinghouses and contact points for all things diverse on campus. That is, colleges and universities that support equity offices and other similar administrative departments now have an institutional resource to help address broad-based issues relating to student diversity in general. While the experience of many is that such offices do indeed effectively advance the interests of specific target populations, a significant risk exists in providing such a service. With a "one-stop diversity shop" for students, staff, and faculty, other administrative and academic departments can all too easily defer individual cases, responsibility for policy administration, and by consequence, any responsibility for creating an inclusive learning environment to one office alone. The problem becomes that – whether due to fear of the consequences, unfamiliarity with specific concerns, or a lack of the skill and competence required to deal with the needs of these under-represented populations – other academic and administrative departments might deflect addressing issues of diversity. In some cases, even the bare minimum expectations, as outlined by institutional policies, can be challenge enough for individual departments to accomplish. Consequently, they turn too quickly to the campus diversity or equity officer to address and take responsibility for the issue at hand.

In order to overcome or avoid this centralizing of diversity issues within a single equity office, it is critical for campuses to infuse the concepts of equity and inclusion at every possible opportunity. Colleges and universities must move beyond simply articulating equity policy and toward identifying specific responsibilities, expectations, and outcomes for all campus constituencies with regard to these concerns. Responsibility for equity and diversity must be shared by all members of the campus community, and all departments should develop a capacity to adequately respond to and address the needs of students from diverse and under-represented backgrounds. For example, the Department of Student Housing and Residence Life at the University of Toronto Mississauga took a number of fundamental steps to embrace its responsibility for creating an inclusive community. Some of these basic practices include:

• Articulation of active commitment to the principles of inclusion and equity in the departmental statement of mission and objectives

- Provision of an average of ten hours of training for professional and paraprofessional staff and student leaders on understanding the many dimensions of diversity and basic competency building on how to advocate for under-represented student rights and responsibilities
- Establishment of explicit statements of student behavioural expectations in the residential code, including expectations around common respect and openness to difference
- Creation and broad distribution of diversity awareness campaigns on an annual basis, including the provision of resources to students-at-large on how to develop a lexicon of inclusive language and practice
- Allocation of financial resources on an annual basis to renovate and retrofit residence rooms to respond to the individual needs of students with disabilities
- Internal administration and screening of requests for special consideration for students with disabilities and transgender/gender variant students, to reinforce the relationship between the student and the residence as primary service provider and the equity officer as resource and support personnel
- Implementation of institutional programs encouraging students to become allies for social justice issues and provision of opportunities to discuss the responsibility associated therein

These examples illustrate how a series of small and relatively inexpensive steps can contribute to the creation of a departmental culture that embraces its responsibility to its student population for equity and inclusion. While not made overnight, these subtle changes and evolution of professional practices have the potential to reach much further in realizing equity on campus than any simple policy can achieve alone. All offices engaged in direct service to students might benefit from an audit of current practices to evaluate where changes are warranted. Regardless, the goals for every office committed to equity remain to raise consciousness of group identities, minimize institutional and attitudinal barriers, and provide ongoing support and intervention for students who seek their services. Individually, diversity offices can begin to help institutions accomplish these goals; however, it is the responsibility of the entire campus community – faculty, staff, students, and administrators – to ensure that members from all backgrounds and experiences can find a sense of place and achieve success at college and university.

# 13

# Organizing, Leading, and Managing Student Services

BRIAN SULLIVAN

Student services represents a significant investment of resources and personnel in any college or university. Beginning with enrolment and orientation to the institution, proceeding through accommodation services, guidance from various counselling and advisement offices, and engagement in campus leadership experiences, and concluding with arrangement of internship opportunities, job placements, and alumni connections, student services facilitates students' entry, matriculation and, ultimately, success in the sometimes challenging world of post-secondary education. How are these services organized and funded? How are they best managed and led for student success? This chapter engages these questions through a conceptual frame and understanding based on experience and offers insights that bridge the historical and theoretical overviews of student services in Canada and the descriptions of its specific forms presented in the previous chapters.

This chapter is organized in four sections. It begins with an overview of how student services is organized at Canadian post-secondary institutions and the influences that have shaped it. Second is a discussion of the strategic processes that guide the leadership and management of student services, with particular emphasis on the role of the senior student services administrator in supporting student success. The third section highlights key issues that challenge the implementation and advancement of student services in Canadian higher education, and the chapter concludes with suggested resources essential to the professionalization of the field and the continued development of these services.

## ORGANIZING AND FUNDING STUDENT SERVICES

As reviewed in chapter 1, well-developed student services have existed for a significant period of time in Canadian post-secondary education, and today's units are similar in function to those found in other countries

(Sandeen 1996; UNESCO 2002). The Canadian Association of College and University Student Services (CACUSS) enumerated four categories of programs, services, and activities that constitute post-secondary student services: educational, supportive, regulatory, and responsive (Canadian Association of College and University Student Services). The key organizing considerations noted at the time were the extent to which student development was emphasized, along with whether the senior student affairs officer reported to the president or senior academic officer. To a degree, that observation now seems surprising, since the composition and organization of the student affairs portfolio was quite similar across institutions (See figure 1).

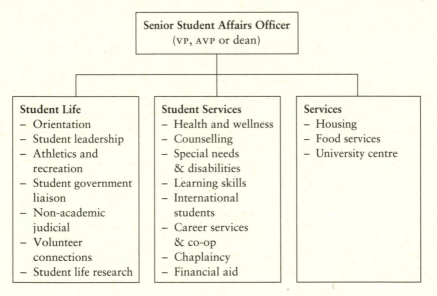

Figure 1
Organizational Chart for Typical Canadian Student Services Portfolio, (circa 1990)

Driving the prototypic organizational chart of that period was the fact that colleges and universities did not have residential populations and their student services organizations responded accordingly, although they more often had greater responsibilities for direct academic support programs, including student advising. Four developments since then have enlarged the scope of student affairs involvement and generated additional organizational options.

First, publication of the *Student Learning Imperative* (American College Personnel Association 1994) and *Learning Reconsidered* (Keeling 2004) has signalled the student affairs field's renewed emphasis on student learning. Such documents have challenged student services to contribute to an institutional consideration of learning outcomes and determine its part in enabling students to achieve those ends. The development of over-arching learning objectives at the University of Guelph, and the response of its student services division with expanded academic readiness programs, peer-assisted learning groups, and formation of a learning commons, is one such example. Academic readiness evolved beyond remediation to assist all students, including the highest performing, in maximizing their post-secondary experience. Implementation of efforts focused on supporting and enhancing student learning has meant much more partnering with faculty and a deeper commitment to assessment. Such features have in turn influenced unit groupings and internal relationships within student services divisions. They have also been accompanied by increased professionalization and specialization of those staff involved in student learning efforts.

A second prominent change was the emergence of strategic enrolment management as a way of thinking about students, and institutional relationships as an organizing vehicle. To date, this has taken a softer form in Canada than in the United States because the system is public, the institutions are all more closely comparable (public, non-profit, comprehensive), articulation and transfer are largely standardized, adequate student demand has enabled institutions to meet financial targets, and the ranking frenzy and inter-institutional jockeying evident elsewhere have not been dominant drivers in this system. However, this is changing somewhat, with competitiveness now on the increase and a buyers' market developing from a student point of view. This enrolment management focus has expanded the range of student service activity at some institutions to include recruitment (domestic and international), admissions, classroom services, student Web services, student information services, and in some cases, academic advising. Partnerships within institutional planning are also much closer. A key driver in this emphasis is the recognition of students as customers, as well as learners, clients, and citizens. Since 2000, Red River College, York University, University of British Columbia, and Université de Montréal, to cite a few examples, have all moved responsibility for enrolment services and registrar functions into the student affairs portfolio. As with student learning, this has been accompanied by a growing professionalization of staff in those roles.

A third major development impacting the nature and organization of student services on campus has been the renewed attention to vision and strategy at the institutional level. Student services units can no longer stop at professing student–centredness; post-secondary settings are now asking those units to help advance institutional aims more directly and to provide evidence that they are accomplishing that intent. This is resulting in many

new program engagements and institutional initiatives, including interna-
tionalization of the campus, student mobility, "building" the entering class
for certain attributes, undergraduate involvement in research, professional
development for research graduate students, community service learning,
industry and association mentoring programs, alumni relations, sustainability efforts, citizenship education, proposing and recognizing students
for external awards, providing services to university town residents, helping
implement and act on institutional surveys such as the National Survey of
Student Engagement (NSSE), and partnering on fundraising goals. This
explicit expectation to serve the institution and its mission, as well as students and faculty, is also changing the scope, organization, and delivery of
student services. Recent strategic plans issued, for example, by Ryerson
University (2008), Mount Allison (2007), Fanshawe College (2008), and
University of Alberta (2008) all illustrate this contribution of student affairs
to institutional advancement.

Finally, the emergence of a more diversified funding base has also shaped
student services across the Canadian post-secondary sector. The TD Bank
Financial Group 2004 reported that the percentage of direct funding from
government decreased from 80 per cent to 63 per cent between 1989 and
2003 – a trend that is apparently continuing. This has also generally
been accompanied by an increase in the tuition and fee share borne by
students; third-party funding sponsorship, including research overhead;
fundraising; and training contracts. Organizational responses to these phenomena have included new advisory councils (e.g., students, employers,
industry sectors, the community), formal and mandatory student consultation processes, community engagement officers, employment outreach coordinators, guidelines for strategic alliances, regular accountability reports to
various stakeholders, and hiring of fund development professionals within
student affairs. The time and resources devoted to managing the issues and
relationships that follow from broadening the funding base are significant.
In a typical issue of the monthly *NewsWire News* compiled by the Canadian
Association of College and University Student Services, one-third to one-
half of the topics relate to these aspects of student affairs practice.

Figures 2.1, 2.2, and 2.3 depict contemporary student services organizational structures for a medical-doctoral university (University of British
Columbia), a comprehensive university (University of Guelph), and a large
urban community college (Mohawk College), respectively. The student
services divisions at all three institutions are well regarded. Compared to
their relatively uniform organizational arrangement of twenty years ago
(See figure 1), there has been significant differentiation of functions and
organizational forms. Five key considerations guide local choices for each
institution. A brief discussion related to each follows.

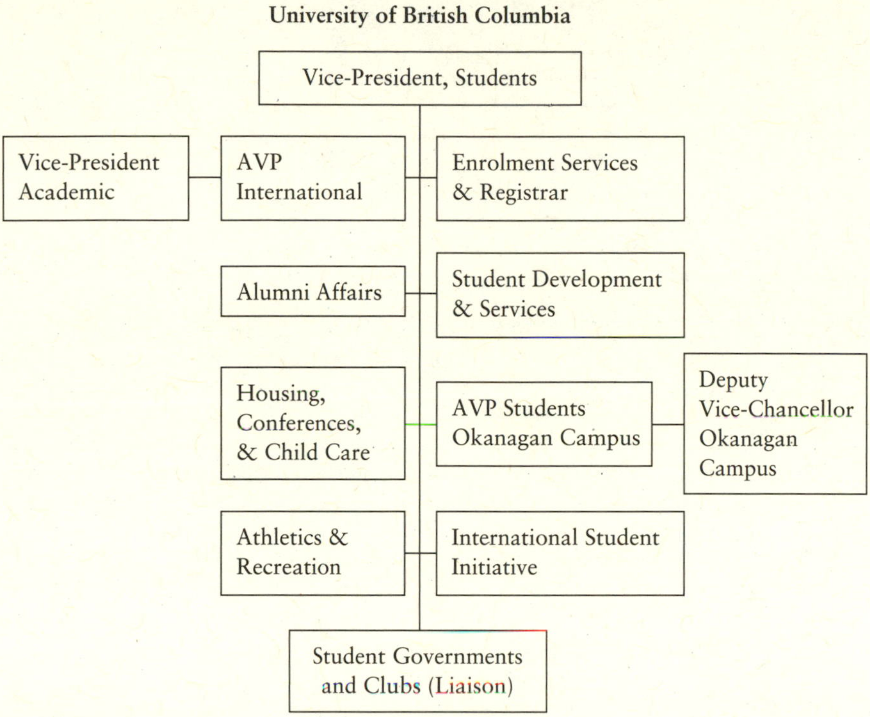

**University of British Columbia**

```
                    ┌─────────────────────────┐
                    │ Vice-President, Students │
                    └─────────────────────────┘
┌──────────────┐  ┌──────────────┐  ┌──────────────────┐
│Vice-President│  │ AVP          │  │ Enrolment Services│
│Academic      │  │ International │  │ & Registrar      │
└──────────────┘  └──────────────┘  └──────────────────┘
                  ┌──────────────┐  ┌──────────────────┐
                  │Alumni Affairs│  │Student Development│
                  │              │  │& Services        │
                  └──────────────┘  └──────────────────┘
    ┌──────────────┐ ┌──────────────┐ ┌──────────────────┐
    │Housing,      │ │AVP Students  │ │Deputy            │
    │Conferences,  │ │Okanagan      │ │Vice-Chancellor   │
    │& Child Care  │ │Campus        │ │Okanagan          │
    └──────────────┘ └──────────────┘ │Campus            │
    ┌──────────────┐ ┌──────────────┐ └──────────────────┘
    │Athletics &   │ │International  │
    │Recreation    │ │Student       │
    └──────────────┘ │Initiative    │
                     └──────────────┘
              ┌─────────────────────────┐
              │ Student Governments     │
              │ and Clubs (Liaison)     │
              └─────────────────────────┘
```

Figure 2.1
Student Services Organizational Chart

## Residential Mix

Residential campuses devote greater per capita resources and attention to campus life, health, safety, counselling, non-academic judicial concerns, and orientation. Student services on commuter campuses pay particular attention to retention, the needs of mature and part-time students, student financial assistance, and furthering a sense of engagement.

## Enrolment Management

A student services portfolio that includes enrolment management will look and feel different from one that does not. The organizational culture best suited to accomplishing enrolment management functions (i.e., customer-, data-, and procedure–driven) is different than the traditional student services organizational culture (i.e., client-, experience-, and practice-driven). Having

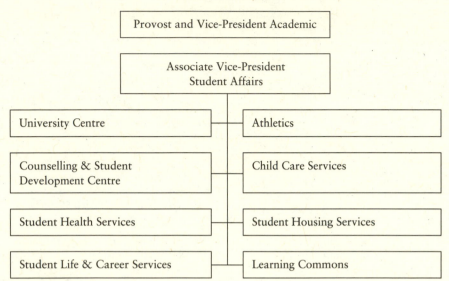

Figure 2.2
Student Services Organizational Chart

these two broad functions together in a portfolio can generate important synergies for student success and reduce waste due to boundary battles, but does require sustained attention to the different organizational requirements of personnel in those functions and to the forging of common cause at the portfolio level.

### Funding and Entrepreneurship

Student service divisions include units from those operating with no reliance on government or tuition funding (e.g., housing, childcare, and health services) to those often funded exclusively from such sources (e.g., student financial assistance, orientation, access and diversity, assessment/research, learning services, peer helping, and student leadership). Some units, such as athletics, counselling, and career services, are typically funded through multiple sources, each with its own expectation and accountability demands. Of particular note is the growth since 1995 in the proportion of student services funded through compulsory ancillary fees. This is most pronounced in Ontario, where at some institutions (e.g., University of Toronto), nearly all of the salary and non-salary operating costs of units such as counselling,

**Mohawk College**

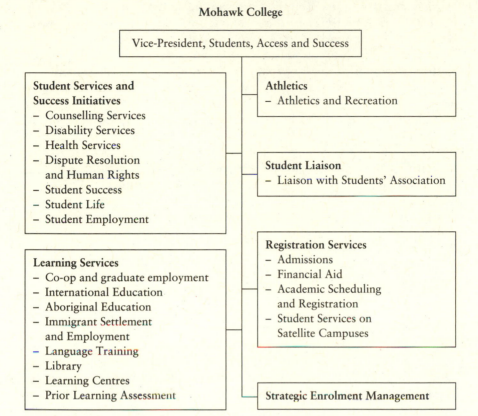

Figure 2.3
Student Services Organizational Chart

careers, advocacy, student leadership, and campus life are funded directly by students. As the provinces continue to restrain tuition increases, even as the demand for such student services is increasing, the proportion of service funding from this fee source will probably increase.

*Reporting Relationships*

As referenced in the Canadian Association of College and University Student Services' mission statement, the choice of whether the senior student services administrator reports directly to the president or to the senior academic officer is an important one, with both options having strengths and limitations. Colleges and some universities are focused almost exclusively on the undergraduate experience and have a more naturally holistic view of student learning and development. In these institutions, a direct report to the vice-president (academic) may be quite natural. An exception usually revolves around enrolment management issues. If a student services portfolio includes enrolment management responsibility, and that area is of particular concern to the institution, one will often see a direct report to the president.

Whatever the report, two considerations are key. First, the goal is to have a seat at the cabinet table. If the president also functions internally as senior operating officer (SOO), a direct report to the president is advantageous. If the vice-president (academic)/provost serves as the SOO, a direct report to that individual may be quite satisfactory and even advantageous, in terms of budgetary support and linkage with faculties and the institutional planning unit. Second, it is important to be a full member of the committee of deans and directors. Promoting student learning, strategic enrolment management, and other institutional aims requires effective and enduring partnering with deans and their faculties. Having credibility within that colleague group, along with carrying and communicating the student affairs mission, is the most important emerging leadership requirement for senior student affairs officers.

## Preparation of Personnel

Until the late 1980s, it was customary and sufficient for student services staff in Canadian institutions to have grown into their roles from experiences of student leadership in various units (e.g., residence life, orientation, recruiting/advising, advocacy) or to have immigrated into them from beyond the educational system with established professional credentials (e.g., health, personal counselling, learning skills, career education). This was largely true for senior student affairs officers as well, who were often tenured faculty. Since institutions had no access to Canadian student affairs professional preparation programs at the graduate level, this form of training was natural and convenient. However, emerging influences such as those noted above have placed new challenges on those roles, and the lack of a pool of qualified candidates at many institutions with training in the broad field of student development and student services and enrolment management is limiting the capacity to deliver on those new expectations. A number of schools have shaped their organizational structures to develop their own broadly prepared staff – through sponsored institutes, internships, job rotations, and educational leave programs – and to take fullest advantage of those with formal training. While the dearth of student services staff, particularly managers formally trained in the field, is a concern, some advances are being made in developing Canadian educational programs and strong efforts are being taken to repatriate Canadians who do graduate student services training elsewhere.

## LEADERSHIP IN STUDENT SERVICES

The institutional success of student services also depends on the senior executive's understanding of the leadership-management distinction. As depicted in figure 3, the leadership and the management of student services require different strategies and processes. Whereas leadership entails the purpose and direction of services, management focuses primarily on their implementation and evaluation. *Leadership* of student services on campus involves visioning, goal setting, supporting change, and establishing partnerships; *management* assembles and allocates resources, mobilizes staff involvement, and assesses the effects of various initiatives and programs. The resultant outcomes are academic achievement, student learning, and student development, all of which are tied to institutional advancement as well as student success.

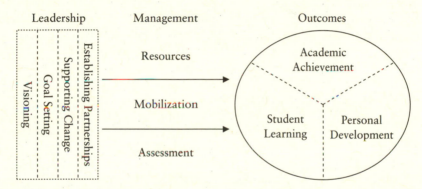

Figure 3
Leading and Managing Student Services

Leadership in student services begins with visioning. However, vision is untethered, absent of knowledge about one's students and institution, lacking in concrete description of the current situation and the desired future state. Goal setting follows and brings the particulars to vision: What outcomes are essential? What resources are needed to implement it? With whom must we work, where, and how? This process specifies what will be done to enact the vision in real and observable ends. Action on the vision then requires a third process: supporting change, including how to make the case for student success. The final leadership consideration in this sequence is establishing partnerships. The organizational alignment needed to enhance student success in post-secondary institutions proceeds from partnerships, especially with parties beyond student services units.

*Visioning (Telling Our Story)*

Vision is an image of the future we wish to create. Practical and focused on results, vision turns the direction described by the mission and sense of purpose into a destination. It transforms a description of what is held in common into a story about what will be accomplished in common. This requires an unflinching understanding of the institution within which it is to be enacted and the students it is to serve.

Learning about the historical roots and origins of our institution and its journey is a critical prelude to the process of visioning. Read about the institution; almost all colleges and universities have published histories. Listen to what it might tell you; seek out alumni and available reports that inform its workings. Dig into back issues of the student newspaper and the photo archives; appreciate the long-term as well as the short-term view. Use the following questions to reflect on the attributes of your institution and what they might imply. How does its sponsorship, public or private, shape what it does? Is it primarily undergraduate in its focus or oriented more toward research and advanced graduate studies? How does its location (i.e., rural vs. urban) set a context for its mission? What do these features infer about stakeholders and accountability? Are the organizational expectations in use rational and bureaucratic (Barr and Associates 1993, 96)? Alternatively, are they collegial, political, or less conventional (e.g., organized anarchy or a learning organization) in practice (Komives, Woodard, and Associates 1996)? What are key features of the physical, human, organizational, and constructed dimensions of the institutional environments (Strange and Banning 2001)?

Understanding one's institution also entails an understanding of its strategy. What guides goal setting and major decisions? Is there a declared strategic plan and is it followed? If not, what does the institution follow? How is progress assessed and do results influence what happens subsequently? Is the strategy broadly understood and how deep is the ownership of it?

Student learning and development happen at the intersection of the student story and the institutional story. There are many aspects to approaching the question, "Who are our students?" Building the capacity within student services to source this information in a variety of ways is critical. Surveys at several points in time are indispensable (e.g., National Survey of Student Engagement (NSSE), Canadian University Survey Consortium (CUSC), National College Health Assessment (NCHA), Cooperative Institutional Research Program (CIRP) Freshman Survey, and cohort studies have particular power (e.g., BC Council on Admissions and Transfer and the BC Provincial Follow-up Survey of Graduates). One aspect of this information is demographic; the second is student self-report. Some of the latter comes through surveys, but much of the information on student characteristics, needs, service use, and perception that is helpful for organizing student services comes via focus groups.

A third type of knowledge about students comes from direct engagement. One of the single most powerful interventions a student services professional or educator can have with a student is to ask what he or she is learning, whether in a specific course or a co-curricular experience. Student peer helper staff members perform a very important role in this regard by sharing with staff current information about students. One can also learn who our students have become by spending time with alumni and listening to their observations, assessing the learning and development outcomes they have experienced, and polling their perceptions. Constant attention to ways of building knowledge about students must become a mindful habit if their expectations of success are to be understood.

### Goal-Setting (What Really Matters)

The creative tension established between a specific vision and an honest depiction of current reality leads to goals, choices, and tactics. A simple but powerful way to describe goals is: either "more good things" or "fewer bad things" (See figure 4). As crude as it may sound, these two outcomes describe how the success of a particular undertaking is often judged.

Students have a large stake in the attainment of institutional goals and they need a voice. Typically, they can find that voice but, like any developmental task, the process needs to be built for success. Students are often brought into higher education systems without adequate orientation, data, mentoring, or feedback. More recently, however, consultation expectations are being embedded in policy to assure that student leaders have access to appropriate and adequate information in the decision-making process prior

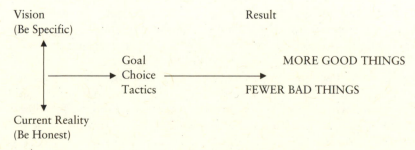

**PRODUCTIVITY**

Vision                                              Result
(Be Specific)

                          Goal                          MORE GOOD THINGS
                          Choice
                          Tactics                       FEWER BAD THINGS

Current Reality
(Be Honest)

Figure 4
Leadership and Goal Setting

to recommending one action or another (e.g., enactment of student fees in Ontario and tuition increases in British Columbia). Such a provision has helped clarify expectations and processes.

Attention is generally paid to whether students are adequately "cared for," but staff members are all too commonly taken for granted. Most post-secondary institutions under-invest in their staff, and scarce professional development resources are often the first to disappear in a time of retrenchment. In addition, college and university managers are typically very under-prepared in the skills of training and coaching, the management development approaches shown to be the most effective in securing employee engagement and commitment.

One approach of particular promise is student peer-helping programs: following a period of orientation and training, and under supervision, juniors or seniors support and serve fellow students. Properly designed and executed, the potential for leveraging service extension with student learning and development is enormous, and the areas of possible application (e.g., counselling, alumni, equity, service learning, and sustainability) go well beyond those traditionally considered, such as orientation, academic support, wellness, leadership, and careers.

### Supporting Change (Getting Traction)

As vision is articulated and translated into goals, and staff and students become engaged in the achievement of those ends, change is inevitable. Several dimensions then require explicit attention to achieve a critical level of momentum. If the vision is not communicated and understood, the result is often confusion. If staff members do not have adequate skills to implement the vision, anxiety can paralyze the process. If incentives and resources to support the change are not sufficient, the pace of change can slow or even come to a halt. Finally, if an action plan is not clearly articulated, it will lead to many false starts.

Successful change management often means thoroughgoing analysis of our own organizational situations – not a common enough occurrence in institutions committed to critical inquiry. At one unnamed institution, for example, counselling services was aware of a growing tension and some dysfunction as it entered the budget planning cycle. The usual incremental tweaking was not achieving what was needed. In the absence of an explicit formulation, however, none of the ways forward seemed obvious or attracted much support. After a relatively short group process with some facilitation on the interaction of institutional story, student story, and the principles guiding service delivery, the unit conceptualized a set of shifts it was experiencing (See figure 5). This was enough to loosen the temporary paralysis and for the staff to select likely action points, test through consultation, and then put a plan in motion.

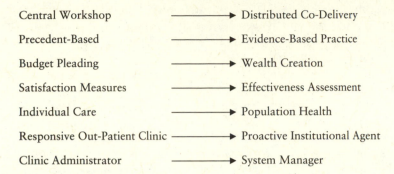

Figure 5
Characterizing a Counselling Service Shift


Organizational politics shape resource assembly and allocation. They can be rational or not, self-serving or not. Student services professionals must embrace the power dimensions of reality and become effective institutional politicians. Students count on it and deserve it. Key attributes of those who successfully lead in this sphere include being competent, understanding organizational positioning and timing, accepting conflict, and maintaining integrity. As institutional change unfolds, various arrangements and distributions may be at risk, and it is natural for current stakeholders to resist change on behalf of the status quo. Recognizing that investment, and the power that maintains it, is an important step in bringing others along. In that regard, ideally, any proposed state becomes at least as attractive as things remaining the way they are.

Few things are more effective in support of desired change than a well-crafted policy, grounded in solid organizational analysis and aligned with the unit's vision and key operating values. Conversely, few things pose a greater impediment to real change than a situationally convenient and idiosyncratically derived policy that rapidly becomes the source of a larger set of problems. Freedom of speech or harassment/discrimination policies spurred by particular incidents are notorious in this regard.

### Building Relationships (You Are Not Alone)

Despite concerns that post-secondary education is becoming more privatized, economically and psychologically, it is becoming more and more clear that we do not do anything on our own. The goals may be settled, the case made, and change requirements anticipated, yet it is still all about systems: learning is socially constructed and organizing only happens with and through others. Partnering is a basic operating principle in the institutional leadership process and explicit attention to building key relationships is foundational to effectiveness. From the perspective of student services, essential partnerships must include student groups, academic units, and community constituents.

## STUDENTS AND STUDENT GROUPS

Showing up is everything in conveying to students a desire to understand and respond to their needs. As the saying goes, "You have to be there." Processes with Canadian post-secondary student groups, particularly elected governments, tend to be informal and agendas are heavily influenced by individual personalities. "Being there" encompasses understanding, empathy, and presence. Be aware of the main features of your student government: Is it unaffiliated or a member of the Canadian Alliance of Student Associations (CASA) or the Canadian Federation of Students (CFS)? What is the policy platform of the particular national organization? Are candidates nominated in slates or do they campaign independently? Are fees based on a referendum or can the elected council approve them? Does the student government have its own building? What is the student government's overall fiscal health and how dependent is it on retail enterprises and alcohol sales? How do constituent student groups at the faculty level relate to the central student government? What is the role of student association professional management staff and how have they constructed their relationship with the college or university administration?

Listening, respecting, suspending judgment, and honouring the highs and lows that student governments experience are behaviours to which student organizations are extremely attuned (See chapter 7). A student services practitioner or unit lacking in this regard will not have real legitimacy, whatever the formal mechanisms. "Being there" also means presence: physical presence on a drop-in basis and when asked; responding quickly to email and routinely forwarding information without being prompted; encouraging colleagues to participate in events and student planning processes; creating physical spaces where students can gather and interact informally with faculty, staff, and alumni; and being a voice for students within the institution on those occasions when students may not have an opportunity to raise their own.

The same broad approaches apply to unelected student groups and clubs and to the many less formal student assemblies. It is as much about attitude as it is about strategy. For example, many staff commute on public transport. Consider how they spend that time: some immerse themselves in newspapers and incident reports; others habitually connect with students, asking how things are going and what they are learning. There is a difference.

For student services managers, surveys can be significant in building relationships when jointly developed with student groups, often accelerating action planning. Focus groups offer similar benefits in that they tap a stream of student sentiment often not represented through formal elected or student group channels. Students, as individuals and in groups, are not only the recipients of our services but also critical partners in the achievement of institutional goals.

### ACADEMIC UNITS

We work in academic institutions, and academic units and programs are the primary interface for most students. Furthermore, the individuals most directly able to influence student success are faculty and instructional staff. Student services cannot be effective in promoting student success without robust and mutually supportive relationships with faculties and degree programs. Key to this relationship is generally someone at the associate dean level with formal responsibility for students.

The overlap of an associate dean of students portfolio with topics of concern for student services professionals is significant. To cite a few, they include enrolment management; student characteristics, needs, and outcomes; need-based financial assistance and merit-based awards; academic progress; experiential educational opportunities such as co-op, international mobility, and service learning; career development and job placement; behavioural incidents; and connections with alumni. Student services primarily serves students, yet faculty and faculty units are also critical clients. This point requires deeper appreciation on the part of student services administrators if supportive faculty alliances are to be achieved. The creation of a faculty service centre, for example, within student information systems is a welcome move in this regard.

Universities and colleges are complex systems, and the ability to do what is important to support student success improves as our knowledge of the system as a whole advances. Unions, the office of legal counsel, plant operations, and environmental health and safety are all examples of units that bear directly on student success, but are often alien to student services managers, much less individual staff. Leadership in the student services portfolio must recognize this and take steps to build shared understanding and personal familiarity with these units.

### COMMUNITY GROUPS

Goals such as "broadened community engagement," "student citizenship development," and "collaboration to advance the public good" are appearing with more frequency in institutional mission statements. In addition, academic programs and individual students are looking for experiential learning opportunities that go beyond the direct purview of the institution. This presents student services professionals with new opportunities and responsibilities. Through recruitment and admissions we are in touch with secondary schools and other educational partners. Through international education we come to know local consular offices, and career centres develop extensive networks with employers. We have formalized opportunities with a broad range of community groups and agencies to engage interested student volunteers, and we have established programs with community mentors, many of whom are alumni/ae. Our expertise in community networks needs to be forcefully brought to the attention of those looking to expand institutional community engagement. Advisory councils, such as those some institutions have convened with secondary school guidance counsellors, open up new connections across programs and fields; council members are a valuable and unique source of feedback on the institution and on the capabilities of students and graduates.

## MANAGEMENT OF STUDENT SERVICES

Returning to the model in figure 3, it is clear that achieving student success in post-secondary education requires not only solid leadership competencies but also a set of management skills essential to implementing a vision and goals. As depicted, these can be characterized as assembling and allocating resources, mobilizing staff involvement, and assessing the effects of various initiatives and programs.

### Resources

Love and Estanek (2004) urged student services practitioners to move beyond the usual considerations of money, space, time, and personnel in thinking about resources and to think instead of awareness, effectiveness, and organization. In their view, awareness of resources is often too limited, a prime example being the way individuals tend to focus on faculty, staff, and students when considering "people." Many of the most innovative ways of expanding resources involve volunteers, parents, alumni, and members and groups from the broader community. Relationships are also under-appreciated as a resource component. Much of the current work that needs to be done to support student success can only occur through new partnerships. The process is the same whether it be community placements for experiential learning, seeking potential donors, community building with the police, or working with plant operations around deferred maintenance for classrooms. The management challenge is which relationships to invest in and how to work across boundaries.

Expanded awareness of resources also extends to the staff group. Some student services units, after defining an issue, have put out the equivalent of a request for proposals within their own organization to tap resources and expertise of which management is not aware. This can be liberating, and often opens a very different window on what staff training and development programs can be about and can provide an impetus for mini-experiments in job–sharing, temporary reassignment, and skill banks.

Improving resource effectiveness can be particularly challenging in student services, as there tends to be a strong allegiance to doing what has previously been done. Suggestions for re-examination are often received as veiled attempts to shift resources away from supporting students toward less student-centred institutional objectives. Case studies and other stories from "outside" are often the best way of introducing constructive reframing. Web-based service provision, student peer-helping programs, and intentional activities with alumni in support of students are approaches to service delivery that expand available resources at very modest incremental costs, build skills of self-reliance and lifelong learning in students, increase the sense of institutional affiliation, and promote citizenship development.

A broadened view of resources leads to an abundance, rather than a scarcity, mindset and one begins to see and experience possibilities for augmented resources in many areas. Some of the "technologies" related to this are relatively new to Canadian student services work. For example, the culture around being an alumnus/a is different than in many universities and colleges in the United States. Consequently, in Canada, alumni/ae activities have tended to be under-resourced. With the possible exception of athletes, little emphasis has been put on cultivating student subgroups in alumni/ae terms (e.g., elected student leaders, residence life staff, student journalists). Alumni/ae are an under-utilized resource. One of the main opportunities for student services resource augmentation is to work closely with alumni affairs and development professionals, beginning with joint programs centred on current undergraduate and graduate students. Finding ways to help alumni/ae connect with each other and with the institution can generate enormous dividends.

Related resource augmentation technologies are fundraising, grant writing, and community compacts. Resources from private individuals, foundations, government agencies, or NGOs (non-governmental organizations) are more available than is often presumed. However, any such request must be grounded in clear divisional and institutional priorities. Grants must be looked at realistically, as they consume resources (e.g., time, people, space, facilities) potentially available for some other use. That said, third-party grants represent a very effective way of seeding new initiatives.

### Mobilizing Knowledge and Energy

Mobilization is the management activity centred on building capacity across key domains and then creating conditions to maximize the ability to access, sort, and apply resident expertise to the problem or opportunity at hand.

Knowledge is one key capacity in this activity. Post-secondary institutions function in complex and turbulent environments: uncertainty is high and the organizational whitewater flows constantly. Knowledge exchange opportunities need to be embedded, habitual, and reinforced. Some have made a beginning in this regard by concluding a meeting or organizational episode with each participant taking time to reflect on: "How was this experience and what did I learn?" We ask students what they have been learning; routinely asking the same of each other could have enormous dividends.

Approaches to building knowledge must move in concert with building involvement. Knowledge has no real currency until it is exchanged, and student services personnel need to be practiced in various forms of building student involvement. This begins by finding out how students wish to engage a topic (e.g., face-to-face, Web, open forum), where (e.g., classroom, social space, residence, student union), and when (e.g., during the work week, evenings, weekends).

Team management is another essential mobilization capacity. The word "team" implies a common vision, member inter-dependence, and a system of recognition and reward. Attention is needed to ensure that system aligns in the same direction as the desired team output. Higher education teams, be they a group to advise on academic readiness programs or the executive team of the student services portfolio, need to be intentional in their operating principles in order to achieve cohesiveness and efficiency. For example, at one unnamed division, the management team has adopted the following rules of engagement: (a) generous listening, (b) being on each other's side, (c) straight speaking, and (d) managing each other's reputation. Articulating and adhering to a shared value platform such as this is often liberating and up-building.

Ironically, given the typical reaction to policies and procedures, they have enormous power to mobilize resources by building common purpose and maximizing efficient use of energy. Some institutions have undertaken policy audits, often with the help of involved students, to identify policies and procedures that can be eliminated or overhauled. Review of alcohol and release of information policies, for example, lend themselves well to this.

### Assessing Learning and Improvement

Assessment is the third management process highlighted. It is about learning and improvement, at both the individual and organizational level. Effective units oversee the resources, mobilize and maximize system capacity, and then assess outcomes to determine impact, stimulate learning, and guide continuous improvement. Intentional and ongoing assessment of student learning and development and program outcomes should be part of each student services professional's mindset and of the institutional culture. Assessment results are crucial to priority setting, resource allocation, and improved student success and service outcomes.

Upcraft and Schuh (1996), Bresciani, Zelna, and Anderson (2004), and Whitt (1999) offer excellent reviews of comprehensive frameworks for assessment. Typically, the questions of interest are positioned as an assessment cycle:

1 What are we trying to do and why?
2 What is my program supposed to accomplish?
3 How well are we doing it?
4 How do we know?
5 How do we use the information to improve
  or celebrate successes?
6 Do the improvements we make work?

Distinguishing between different kinds of outcomes – program outcomes, student learning and development outcomes, input outcomes, student needs outcomes, and service utilization outcomes – is important. Assessment also occurs at different levels within the organization: individual student or staff, program, unit, portfolio, and institutional. A range of assessment tools and skills are required.

The first set of basic questions guiding assessment relates to intent: What is the objective of interest? What is the purpose for assessing it? Who or what is the object of the assessment? The next set of questions relates to assessment tools: What is the best assessment method? How should the data be collected and who should collect them? What instruments should be used? How should the data be recorded? Key criteria in choosing tools and methods should include input from the assessment client, the capabilities of those to be involved, resources available to conduct the assessment, the prescribed timeframe, how results will be reported, and who will have access to them.

Paying careful attention to ethical considerations related to an assessment project is also critical. Failure to do so can give rise to questions of legitimacy, where there is already ambivalence about whether student services professionals qualify as "investigators," and where the ethics review boards may have limited understanding of assessment approaches akin to research but administrative in their focus.

Generating a quality assessment plan is only half of the challenge; the other half entails teaming up with the assessment client to elicit an endorsement of the results when they are delivered. A partner-like relationship is key to ensuring that the assessment effort is related to objectives that are meaningful and important to all involved. In addition, the focus should be on using assessment as an aid to living into a desired future, rather than as a blade to dissect what has already happened. Such positive and intentional engagement from the outset can increase the probability of relevance and the adoption of results once the assessment is completed. Well-designed focus groups with students, early in the project, can help clarify areas to be addressed in the assessment and heighten student government and student groups' awareness. Unit or organizational level assessment will typically involve student services personnel coming together with academic administrators, faculty, and other constituents, both on and off campus; the secondary gains for student success arising from such collaborations are often significant. The goal of a partnership approach is to support a positive impact.

Collaboration should continue throughout the assessment project. Assessment data should either inform continuous improvement decisions or specifically test a proposition. Being clear on the purpose, rather than the object, of the assessment is very important. Specifying whether that purpose is program performance, unit mission, better decision-making, resource reallocation, or policy formulation will improve the assessement's intended impact. A University of Toronto report, *Measuring Up* (2005), which utilizes National Survey of Student Engagement (NSSE) data to assess progress toward identified student experience objectives, illustrates one such approach incorporating these basic assessment elements.

## ISSUES AND CHALLENGES

This chapter began with an overview of changes in the external environment that prompt organizational reconsideration of student services at Canadian post-secondary institutions. Some of those influences continue and new ones arise in the form of those highlighted below.

### Enhancing Student Academic Success

Feedback from individual students, alumni, employers, and surveys such as the NSSE suggest that there is considerable room for improvement, especially in the instructional experience that students report. The emerging buyers' market for places in institutions and the pressure for a good return on the increasingly expensive public and private investment in post-secondary education suggest that a higher priority is being placed on ensuring that students succeed if at all possible. Student services divisions are being challenged to have current assessment data, to move beyond individual programming to group and systemic interventions, and to find new ways of collaborating with faculty colleagues to improve the learning experience for students. Innovations such as cost-sharing student development officers with faculties and locating them in academic units are increasingly seen as a way to share skill sets and data, and build ongoing partnerships. Whitt (2006) offers a constructive and comprehensive set of "lessons" for thinking about the student services contribution to academic success, and James (1999) reviews operational considerations for learner support and success, particularly in the context of Canadian community colleges.

### Safeguarding Access

It is a time of uncertainty in the government student loan landscape. The proportion of assistance in the form of grants is being reduced; tuition and costs have risen significantly in many jurisdictions; and for increasing numbers of students, the necessity of part-time employment is impinging on their ability to have a full educational experience. For many second-degree programs, such as law, dentistry, and medicine, reluctance to take on more debt is skewing the class profile and exerting a powerful steering effect on the choices many students in the program make as to what and where to practice. Student services divisions play a key role in developing homegrown financial support mechanisms, providing education toward financial literacy, and advocating strongly with students at the provincial/territorial and federal government levels for a more coherent and responsive financial assistance program.

### Serving Aboriginal Students

Much needs to be learned and done to make our post-secondary institutions inviting and supportive for Aboriginal students. This will involve working directly with local secondary school systems and First Nations or urban Aboriginal communities; using fresh processes for planning and consultation; exercising flexibility in the application of established standards, while still ensuring quality; having more Aboriginal staff at our institutions; and providing training for all staff with respect to the opportunities and challenges faced by Aboriginal students.

### Branding and Marketing

As well as building support in the broader community and achieving their business plan goals, institutions are striving to be distinctive and to show how they add value. The amount and type of student engagement, the quality of the co-curricular experience, and what alumni have to say about the institution are all becoming more pressing student services division concerns. Those with enrolment management responsibilities have the additional job of packaging the university's story in an appealing manner while being genuine about the experience of their current students.

### Preparing Citizens of the World

The Canadian post-secondary system is being called on to prepare our students to be global citizens and agents for positive change. With established programs in leadership, sustainability, student mobility, and community engagement, student services divisions have an unparalleled opportunity to help their institutions meet these educational goals. Importantly, this includes the challenge of identifying outcomes that are relevant and measurable.

### Serving Our Alumni

Alumni/ae services are very underdeveloped at Canadian universities and colleges. It is now becoming apparent that many institutional aims can be accomplished more powerfully and expeditiously if connected alumni/ae are mobilized in their pursuit. In the long term, positive alumni/ae relations are a product of students having a good educational experience while at the institution. Student services programs can contribute expertise about how to help current students begin thinking as "alumni/ae in residence" and seeing graduation as a process of joining something for life rather than departing the institution.

### Serving Graduate Students

As the competition for the best and brightest students heats up among institutions with graduate programs, the quality of the experience for those students is paramount. Graduate students in research and professional programs are increasingly impatient with our traditional support mechanisms and anxious to receive broad-based professional development, career guidance, and assistance toward timely completion, and to have a respectable quality of life while in their programs. In this regard, one challenge particular to Canadian student services is to ensure that a number of staff have had a graduate student experience so that there is a deeper understanding of the educational context for those students.

### Paying for Things

Beyond the usual concerns of meeting enrolment targets and budget parameters are particular issues of sustainability in student services systems. Prime among these are the research and development and ongoing maintenance required to sustain a student information system, resources to support the voracious demand for new and updated Web-based applications, and the growing expectation that increased staffing costs for services such as careers, personal counselling, and health will be met through revenue streams generated by those services rather than through core institutional funding. An even harder push may come as to whether an institution needs to "make" a particular service or can outsource or buy it from elsewhere.

## Developing Our Staff

Given the current foci on learning, strategic enrolment management, and advancement of institutional aims referenced earlier in this chapter, the skill sets being demanded of student services staff are changing and intensifying. In addition, the way in which traditional-age students now access and organize their personal and learning experiences, particularly in the context of electronically facilitated modes of relating, has opened significant gaps between the experience base of many student services managers and that of the students they serve. Students are less and less interested in "getting with our program"; more junior staff, adept in these newer ways of operating, are serving an indispensable translation function and need to be legitimized in that role. Also, more intentionality is needed to ensure that our students see themselves in the racial, ethnic, religious, and international attributes of our staff.

## Balancing Market Place Demands

Third-party funding other than traditional government and tuition sources is increasing in strategic value, and many institutions now depend on such sources to fund core activities. There are important ethical, policy, political, and practical considerations around this evolving dynamic. Student services is often called upon to be a conscience in this dance between the objectives of marshalling additional resources and of safeguarding free inquiry. Institutions will be depending heavily on the student services division to have sufficiently robust relationships with student government, alumni/ae, and local community constituencies that it can undertake consultative processes in these areas of creative tension and help build both responsibility and appropriate relationships.

### INFORMING OUR PERSPECTIVE

Remaining current on the leadership challenges of the senior student affairs officer is essential, and the list of resources foundational to the task is extensive. Although not complete, what follows is an informative, helpful, and inspirational selection. They cover a range of materials that examine both the specific and general contextual considerations that impinge upon this role, with some addressing the functions and purposes of student services, others current trends that affect their implementation, and last, those that give insight to various leadership needs and approaches.

In addition to this book and among the foundational resources is *Student Services: A Handbook for the Profession* (Komives, Woodard, and Associates 2003). This volume offers a straightforward treatment of the core professional principles, theories, and competencies central to organizing and managing student affairs programs and services. Although grounded in the US post-secondary experience, many units are highly transferable to the Canadian context. In *Where You Work Matters: Student Affairs Administration at Different Types of Institutions*, Hirt (2006) utilizes a creative and practical taxonomy of institutional types to illustrate the varying roles and challenges of student services work in different kinds of post-secondary institutions. Manning, Kinzie, and Schuh (2006), in *One Size Does Not Fit All*, use a different taxonomy, centring on locus of activity, that draws out important organizational design considerations. While all the institutions in these two reviews are in the USA, the Canadian post-secondary system can draw lessons as it moves in the direction of greater differentiation and seeks to illuminate the new situations being faced by Canadian practitioners. Gilbert, Chapman, Dietsche, Grayson, and Gardner (1997) also add to the mix in offering a useful history of Canadian student services from the first-year experience point of view (See chapter 5). The profiles provided of programs and organizational structures at a large variety of institutions are very helpful in familiarizing oneself with the Canadian context.

Key purposes of student services are addressed in several comprehensive resources. First, Hamrick, Evans, and Schuh (2002), in *Foundations of Student Affairs Practice: How Philosophy, Theory, and Research Strengthen Educational Outcomes*, use abundant examples to emphasize institutional-level considerations in student affairs. Their point of departure is student learning, as they highlight key student outcomes such as democratic citizenship and life skills. Several other authors (e.g., Harvey-Smith 2005; Whitt 1999) embrace this end goal for student services by exploring, for example, the mental models that guide our work, what it might mean for the student affairs enterprise to be more learning-centred, how we can form partnerships with our academic colleagues, and what we need to know and be able to do to foster student learning or what it means for an institution to adopt a thoroughgoing focus on being a learning organization for the transformative support of the learning paradigm. In *Learning Reconsidered:*

*A Campus-wide Focus on the Student Experience* (Keeling 2004), a joint effort of the National Association of Student Personnel Administrators (NASPA) and the American College Personnel Association (ACPA), a discussion of the context, process, and content guides integrated use of higher education resources in the service of learning that is transformative and responsive to the whole student. It offers a shared vocabulary and guide for student affairs–academic affairs partnerships striving to focus on student learning outcomes. *Assessing Student Learning and Development: A Handbook for Practitioners* (Bresciani, Zelna, and Anderson 2004) provides techniques to determine success by outlining processes and methods for assessing student satisfaction, personal development, and learning outcomes, and by including a discussion of best practices, benchmarking, and peer review.

Leadership of the student services institutional portfolio is the focus of several resources that speak, directly or indirectly, from the management literature as well as from personal testimony to the support of strategic decision-making in the context of student affairs. For example, Love, and Estanek (2004) utilize recent insights from organizational theory to help student affairs practitioners understand and work with organizational structures and processes. They argue convincingly for a fresh way of thinking about organizational power, leadership, resources, assessment, and technology. Brand (1999), author of *Whole Earth Catalogue,* offers a surprising treatise on time and responsibility in the form of a series of meditations for managers. In the author's view, the ever-shorter attention span and opportunistic stance we cause and accommodate – *kairos time* – is creating a colossal societal shortsightedness. He suggests that we owe it to our students, our institutions, and ourselves to recover what it means to take the longer-term, wise view – *chronos time* – and accept our big-picture responsibilities. Looking honestly and respectfully at the inherent conservatism of institutions of higher learning and teasing out what is unresponsive and deadening from what is faithful stewardship and wisdom is a truly worthy calling and a contribution that student affairs is uniquely qualified to help make. Fullan (2001) stresses the importance of the personal attributes of the leader, including enthusiasm, energy, and hope in leading change and strategic management at the organizational level. Authored by an experienced educational administrator and researcher, the theoretical constructs in this volume are accessible and replete with educational institution illustrations, and offer a helpful vocabulary for shared meaning. Similarly, Ellis (2003) addresses many of these points in her chapter for *Dreams, Nightmares, and Pursuing the Passion: Personal Perspectives on College and University Leadership.* This is an engaging and instructive personal reflection on the first two years of the author's student affairs vice-presidency at the University of Nevada-Reno. Journal entries are clustered under headings such as "Connecting with the Faculty," "Seeing Through Students' Eyes," "Navigating the State System," and "Being Myself." Some very helpful illustrations for the management topics of relationships and resources are introduced, bringing the concept of personal agency to life.

An appreciation for the current context of these challenges is found in the recent work of several Canadian authors. For example, Andres and Finlay (2004) feature an edited collection documenting changes in the social field of Canadian post-secondary education, and institutional responses in the face of such change. The contributions are largely based on college and university survey findings from recently completed graduate theses, and many of the authors are currently working in student affairs. This volume gives fuller meaning to the context and impact of the change drivers cited above in this chapter.

A 2004 TD Economics Special Report, *Time to Wise Up on Post-Secondary Education in Canada,* is a clear-headed analysis of post-secondary public funding and tuition levels in constant dollars. The report expresses concern at the increasing reliance on private (student) funding, suggesting the urgent need for student financial assistance reform. Eastman (2003) focuses on the strategic responses available to Canadian universities as they increasingly engage in marketplace activities and concerns to outperform competitors. Thorough consideration is given to topics such as budgeting options, the role of the (administrative) centre in a decentralized institution, and constraints on strategic management at the faculty level.

The effectiveness of senior leadership in post-secondary student services depends a great deal on being attuned to trends and events that shape the day-to-day operations of an institution; connection to current issues and best practices in the field is mandatory for anyone seeking to provide strategic leadership to a division as diverse in purposes as student services. An excellent resource is *Communiqué*, the national journal of the Canadian Association of College and University Student Services (CACUSS). Often thematic in content (e.g., mental health on campus), each issue serves as a handy barometer of current concerns and initiatives in Canadian post-secondary student affairs. Furthermore, it offers an opportunity for perspective sharing on important topics and provides a venue for relevant program descriptions and successful outcomes.

In conclusion, student services in Canadian higher education has evolved into a complexity of challenges demanding a well-informed approach that capitalizes on the emerging body of professional literature that informs what it does. Promoting the continued success of students entails an advanced appreciation of this knowledge base and the ability to implement these ideas into solid programs and practices. Effective strategy in all this demands a vision grounded in the best ideas, credible research, and most-proven experiences. Student affairs can expect nothing less from its campus senior-level leaders.

Success is a metric applicable to whole institutions and their divisions as well as individual students. While each of the various offices typically affiliated with student services contributes an important piece to the overall success of the division, and by extension that of the institution, it is the synergy of their collective action that most readily assures the college or university's performance when it comes to supporting student success.

# PART THREE
# Institutional Mission and Context

The organization and delivery of effective student services depend much on the type of institution that sponsors the services, the personnel and operating resources available to support implementation, and the profile of students being served. Such features are typically a function of institutional mission. Historically, in Canadian post-secondary education, the evolution of institutional design and purpose has generated a varied system of provincially/territorially sponsored public universities, colleges, and university colleges that share a common interest in promoting student success, but accomplish it through very different emphases, structures, and programs. While colleges exercise their strengths in serving the career, technological, and vocational interests of a diverse constituent, through wide-ranging certificates and diplomas, universities focus their resources on the generation and transmission of knowledge, preparation of degree-seeking candidates, and service to sponsoring communities. Although such purposes have traditionally been accommodated mostly by local and resident colleges and universities, a third option – distance education – has emerged in recent years at both types of institutions as a significant addition to the mix, requiring newer models to meet student needs.

This section focuses on the integration of student services in these three post-secondary options – colleges, universities, and distance education programs – giving attention to their unique features, typical students served, and some of the defining issues that shape the design of their programs and services for student success. Chapter 14 addresses the systems and challenges particular to the community college context, with emphasis on its institutional goals, limitations, and its unique contributions to the Canadian system. Chapter 15 considers many of the same concerns, but from the perspective and dynamics of comprehensive and research-based universities. Chapter 16 focuses on the organization and delivery of student services at a distance, considering the challenges of designing and implementing online systems to respond to growing student needs.

# 14

# Student Services in College

TED JAMES

At the heart of most colleges in Canada is a vision of increasing access to higher education through opportunities for social and economic advancement, most often for those disadvantaged by location or previously limited education. While this is but one aspect of the college mission, the access imperative has always sought increased success for students who otherwise would face fewer career and life options. Indeed, many personnel, especially those in student services, are drawn to work in colleges precisely to effect that goal (Mathews and Freeland 2006). In that context, student access and student success have usually been synonymous.

However, as colleges have matured and strived to deliver on their promises, greater differentiation has occurred between these two concepts (Drea 2003). Today, student success in college is a much more multifaceted concept, and one which is moving increasingly closer to becoming a strategic advantage for such institutions, if its opportunity can be realized. This chapter focuses on student services in Canadian colleges, illustrating the role it plays and how it is organized to foster student success. Also examined are some of the issues and challenges the field faces in continuing to create opportunities to spur student access and success.

## COLLEGES IN CANADIAN HIGHER EDUCATION

The expression "college" has a variety of meanings, often being a general term for any type of post-secondary institution. Perhaps nowhere does the term have most variety than in Canada, where a multiplicity of types of colleges exists within the landscape of its higher education system (Holmes 1992). Nonetheless, the majority of these colleges – especially public ones – were created within a relatively short period, in the 1960s and early 1970s, in response to a dramatic public policy initiative to increase access to post-secondary education, particularly for those from lower socio-economic groups (Dennison and Gallagher 1986).

The growth of this sector is impressive. The Association of Canadian Community Colleges (ACCC), created in 1972 to represent colleges in Canada, today lists 175 members across the nation with names that include descriptions such as technical college, provincial institute, polytechnic, university college, regional college, and CÉGEP (in Quebec). ACCC estimates its member institutions represent student populations of 900,000 full-time and 1.5 million part-time learners. Canadian colleges employ in excess of 30,000 faculty members across more than 900 campuses (Association of Canadian Community Colleges). In addition to public colleges, private colleges also offer an extensive catalogue of career programs, ranging from hairdressing and graphic design to urban language schools that cater to international students and immigrants.

Since, under Canadian confederation, post-secondary education is a provincial or territorial responsibility, colleges can vary widely in size, mission, and governance from one province to another (Skolnik 1991; Jones 1997). Public colleges in Canada oversee budgets varying from $9 million to $120 million annually. While all receive the bulk of their funding from government sources, the proportion can range from 45 per cent to 80 per cent of their revenues. Student fees (up to 20 per cent) and fee-for-service industry training contracts (up to 30 per cent) make up most of the difference.

Originally, colleges were limited to offering credentials in one-year certificate and two-year diploma programs, typically in fields of health, social services, business, applied arts, and applied sciences – though some included trades training and apprenticeship. Most colleges offered adult education programming, including skills upgrading and college preparation, as well as some community education and non-credit courses. Institutions whose origins reflected the American junior college model offered two-year university transfer programs that assisted access to baccalaureate programs. In British Columbia, the introduction of the university college represented a major evolution in the college concept (Dennison 1992), converting former regional colleges into degree-granting institutions, which focused initially on undergraduate teaching but lately have embraced research projects and added graduate-level programs. Since 2000, some provincial/territorial governments have extended degree-granting mandates to colleges to meet increased marketplace demand for this level of credentials. As of 2007, nearly forty colleges in Canada were offering degrees or applied degrees (Millar 2007), and both the number of institutions and degrees continues to grow, with implications for broadened student services (Conrad 2005; Reed 2006).

While this mandate continues to widen, most colleges remain grounded in local or regional communities and are more and more seen as vehicles of economic development and labour force adjustment, with an increasing number of industry partnerships and contract training opportunities. This has spurred a growing entrepreneurism within these institutions (Knowles 1995) and even competition among local providers (Dennison and Schuetze 2004). In addition, many colleges have embraced international education, recruiting greater numbers of foreign students, pursuing consulting or training contracts delivered abroad, and responding to opportunities within a globalized environment (Jones, McCarney, and Skolnik 2005; Levin 2001). Also, the number of colleges offering degree-level programs has increased college involvement in research and innovation (Goho, Hoemsen, and Webb 2005). All of these changes are altering the mission of colleges and blurring their distinction from universities in some provinces, leading to added pressure on student services (Drea 2003; Conrad 2005). However, many of the unique features of colleges remain, especially those aspects that promote the promise of student success.

Colleges still tend to offer students easier access through open admission policies and more inclusive entry criteria. Even with a doubling of tuition fees since 2005 in some provinces, colleges still charge substantially lower fees than universities. They also offer much smaller class sizes and greater student contact with faculty. College faculty are hired primarily as instructors, not professors, and consequently have heavier teaching loads per semester. The ratio of campus space devoted to laboratory use tends to be higher in colleges as well, and programs tend to be career or vocationally focused. The student population is more likely to be drawn from local communities, and although some colleges do provide student residences, the proportion of students and faculty commuting from off campus is generally higher than at universities. Colleges attract greater numbers of mature students, including some "back-transfers" – university graduates seeking to acquire employment skills. Full-time college students average between twenty-six and twenty-eight years of age.

As the demand for post-secondary education and training increases within a more competitive global knowledge economy, the scope of Canadian colleges is likely to evolve even further. Colleges seem well positioned to respond to changing workforce development needs and to become preferred comprehensive providers of learning opportunities within local communities. To underscore this competitive advantage, ACCC, for example, is promoting its organization of colleges as a "national training network" for Canada, including the marketing of its network abroad.

## ROLE OF STUDENT SERVICES IN COLLEGES

College-based student services evolved from origins that differed from universities established before 1900 (Rhatigan 2000). It was not rooted in a tradition of paternalism or *in loco parentis* as in other institutions. It arrived on the post-secondary scene years after the well-defined university student personnel movement that extended from the mid-1920s to the beginning of the 1960s (James 2005). College student services was established with an institutional mission to focus on a new diverse mix of students. As Dennison and Gallagher (1986, 70) emphasized:

> colleges were first characterized by the comprehensiveness or multi-purpose of their dimensions of their curricular. The principle of comprehensiveness required they offer a mix of different programmes, for a mix of students with different abilities and past achievements, with a mix of educational goals, within a single institution, usually on a single campus. The mixes differed from province to province and from institution to institution, but the mixes were designed and deliberate, not the result of programme evaluation or historical accident.

From the start, colleges attracted a heterogeneous student body comprised of a much wider cross-section of the community than those admitted to universities or single-purpose institutes (Uhl and MacKinnon 1992). These included more part-time, mature, ethnically diverse students from a wider band of socio-economic strata (Adams 1998). This was viewed not only as a strong push for the democratization of higher education in Canada but also as the development of institutions with more responsive delivery systems. To meet such needs, colleges adopted open admissions policies; permitted students to change programs easily – even to "try out" different programs; and offered classes days, evenings, and weekends – often for a full twelve months of the year – to meet the different schedules of employed students, student parents, swing-shift workers, and others (Dennison and Gallagher 1986).

Within this context, student services quickly became a well-respected, comprehensive, and integral part of most colleges. To ensure that they were able to meet the needs of a wider mix of students, colleges supplied the non-instructional support services to ensure that students would be successful following their admission (British Columbia Ministry of Skills, Training and Labour 1995). For instance, Dennison and Gallagher (1986, 75) described how the role for counselling services in a college environment is an example of the new-found importance of student support:

> In other post-secondary institutions, professional counsellors were viewed as necessary for dealing with problem students, if necessary at all; in the new colleges, counselling – and then a whole range of other student services – was not seen as peripheral but as integral of this kind of institution; all applicants ... were to be able to receive professional

advice and assistance in career and educational planning, and this service was held to be just as important to the success of the students and the institution as the teaching services provided.

As colleges grew and their student populations diversified even further, the size and scope of services available in them expanded to meet the broader base of student needs. Financial aid offices provided budget planning and management advice; on-campus employment services designed work study and co-operative education opportunities; specialists in learning assistance were hired to support the needs of students with disabilities and learning difficulties; and centres were opened to serve as social support structures for minority students.

## ORGANIZATION OF STUDENT SERVICES

Student services in colleges are generally organized into a separate division headed by a senior administrator responsible for such support, as well as registrarial functions, library services, and increasingly so, the provision and maintenance of educational technologies. In contrast to the models found in universities, colleges typically feature a more centralized organization, much to their advantage in maintaining a consistent approach for the delivery of services and ensuring a level of budgetary support (BCSSAC 1981). Alternatively, their more dispersed locations, their lower level of overall funding, and their smaller size of operation leads to lower economies of scale in colleges and less consistency in the level of services available, especially in outlying campuses (James 1999).

The expression *student services* can cover a wide range of different units and activities in colleges, including:

- Registrar's office services
- Academic advising
- Assessment services and prior learning assessment
- Library and learning resources
- Counselling and career services
- Student employment/co-operative education
- Wellness and health services (sometimes medical services)
- Financial aid services
- Learning assistance and tutoring
- Disability resource centres and services
- Aboriginal student services and access programs
- Distributed learning services and support
- Child care services
- Computer support services

- Human rights/harassment services
- Gender-specific services (e.g., women's centre)

Increasingly, student services in colleges is being re-organized into a "one-stop" facility, housing most services under one roof and staffing it with cross-trained professionals to minimize any frustration associated with having to visit several different offices. With the Saskatchewan Institute of Applied Science and Technology (SIAST), for example, this involved a province-wide review and integration of student services delivery to promote improved student success (Jensen 2002).

Student services in colleges is generally funded from institutional budgets rather than from separate fee levies, although that trend appears to be shifting. Services offered by colleges are generally distinct from those provided by student societies. Where residences exist, campus life services mirrors that available at universities. On commuter campuses, however, student life is much more truncated.

Canada has a variety of professional associations that attend to the learning needs of those who staff student services. One major national organization is the Canadian Association of College and University Student Services (CACUSS) and its various divisions (e.g., Canadian Association of Disability Service Providers in Post-Secondary Education). CACUSS holds an annual national conference each summer and publishes a magazine called *Communiqué*. Other national bodies serving various student services subgroups include the Canadian Association of Student Financial Aid Administrators (www.casfaa.ca) (See chapter 4) and the Canadian Association of Career Educators and Employers (www.cacee.ca) (See chapter 11).

While these national organizations serve various types of institutions, the interests of colleges per se are served primarily via the Association of Canadian Community Colleges (www.accc.ca), which includes affinity groups focused on student services. Regionally, bodies such as the Committee on Student Services of the Association of Colleges of Applied Arts and Technology (www.acaato.ca) or the Atlantic Association of College and University Student Services (www.aacuss.ca) promote best practices and professional development opportunities.

The field is further served by other professional development opportunities such as the Canadian Institute on Student Affairs and Services (www. cacuss.ca/en/07-cisas/index.lasso) offered by the Centre for Higher Education Research and Development at the University of Manitoba (www.umanitoba. ca/centres/cherd/development). *College Quarterly*, an electronic journal hosted by Seneca College (www.senecac.on.ca), offers regular articles on aspects of student success in colleges; additional research reports and other scholarly articles on this topic appear in the *Canadian Journal of Higher Education*. Nevertheless, the role of Canadian colleges in general, and of student services in particular, is not well reflected in Canada's limited higher education literature. While seminal works, such as *Canada's Community Colleges* (Dennison and Gallagher 1986) and *Challenge and Opportunity* (Dennison 1995), provide college-specific analyses, and articles by Andres (2001), Dietsche (1990, 1995, 1999), and Jones (1997) speak to the needs and experience of the college sector, few writers have focused on the imperatives of student success in these institutions. Notable exceptions are the ACCC (1997) and James (1999), along with several graduate studies (Campbell 1998; Erland 2003; Kirby 2000; Krakauer 2001; Maw 2005; McWilliams 1998). More recently, a large-scale pan-Canadian study of college students (Dietsche 2006) is helping to paint a more accurate picture of the college student experience and suggest ways it can be enhanced.

## STUDENT SUCCESS IN COLLEGES

Even though colleges early on adopted an open admissions policy to increase participation, concerns existed about whether this simply increased access to failure (Clark 1960) and confusion (Dippo 1994) for those not destined to succeed anyway. Yet, the academic standards required of students in college remained unchanged, or perhaps were raised somewhat in response to greater demands by employers for quality college credentials (Kilian 1995). By the 1980s these seemingly contradictory missions of colleges were readily apparent:

> Community colleges, especially today, are faced with a fundamental dilemma. On the one hand, they want to keep their doors open to everyone; on the other hand, they want to offer quality and academic excellence in their programs. The open-door, open access, right-to-fail mentality of the '60s adds to the dilemma of the '80s. (Roueche and Baker 1987, 37)

One solution to this dilemma was to place more emphasis on student success, to help more students overcome previous underachievements (Beatty-Guenter 1988).

While the term *student success* has always been nebulous (Losak 1986), most colleges focused their early efforts on maximizing student program completion and reducing student attrition (Beatty-Guenter 1988; Dietsche 1990; UCFV 1992; Ungar 1980). Drawing upon a growing USA literature on voluntary student departure (Gilbert and Gomme 1984, 1986; Grayson and Grayson 2003), this strategy mirrored the university approach toward increasing student success rates. One model in particular (Tinto 1987) focused on the lack of academic and social integration with the institution as principal contributors to student departure.

Not surprisingly, though, this model had limited application to small-sized colleges, with large numbers of students who were commuters, part-time, and disadvantaged; often there wasn't much to integrate with (Corman, Barr, and Caputo 1992). Moreover, the goals and motivation of the student were frequently missing from such analyses (Erland 2003; McKeown et al. 1993). Even more problematic was the apparent lack of amelioration possible by institutions of any type to reduce student attrition rates significantly (Grayson and Grayson 2003).

Nonetheless, concern for student success continued, especially among student services professionals, many of whom carried the torch forward, seeking new ways to aid students (Dietsche 1995, 1999) and refusing to subscribe to a sink-or-swim philosophy. One legacy from those efforts is the student success course or seminar, partly imported from the spreading First-Year Experience movement in the USA and partly homegrown from study skills workshops and other services traditionally delivered by college counsellors and learning specialists (Beales 1998; Gilbert et al. 1997; McWilliams 1998). However, during the 1990s, the focus on student success broadened from concentration on the attrition of *some* students to documenting the achievements of *all*, as stakeholders – government, industry, local communities, and their own students – called on colleges to evaluate their effectiveness, particularly the success of their student outcomes (ACCC 1997).

Early Canadian studies of college impact (Dennison et al. 1975) focused on the profile of the students and their aspirations. These studies found that colleges were successful at widening the franchise of access, having enrolled students with significantly lower academic ability, with more years away from formal education, and from lower socio-economic backgrounds. But the promise of higher education was largely unfulfilled for the many disadvantaged students who lacked the financial and social support to attend or remain in college (Butterworth 2005; Gallagher 1995).

Later attempts to expand remedial education programming and provide support services tailored specifically to the needs of student subgroups, such as single parents, Aboriginal students, income assistance recipients, and the chronically unemployed, achieved mixed results, particularly in the mid-1990s when federal and provincial/territorial governments brought in welfare reform and various unemployment reduction initiatives. Studies of these efforts show that much remains to be done by colleges to better serve the needs of disadvantaged adults (ACCC 2005; Andres and Findlay 2004; Campbell 1998; Kershaw 1998; Holmes 2005). Despite this, based on either self-report follow-up surveys or career-path tracking of former students, outcomes for most college graduates were highly positive. Studies revealed, for the most part, a picture of students being solidly satisfied with their college experiences, particularly the quality of instruction. College graduates usually made easy transitions into the workforce and pursued careers in their field of study (Allen, Harris, and Butlin 2003; BCOWG 1999; Finnie 2000).

One crucial transition role played by an increasing number of colleges was facilitating transfer to university. This function received considerable research attention, especially in Western Canada (Andres 2001). Studies sponsored by the British Columbia Council on Admissions and Transfer (BCCAT), for instance, revealed that comprehensive articulation agreements among provincial/territorial institutions encouraged large numbers of students to transfer after one or two years of college. More important, since their academic performance at university graduation was indistinguishable from non-transfer students, colleges thus demonstrated considerable success in developing an alternate access route for students who had been denied direct entry to university from high school (Pendleton and Lambert-Maberly 2006).

Also starting in the 1990s, and gaining momentum in some provinces, student success in college was scrutinized through government accountability frameworks introduced in response to general quality assurance movements in society (Dietsche 1995; Drucker 1992; Miner 2004). Elected college boards and industry advisory committees (Warkentin 2005) had always held colleges accountable, but governments also introduced various key performance indicators and delivery targets as additional measures of college performance (Freed and Klugman 1997; Jones 2004). Some embraced the challenge with implementation of an institution-wide continuous improvement model; in the case of St Lawrence College, that led to ISO certification in 1996 by the International Organization for Standardization in Geneva – the first college in North America to achieve that (Consensus Canada 1996). Other schools objected to the imposition of "corporate" methodology and "customer service" language that seemingly belied the nature of the educational enterprise and the didactic relationship between colleges and their students. Consequently, many colleges struggled to find ways to make the accountability serve internal as well as external agendas.

Since the mid-1990s, another approach to accountability for colleges has emerged from the "learning college" concept in the USA. O'Banion (1997, 47), building on Barr and Tagg (1995), defined the concept thus:

The purpose of a learning college is to place learning first in every policy, program and practice in higher education. Not research, not politics, but learning. In this transformation, everyone ... becomes focused on improving learning. Not grades, not grants, not publications, but learning ... The time-bound, place-bound, efficiency-bound and role-bound institution is not sufficient to the tasks facing us in the 21st century.

In Canada, the efforts of Humber College, as a vanguard institution of the League for Innovation in the Community College consortium, have led the way in realigning the college mission with learner-focused and learning-centred post-secondary education. This vision has spread widely and has been embraced by numerous institutions as a strategic direction for renewal, a stellar example being Nova Scotia Community College. While pioneers such as Krakauer (2001, 2005) have searched for ways to apply and assess a more learning-focused approach at the macro-level, in practice, gains can be more forthcoming when exercised by micro-level change agencies such as SUCCESS@Seneca (Fishman and Decandia 2006). Interestingly, student services in colleges were early adopters of the learning college concept, seeing this as a natural extension of their philosophy (Harvey-Smith 2003; James 2005).

## ISSUES AND CHALLENGES

Colleges face several issues trying to maintain and improve services for students. How successfully they meet these challenges may be critical to the future of the institutions themselves in Canada. Perhaps more than ever before, the ability of colleges to remain comprehensive, flexible, and responsive to diverse needs of the community may rest largely on their expanding the expertise and student-centred philosophy traditionally residing in student services.

While the profile of students and their expectations are changing in all institutions of higher education, the impact in colleges is profound, and student services as a college campus service provider is often the first to respond to these impacts. Rising tuition costs and declining disposable income among parents of the college-bound have forced more students to work, often long hours, while attending school, thus reducing time available for study. Colleges are responding with more bursaries and campus employment opportunities, as well as financial management services. Students with learning disabilities and mental health problems are also attending college in ever-greater numbers, straining counselling and disability resource centres (See chapter 9).

Colleges are also striving to meet the needs of students from other special groups – for instance, those of Aboriginal ancestry (Hampton and Roy 2002), for whom Canadore College has partnered with Nipissing University to facilitate their college to university transition (McLaren and Chum 2006). In addition, colleges are responding to Canadian immigration policy by increasingly serving learners from multicultural origins (Kilbride and D'Arcangelo 2002) and foreign markets (Levin 2001). In doing so, they are realizing that the strategies and best practices involved improve student success for the student population as a whole (Asuncion et al. 2005).

Students are more demanding of educational technology, having grown up with easy access to computers, electronic games, and cellphones. Refitting campuses with computer labs, smart classrooms, and wireless networking has drained some college budgets, often diverting resources away from other service areas (Noam 1995). Administrators have faced difficult decisions trying to rationalize what services should go online and how to staff multiple points of student interface. Student expectations of 24/7 service, with immediate response times, have forced many service personnel to acquire improved technology skills and colleges to provide more self-service, online access (Cross 2000). While many young services providers embrace the potential of these new technologies, others – older and accustomed to providing hands-on and one-to-one service – are less keen to change, especially as retirement nears. Colleges will need to make a concerted effort to improve in-service training and support for its employees, such as the Supporting Student Success credit course that Nova Scotia Community College offers to college faculty and staff (Boutilier 2001).

Increased consumer expectations among college students (Coaldrake 2001; Dietsche 1999; Miller et al. 2005) are placing greater demands on services providers to develop new standards and operations, more rigorous quality control, and continuous improvement (Belbin 2003; Keith 2005). College students are also willing to lodge complaints, hire lawyers, and contest grades (James 1999). While academic departments may bear the brunt, student services areas are often directly involved in providing counselling and even advocacy programs, particularly where minority students are affected. As a result, harassment advisors and human rights officers are common today on college campuses (See chapter 8). In addition, the health of college students is an area of increasing concern (See chapter 10), including trends toward more incidents of self-harm among students (Cairns 2006). Mount Royal College, for example, has created a multidisciplinary wellness centre for students designed to provide support for their holistic health (McElary 2006).

These changes are also having a transformational effect on the provider-customer relationship between colleges and students, resulting in a number of new student affairs–led initiatives, like the two-day Extreme Customer Service Workshop introduced at Bow Valley Community College (Ansari and Bruckner 2004). As student demands grow, access to information expands, and as competition to serve students deepens, colleges will search more critically to carve out their niche in the higher education market. Some suggest that increasing pressure will force colleges to differentiate or die (Drucker 1992; Noam 1996 Rowley, Lujan, and Dolence 1998). In response, colleges may turn to student affairs expertise as a competitive advantage (Earwalker 1992; James 2002), a point averred by Doucette (1998):

Community colleges should acknowledge what they do well, perhaps better than most other institutions. These colleges have a longstanding commitment to and know-how to support learners ... Rather than competing with Microsoft and Disney, community colleges will prosper if they do what they do best: provide learning support services to help students learn, regardless of where they get their information ... They should draw upon years of experience in student development, student support services and developmental education to become the best learning support organizations in the world. Disney and Microsoft cannot compete in the provision of these services in support of student learning. In their local communities, this appears a winning strategic market niche for community colleges.

The future for most colleges that embrace this challenge is likely to involve a reassessment of the significance of student services as a catalyst propelling colleges toward a more integrated learning-centred environment (Conley 2005; Freeland 2006; Maw 2005; Rekar Munro 2005; Tinto 2004; Tysick 2004). One Canadian example of this trend is the campus-wide focus on new-student orientation at Mohawk College that grew out of a cross-college strategic initiative (Miller 2006). Another promising expression of this approach is the campus-wide focus on the "whole student" experience adopted by USA student affairs personnel in *Learning Reconsidered* (Keeling 2004) and *Learning Reconsidered 2* (Keeling 2006), brief treatises on the importance of linking academic learning and student development to foster transformative education both in and outside the classroom. Such initiatives have the potential to unite service functions and teaching departments in new partnerships (Engstrom and Tinto 2000), the long-sought holy grail of the student services quest for respectability (James 2002). Along the way, service professionals may be well placed to assist teaching faculty to better understand and meet the needs of a more diverse and demanding student body (Willms and Flanagan 2003; Zmetana 2002), as well as assist students to take a more active role in their own education (Alberta Learning 2002; Moore 2004).

A reinvented role for student services in colleges might assume strategic importance if competition for students among these institutions becomes more pronounced. Indeed, the central goal of a college might well become to support learning in ways that rely upon the talents of its student services professionals:

learning colleges should become providers of learning support services and learning expertise. Their principal function will be to inventory learning options and experiences and to guide and support students accessing them, whether as brokers or deliverers of programming. In so doing, colleges will evolve into formal learning support centers ... This vision will have key implications for changing faculty and staff roles – such as the changing role of librarians assisting learners to make sense of information available on the Internet – but it will also move many student support services into mainstream importance in the educational institution. (James 1999, 73-4)

For colleges to meet this challenge, student services professionals need to advocate strongly within their organizations for putting the needs of students first on the agenda of institutional concerns, and organizing internally to fulfill that promise (Krakauer 2001, 2005; Leary 2006). Douglas College, for example, has developed an institution-wide plan for services as a corollary to the college's academic plan, advocating a service philosophy that distinguishes and links *transactional* with *transformational* types of service delivery:

As a learning institution, it seeks to play a transformational role in students' lives. As a learning-centred institution, where its intentions with students are transactional in nature, the service goal is to remove barriers, providing a quick, friendly and convenient service that fosters an environment conducive to transformational learning. Douglas College seeks to deliver services in a developmentally appropriate manner that helps students become responsible, self-directed and self-sufficient individuals (Douglas College 2005, 1).

To meet this challenge services providers need to evolve, communicate, and commit to more transparent service delivery standards than have characterized past decades (Robinson 1999). While student services professionals in the field have espoused principles of service delivery (Canadian Association of College and University Student Sevices), the metrics to evaluate service performance have often gone uncollected, even unidentified. This is one aspect of student success that is well within the grasp of college personnel to improve.

## CONCLUSION

If this chapter's assessment of the future for student services in colleges is accurate, that future is bright indeed. If Canadian colleges continue to promote the concept of the learning college and to strive for more learning-centred education, the future for student success in these institutions is bright. To achieve this vision, however, colleges must embrace new realities while building upon their traditional strengths in an era where funding concerns, stakeholder expectations, and an aging workforce are inevitable.

# 15

# Student Services in University

MICHEL OUELLETTE

The history of universities in Canada dates back to the establishment of the first institutions in Nova Scotia, Upper Canada, Lower Canada, and New Brunswick in the seventeenth and eighteenth centuries (Jones 1997), chartered for the purposes of providing opportunities for young men to pursue advanced studies in the liberal arts and to prepare them for roles within the professional ranks of society (See chapter 1). As specialization increased the number and diversity of potential careers, the role of universities expanded and the development of advanced degrees grew into expert fields of study. The need for graduate schools within the university system eventually emerged and advanced degrees were awarded. As the number of higher degree programs grew (Jones 1997), a need also developed to enhance the body of knowledge within various fields of study, and the research emphasis evolved into a significant component of graduate study and the overall mission of many institutions.

The growth of universities, some at a more accelerated pace than others, and the focus on graduate education and research (Cameron 1997) saw institutions altering student enrolments and the focus of their mission. Thus began a subdivision of universities into (a) *primary undergraduate institutions* with greater attention directed at preparing students for advanced study and professional degrees, along with emphasizing teaching and learning; (b) *comprehensive universities,* which attempted to merge quality classroom instruction and the development of certain graduate programs; and (c) *primary research/doctoral institutions* with emphasis on graduate studies and extensive research.

Altered missions also meant that particular universities were prepared to attract different faculty and students with varying research interests and professional aspirations, and with learning philosophies more aligned with specific institutions. Therefore, faculty members with a greater interest in research gravitated to larger medical/doctoral schools (e.g., University of

Toronto), along with students aspiring to various professional fields. Faculty and students preferring smaller institutions with equal interest in the classroom and preparation for graduate studies were attracted to more mid-sized, comprehensive institutions (e.g., Memorial University of Newfoundland). Finally, those with a focus on teaching and the benefits of a quality undergraduate learning experience found themselves at smaller institutions (e.g., Mount Allison University). Although it is somewhat naive to think that students and faculty would be so easily directed to the institution of their choice, for the most part, universities were able to attract individuals focused on specific areas of interest. In this manner, the university system in Canadian higher education has evolved from a single-minded purpose to a range of institutional types serving a variety of educational missions. Consequently, since its emergence, student services has also diversified in response to the needs of an evolving student population served.

## ESSENTIALS OF STUDENT SERVICES

How did choice of institution impact the range of services available to students? Student affairs officials have long recognized that helping students achieve and assisting them to graduate should be the unit's primary concern. While university recruiters focus on attracting students to the institution and faculty members, to varying degrees and based on their interest in teaching and/or research, provide students with academic competencies to complete degrees, professionals under the banner of student services assist students through the academic and developmental challenges of the university years. In reality, many students reach personal and professional goals with little or no direct assistance from professionals and programs in student affairs. However, one must wonder whether even students requiring minimal aid could have achieved greater results if necessary supports had been available at critical times of the academic journey.

Institutional focus and the degree of student dependence often guide the discussion surrounding the involvement expected of student affairs officials (Hanson and Delworth 1980). Is student services seen in the same way as other campus programs – strictly as a unit staffed by service providers, dispensing aid when students come forward? This model has been the cornerstone of most campus operations. Staff members may be very comfortable in the role and choose not to venture beyond the customer–service provider relationship, responding only when students need assistance. Other universities choose a developmental model in their relationship with students and deal proactively with student issues in a more contemporary approach that focuses primarily on student learning. Such a process ensures that programs deal with issues of cognitive competence, both intrapersonal and interpersonal, as well as the development of practical skills. The most progressive approach to date is the learning outcomes model that examines individual programs and their relative worth and contribution to student learning. This focus combines traditionally faculty-valued developmental outcomes (intellectual) and traditionally student affairs–valued outcomes (affective and moral) into overall learning. Therefore, student affairs officials become more closely linked to the academic mission of the institution (McClellan, Cawthon, and Tice 2001).

## Recruitment, Admission, and Orientation Services

Categories of services to students have traditionally been based on students' abilities to deal with particular academic and developmental challenges. At the beginning, and seen as helping students transition into life at university, are services associated with recruitment and admission, along with orientation and first-year experience programs. Effective recruitment is the initial step in identifying the correct fit of students with an institution and ensuring that a connection develops between students and the right university. This stage highlights the importance of an institution's ability to help students, in general, make a smooth transition to university. Additionally, a range of special services may be required for certain groups of students (e.g., first-generation students, Aboriginal students, students with disabilities) whose needs require particular accommodations and responses.

Once commitment to an institution is secured, the next step is facilitating the transition of students through quality orientation services. Many universities often begin the orientation process following acceptance and prior to enrolment, and include such activities as summer orientation programs, parent orientation initiatives, or even summer reading programs to acquaint students with the rigors and expectations of university life (Abraham and Wagnon 1992). A significant focus for first-year students is an introduction to the academic realities of campus life (Perigo and Upcraft 1989). Thus, a quality orientation program introduces students to a range of available services on campus and becomes a resource centre for assistance in the future. While such services may be commonplace at most post-secondary institutions, the mission of each institution will, in some way, determine the emphasis placed on each service unit.

If helping students connect with the institution is key and first-year student success entails establishing proper relationships, an important vehicle is a first-year experience program (Jewler 1989). Typically, a structured plan of academic and developmental information helps incoming students learn the necessary in-class and out-of-class skills, along with required academic and professional resources, to enhance their chances for success (Gordon 1989).

## Engagement and Support Services

A second group of services is associated with the ability to engage students in the life of the institution. Exemplars include personal and career counselling, health services, services for students with disabilities, and student advising and tutoring. Other services within this category would be student leadership programs, service-learning initiatives, or similar activities that highlight student involvement beyond the classroom. Such programs usually achieve key objectives: allowing students to connect in very concrete ways with the institution, providing students with academic tools necessary for success, encouraging learning beyond the classroom, and ensuring a more complete student educational experience.

Counselling services (See chapter 9) is one unit that transcends the type of post-secondary institution, as any student could encounter personal problems requiring the assistance of skilled professionals. The size of the counselling unit may vary from institution to institution and some universities may merge personal and career counselling into a single unit. Some might argue that comprehensive and medical/doctoral institutions, with greater pressure to succeed, warrant a greater number of trained professionals. In any case, the increase in the number of students with personal and psychological challenges now attending post-secondary institutions, regardless of size or mission, makes counselling services an important cog in any student services wheel.

As well, it is safe to assume that financial aid will be critical and every student affairs unit will have professionals to help students avail themselves of financial resources from provincial/territorial and federal agencies, as well as a myriad of possible scholarships and bursaries (See chapter 4). Aside from helping students manoeuver through the economic hardships of college life – or simply plan a budget – the office identifies difficulties that students might encounter and financial pitfalls that impact a student's ability to achieve and succeed (Lenning, Sauer, and Beal 1980). The emphasis on financial aid and the assistance programs available to students might vary depending on the focus of an institution, its location in the country, and the provincial/territorial student loan system in place.

Greater attention is also directed at the learning and living environment so that students will feel positive and persist to graduation (See chapter 6). Student retention proponents say such actions are reasonable and even moral since the institution was so determined to recruit these students in the first place and should be in position to ensure their success. Opponents argue against an excessive parental role and contend that once students are recruited, assuming a quality orientation program has exposed them to a range of services and programs aimed at success, the responsibility lies with each student to take the necessary steps, find the required resources, and go about the business of learning and graduating (Roberts 2003).

Providing a safe, secure, and comfortable on-campus living environment remains another expectation of student services (Strange and Banning 2001). Whether front-line paraprofessionals in a specific residence or officials responsible for room allocation, professionals in student housing are key contacts (Blimling 1993). With students away from home environments and traditional supports, such individuals can also be of tremendous assistance in crisis situations (Winston, Anchors, and Associates 1993). While officials might discourage an *in loco parentis* relationship with students, the professional model of residence life supports active involvement in their lives.

Larger institutions with professional and graduate programs have residences offering more independent living for students who have experienced the lifestyle of traditional residences, but now seek a mature environment. Demanding academic schedules, access to cooking facilities, and generally a lifestyle that more resembles typical apartment living are reasons that students desire more non-traditional arrangements. Graduate students in medical, professional, and research programs, in particular, along with their families, are also attracted to the convenience and cost of on-campus accommodations and seek universities that will enable their pursuit of graduate and professional degrees while living in a community of like-minded individuals. Proximity to daycare services, schools, and convenient shopping benefits students and families alike. International students are drawn to post-secondary institutions that have large international communities and that recognize the need for residence services that cater to a diverse community and meet the needs of students with different lifestyles, dietary concerns, and customs.

Coupled with an expanded range of living arrangements is the need for sufficient health supports (See chapter 10). Health care professionals listen to student concerns and identify students in crisis, who may need more specialized intervention or the assistance of other campus professionals (Bridwell and Kinder 1993). Such units have also seen an increase in services as the campus population has grown and become more diverse. Once again, the size of the community and the nature of its constituents determine the range of health services provided. The mix of faculty, staff, and traditional, graduate, and professional students, along with tenets of institutional mission, also determine the manner in which such services are dispensed, whether purely prescriptive or more developmental in focus.

Offering tutoring and advising options might be seen as a university going "above and beyond" the range of services normally provided to students. Many institutions only see a limited responsibility in providing such programs – after all, many traditional academicians still adhere to the sink-or-swim mentality for students desiring a university degree. If students are not sufficiently adept, academically or developmentally, to succeed, failing them and/or encouraging them to pursue less rigorous academic programs may be a suitable alternative. However, if the institution is truly committed to student success, providing support over the academic hurdles, particularly in the first few years, is more of an obligation than a service. Some institutions may develop "stand-alone" units, either independently or within student affairs, to look after the academic advising needs of students (Kramer and Spencer 1989). Although faculty members may oppose such an organizational structure as an infringement on the expected role of academics, proponents recognize the specialized knowledge needed to be effective advisors.

While familiarity with academic regulations ensures credibility, the second, more informal advising or mentoring concentrates on personal challenges affecting academic performance and on improving the connection with the institution (Johnson 1989). Such links are often most challenging for faculty because of time demands; nonetheless, informal advising could mean the difference between a student doing well in a particular course, choosing the right career path after university, or simply making appropriate personal choices.

Supplemental instruction is another service that faculty can assist with in helping students. This strategy has roots in the mid-1960s at the University of Kansas City, where academic assistance programs were developed to aid students who were having difficulty in several courses, in first year and beyond, that required greater faculty intervention. Such programs provide students with additional specialized instruction: peer-assisted learners are assigned to particular courses, attend class on a regular basis, organize tutorials and extra instructional sessions for students, and are generally an added resource for students (Widmar 1994). Supplemental instruction programs are offered to all students, providing additional assistance for various aspects of a particular course, enabling more individualized instruction and support than available in the classroom, and allowing students to get the most out of their programs.

Finally, co-op programs that incorporate hands-on, real world, paid internship experiences can provide another opportunity for faculty to help students succeed (See chapter 11). Such initiatives offer a change of pace, allow a number of semesters to be spent in a workplace environment, enable concepts learned in the classroom to be applied experientially, promote the acquisition of job-related skills, and generally provide a broader educational experience than is otherwise available in the classroom. Co-op programs are good opportunities for students to gain exposure to the world of work and its expectations. The programs also strengthen students' connection with the institution through its relationship with the workplace.

Student affairs officials also need to be concerned with student retention and the quality of the student experience. Student engagement and involvement are important components and ensure that life outside the classroom contributes to success in class. Upon arrival, during the orientation process, new students are encouraged to get involved in both educational and social activities beyond the classroom. Students living in residence, through various formal and informal activities, are provided various opportunities for involvement and connecting quickly with the co-curricular life of the university.

A louder collective voice has emerged in post-secondary circles advocating greater institutional involvement to support students throughout the years at the institution and provide the assistance necessary to ensure their success. Research supports the need for students to facilitate the connection to the institution by becoming involved early and staying involved throughout the college years. Based on the Involvement Theory (Astin 1984), describing engagement in both physical and psychological dimensions, students becoming involved on a university campus can set the stage for a lifetime of activism. Student leadership opportunities abound on most campuses (Roper and Longerbeam 2002) (See chapter 7). Through positions in residence, within individual faculties and departments, or at the undergraduate or graduate level, students can take an active leadership role, learn about institutional governance, and participate in the decision-making process. Skills learned can be tremendously valuable and can become a significant part of a student's university education. Such experiences can be transferred readily from one leadership situation to another and become marketable skills once students graduate.

Student government, student clubs, and male and female fraternities are other examples of formal university groups that facilitate the student connection with the institution. Most of the groups develop leadership skills and serve as important networking opportunities. Such formal involvement also provides much learning and the acquisition of marketable skills that will be tremendously beneficial as students pursue full-time work opportunities, as well as further graduate and/or professional programs. Time management becomes important as students juggle a demanding academic schedule, leadership opportunities through various student organizations, and a social life away from the institution.

Additional opportunities include work study programs that provide on-campus employment and much-needed revenue for students, but also foster institutional engagement. Work study programs are usually co-funded between a pool of institutional resources and a sponsoring unit and give participating students a limited number of hours of work per week over the course of the semester. The work schedule is determined jointly between the student and the host unit. Even less-structured on-campus work opportunities are beneficial, such as working for dining services, campus recreation, physical plant, or student-led organizations. Their purpose, aside from monetary, is to provide opportunities to become involved, foster a sense of engagement, exact a long-term commitment to the institution, and enhance the chances of student success.

Two other programs have gained increased attention and popularity recently and similarly highlight the importance of skill development beyond the classroom. Student leadership development programs (Komives, Dugan, Owen et al. 2006) have emerged as increasingly important for students, but also for the health of the institution. While many university officials still see the development of leadership skills as a by-product of a quality university education, more people are acknowledging that skills required for effective leadership can and should be taught as formally as competencies required in other disciplines. Therefore, while programs mentioned above provide structured avenues for leadership skill development, oftentimes informally, greater emphasis is being put on formal classroom instruction highlighting various skills required for effective leadership, on related theoretical foundations, and on an overall commitment to providing experiential opportunities.

Service-learning programs look to enhance the university experience by expanding learning beyond the formal boundaries of the institution (Jacoby and Associates 1996). While the concept of helping others is not new, the extension of campus learning through involvement in community projects is still in its infancy, and only recently have universities recognized the significant learning benefits that occur through such community-based activities (Dungy 2003). Some institutions even advocate that a student's education is not complete unless some involvement in service learning takes place as a prerequisite for degree completion. Students can also become involved in service-learning initiatives as a way of meeting people and dispelling negative stereotypes associated with university students (e.g., that they are indifferent to their surrounding communities).

Another student-led program receiving favourable reviews is peer mentoring (Tinto 1993). From orientation and peer-helping programs for first-year students to acting as resource persons within student affairs, the value of students helping students through the difficulties of the university experience should not be overlooked. Peer-assisted programs can be structured through faculties or other service units, or less formally through casual meetings among students. Even senior students can benefit from the assistance of peers helping them through various academic and personal challenges.

Some students deem such formal involvement as too demanding and may choose less visible ways to contribute to campus life. Whether participating in a residence event, attending a social function organized by the student government, volunteering at a charity fundraiser, working on campus, or playing intramural sports, the degree of participation remains with the students. However, institutional officials must create such opportunities and market student involvement as an integral part of student development (Kuh, Schuh, Whitt, and Associates 1991). Many institutions have formalized student leadership and recognize participation in university activities by developing programs that aid students in acquiring skills necessary to become effective leaders. The reasons are not simply altruistic, as campus officials recognize that "success breeds success." If students feel valued, involvement is likely to continue, other students are encouraged to participate, regard for the university experience increases, and alumni support of the institution expands.

The connection generated through such involvement can only be strengthened if a legitimate partnership exists between students and the institution's academic and administrative leadership (Schroeder 2003). Students in the twenty-first century come with higher levels of maturity, worldliness, and expectations for respect than in previous eras. More important, given the average age and the relationship with the institution, students see themselves as partners in campus affairs and aspire to a legitimate role in institutional decision-making. The partnership demands a level of disclosure allowing for more informed decisions and enables students to take a more active role in institutional governance. Such openness may be uncomfortable for university officials; however, the relationship between the institution and its students can only be strengthened.

## Graduating and Career Development Services

A third group of services supports students as they move from university to the workplace, graduate studies at another institution, or preparation for careers in various professional fields. Career and placement services, co-op and internship activities, and fourth-year experience programs are typical initiatives provided for graduating students (Gardner, Van der Veer, and Associates 1998) (See chapter 11). However, institutions are becoming increasingly interested in maintaining a connection with students following convocation. Therefore, greater importance is being placed on alumni and development programs so students' association with the institution is not severed, and the university can turn to these graduates for financial support and as key stakeholders in new programs and initiatives.

Few institutional stakeholders would dispute that the major responsibility for student success lies within the student affairs unit (Upcraft and Barr 1990). Yet, faculty members and institutional support staff also have a crucial role to play. Students often comment on interactions with a particular faculty member and the value of such exchanges in helping them connect with the institution. In addition, the community external to the campus continues to figure prominently in helping students forge relationships, both on and off campus. If students are to truly have a meaningful experience, succeed academically, and grow developmentally, student success is not solely the responsibility of a few individuals but that of a host of campus and community officials.

Students must realize that education is multidimensional. Beyond the classroom are various opportunities to gain knowledge, to be part of the institution, and to succeed. Learning takes place within and beyond the institutional environment, in and out of class, and forges a relationship between students and the campus community.

## ISSUES AND CHALLENGES

Concerns expressed over the role that student affairs plays in the lives of students has campus administrators examining the unit and its relationship to overall institutional functioning. Students are arriving on campus with personal and psychological challenges rarely seen fifteen or twenty years ago. Students must now cope with varied learning disabilities; navigate unfamiliar physical, emotional, and psychological surroundings; adjust to a life of semi- or complete independence; and attempt to succeed academically. Various physical health issues may also require institutional intervention. Furthermore, the cost of attending a post-secondary institution requires that student financial aid play a more prominent role in helping students cope with the economic realities of a post-secondary education and adult life (Sandeen 1991)(See chapter 4).

University officials have also divested themselves of many services for students, shifting the responsibility and cost onto students and student governments rather than directly sponsoring the human and financial resources to deal with such needs. For example, off-campus accommodations were a typical service provided to students seeking more independent living away from traditional on-campus student residences. Concerned that university officials were simply providing a listing of available rooms and units, with little attention to the quality of such accommodations, student representatives developed their own listing of available spaces and determined their suitability for student occupancy. Many student governments now operate an off-campus housing service for students. Whether intentional on the part of university officials or a result of diminishing resources to support such a program, the transfer of such services from the university to student government reflects a growing trend on larger university campuses.

The exporting of student services to student governments or even their outsourcing to off-campus providers has raised many questions regarding the impact on the overall quality of the student experience and the integration of in-class and out-of-class learning. When student issues are treated as isolated problems or life challenges, their impact on academics is overlooked, resulting more often than not in interventions aimed at remedying the immediate issue rather than considering how the problem impacts overall student success.

The degree of emphasis on student services by universities is often guided by the size of each institution, but also the focus on the student experience. As universities grow and change their institutional mission, more or less emphasis is placed on responding to the needs of students. As they increase in size and become more concerned with research rather than teaching, services to students are likely to be reoriented to the new mission. For example, less effort might be directed to the incoming student and more to the student preparing for a career in research, either at a private agency or another post-secondary institution.

Student affairs professionals also remain concerned with the relationship to the academic community. Faculty and other academic officials recognize the importance of student affairs professionals in addressing students' personal issues, career development concerns, or overall adjustment to the university environment. However, faculty members dispute the degree of intervention that should actually take place and question if the help and support provided to students is as much a hindrance as a presumed benefit. Should students not learn to cope with the challenges of the university environment? Is failing not part of learning and might students not learn as much from not succeeding as they would if every course, every lab, and every academic pursuit were a successful one?

A more pressing issue is the academic community's view of student services units, particularly in regard to their contribution to overall student learning. While the service component cannot be ignored and is integral to student success, questions arise as to how much of the service component in student affairs is intertwined with the learning taking place in the classroom? If integration of learning cannot be established, what can be done to move the work in the classroom and the efforts of student affairs professionals in a common direction? If the relationship cannot be strengthened, the dichotomy that has existed between student affairs and academic affairs will continue, with the likelihood that the primary focus of academicians and the emphasis of student affairs officials will remain on divergent paths. Some have begun to address this gap in a sequence of monographs titled *Learning Reconsidered* (Keeling 2004, 2006), where the potential for achieving learning outcomes is explored across traditional divisions of the academy.

A related concept is financing of student affairs units – sometimes, as some faculty members have mentioned formally or informally, at the expense of more valuable academic initiatives. The issue becomes more pronounced during budget discussions and decisions on the allotment of funds, and debate may be even more heated at institutions with a mission focused on graduate studies and research. Academicians are always seeking additional funding for new courses, for research, or for additional instructional support.

Similarly, student affairs professionals seek additional funds for new programs, additional staff, and intervention supports. Budget allotments are usually based on the proximity of programs and services to the academic mission of the institution. Until recognition of the relationship between academic affairs and student affairs becomes stronger, and the mission of various components of the post-secondary enterprise are more closely aligned, struggles for funding will always exist and both units will be challenged to co-exist within a common institutional mission.

### CONCLUSION

This chapter has highlighted the involvement of student service units and their influence on the success of university students. Faculty, staff, and peers each play a role in helping students connect, tending to their developmental needs, and contributing to their success. The responsibility is not solely on students, although most people would expect students to play a significant role. However, faculty and staff also contribute to student growth and development.

What can be expected of university student services in the future? First and foremost will be the connection with the mission of the institution. Until significant efforts are made to bond to the institution and its primary focus, the survival and the relationship of student services to the university cannot be assured. Conversely, if student service units see their purpose as aiding learning and enhancing the primary mission of the institution, the units will be seen as contributing to the goals of the institution and helping students achieve personal and professional objectives.

Similarly, student services will be expected to move away from a conventional therapeutic model, where ills are corrected through various formal interventions, to a more wellness-oriented focus where the overall health of students is the cumulative result of various student services units working collaboratively to ensure the most positive learning environment (Strange and Banning 2001). Greater co-operation will be expected between units to ensure that necessary supports are provided.

Therefore, university student services units will be expected to take on a greater learning orientation and ensure that change and adapting to change become integral components of the evolution and growth of the unit. The focus on learning is paramount if the unit is to flourish and contribute to student success. Learning is broadly defined to include content knowledge in both cognitive and affective domains. Integral to this growth is a commitment to learning outcomes and to the various facets of student services playing a contributory role.

Equally important to the growth of student services units are the development of staff and the fostering of professional development opportunities.

Improving effectiveness through a range of formal initiatives that help
student services professionals better serve the needs of the student community directly improves the overall quality of services being provided and
enhances the degree to which units within student services can meet the
needs of students. Whether through regular in-service sessions, professional
retreats, or opportunities to attend conferences and workshops away from
the institution, an investment in the professional preparation of staff yields
many benefits for the institution and its students.

A partnership – involving student services as a whole and various faculties of the institution – is advocated so that student services programs,
activities, and supports are developed in concert with faculties and academic
units to meet their expectations and needs. Secondly, a partnership also
needs to be developed between providers of student services and the individuals being served. Students need to take a more active role in identifying
services of greatest benefit and ensuring that the institution recognizes such
programs as an integral part of student success. Formally, through systematic
input, or informally, through periodic feedback, students have a role to
play in the development of a student services unit at a particular institution
and, ultimately, its contribution to student learning.

Collaboration – a co-operation of roles and responsibilities so students
can rely on various resources during the long academic journey to successful degree completion – is encouraged. Faculty need to extend themselves
beyond the classroom and take a more active role in the lives of students.
Staff can provide a range of specialized services that help students connect
with the institution. The student community must willingly help one another
achieve success. And the off-campus community needs be encouraged to
look beyond the challenges of student conduct and assist students with the
difficulties of being away from home and living in a new community by
ensuring they connect with the neighborhood. Only through such an effective collaboration can students truly feel a part of the institution and belong
to its community of learners. Through such efforts – with all parties taking
responsibility and being prepared to assist — students can commit to learning and focus on success.

The university model in the Canadian post-secondary system has much
potential for nurturing the talents of the best and brightest. Through time
on task in educationally purposeful activities, students succeed as a function of their institutional engagement both within and beyond the classroom.
A core outcome of this process is student learning, and a critical partner
in assuring its effect is student services.

# 16

# Student Services at a Distance

DONNA HARDY COX AND BRUCE BELBIN

With the expressed goal of "empowering the individual student to study independently and to control the time, place, and pace of study" (Miller 1996, 42), distance education has long been among the delivery options of most institutions of higher learning in Canada. Although known earlier as *correspondence, independent, home,* or *open* study, this form of learning has evolved further to capitalize on advances in technology in offering increasingly sophisticated modes that are both accessible to and supportive of learners' needs (Bartolic-Zlomislic and Bates 2000; Cochrane 2000; Daugherty and Funke 1998). Currently, many post-secondary institutions offer courses adapted to a variety of media. Previously printed materials, textbooks, course guides, and other supportive documents are delivered to students through audiocassettes, video streaming, computer files and software packages, email, and podcasts. Contemporary learners also have access to a greater range of technology, enabling them to take further advantage of these more sophisticated modes (Bates 2000; Eastmond 1998; Ludwig-Hardman and Dunlop 2003; Miller 1996; Volery and Lord 2000). In addition, and also facilitative of these opportunities, there is a growing array of initiatives at Canadian colleges and universities, often under the leadership of campus student services, that support the success of those enrolled in such programs.

This chapter examines the student services role in contributing to success for the increasing number of distance education students who are employing computer-mediated technologies to participate in post-secondary learning. In addition to a focus on the basic services and programs developed to serve such learners, this chapter considers how they are organized and what constitutes some of the best practices that support student success in distance education. Lastly, attention is given to current issues and challenges that warrant further consideration from those in the field whose policies and practices shape the distance learning environment for students. First, though, it is helpful to understand the historical context for distance education in the Canadian post-secondary system.

## DISTANCE LEARNING IN CANADA

Beyond Mugridge and Kaufman's (1986) work, there has been little documented to capture a comprehensive history of distance education in Canada (Selman 1994), commonly referred to as *extension services* in its earliest days. However, some have attempted to identify the major initiatives and events in Canada's continuing education history. For example, in 1880, Queen's University began offering distance education courses based on a model developed by the universities of Cambridge and Oxford in the United Kingdom. By the 1890s, *correspondence study* programs were developed in many US institutions to educate rural agricultural workers (Selman 1994), an approach that would later find its place in Canada. By the middle of the twentieth century some Canadian schools, such as Memorial University of Newfoundland, had well-established departments of extension services. The 1970s witnessed significant growth in North American distance learning, in response to an increased emphasis on continuing professional education. Many universities also developed distance options to meet the increasing professional needs of baby boomers and to further support rural services as positive public relations for publicly funded systems (Selman 1994). During this period of growth, the types of educational services that evolved depended greatly on an institution's geographical location and the culture of its clients. While some offered courses with an academic focus, others focused on the applied needs of individuals within the region they served (Selman 1994). Regardless, the need to extend higher learning beyond the campus, providing greater opportunities for access and success to a broader citizenry, has left a legacy of distance learning programs in Canadian higher education, with several achieving recognition in their development of creative approaches and practices.

Three of the most established Canadian institutions in distance education delivery are Alberta's Athabasca University (1970); the University of Quebec's Télé-université (1972); and the former Open Learning Agency of British Columbia (1978), which became Thompson Rivers University, Open Learning (2005) or TRU Open Learning (TRU-OL). Each of these schools has responded at an exceptional level to a common mandate – to extend university services to students in an effort to overcome limits of time, money, and limited prior academic success. Acceptance of this approach is evident, for example, in the doubling of Athabasca's enrolment during one five-year period (1995-2000) (Frank 2000) to reach its millennial level of more than 32,000 students. It is estimated that almost three-fourths of community colleges in Canada and nearly two-thirds of universities offer distance education courses. Consistent with this, in international growth trends in distance learning (Haughey 1994; Potter 1998), Canada accounts for one-fifth of all distance education programs (Srivastava 2002).

The demands of distance learning in Canada, especially as they pertain to online opportunities, have stimulated a number of national initiatives and federal funding strategies. For example, in July 2000, the Council of Ministers of Education formed the Advisory Committee for Online Learning to study the impediments and incentives of online education and "to advise governments, universities, and colleges on a coordinated approach to online post-secondary learning" (Universiy of Waterloo). Similarly, the Association of Universities and Colleges in Canada established a Task Force on Technology Enhanced Learning. Additionally, the federal government (which long ago abdicated its management of higher education to the provinces) has also stepped into the development of Internet resources to support online learners in higher education in the form of online assessments. All of this makes it apparent that distance learning has grown considerably in Canadian higher education over recent decades and has attracted significant investment in its development and maintenance. Clearly, it is here to stay and carries much promise in its extension of opportunities to people and places previously underserved.

## STUDENT SERVICES FOR DISTANCE STUDENTS

Athabasca University has taken much of the lead in Canada on the development of literature on distance education through its publications such as *Learning at a Distance: A World Perspective* and *Theory and Practice of Online Learning* and its development of research institutes, journals, and graduate education programs on distance education (Anderson and Elloumi 2004). This growth in the field of distance education and in researchers is showing a concern for topics such as adult learning styles, access to learning opportunities, reasons for participation, factors related to attrition, and learner satisfaction. Potter (1994, 1998) challenged Canadian higher education to consider the importance of support services to distance education students, addressing the high attrition rate among such students, the assumption that adults need help with advancing technology, the life transition experiences of adults, and the high percentage of women among the ranks of distance learners. Subsequent to this landmark study, shifting demographics have continued to yield a greater diversity of participants in Canadian universities, necessitating a greater understanding of the various groups studying both on and off campus.

To improve the delivery of student services in distance education programs a greater understanding of the needs, interests, and personal demands of students is paramount (Wagner 1995). Assumptions about students, including their motivation to enroll in distance programs, prior skills, personal experiences, and culture and learning styles, must be examined further (Granger and Benke 1995). If distance education is to continue to flourish in the years to come, levels of student support services must increasingly appear to be "seamless" or fully integrated from the perspective of the learner (Miller 1996; Paul and Brindley 1996). Services should be viewed as necessary and integral to course delivery – not as an "add on."

## MODELS OF DISTANCE SERVICE DELIVERY

Three principal models or institutional approaches to online education are emerging in Canada: (a) exclusive, (b) complementary, and (c) integrative. The *exclusive* distance model is exemplified by Athabasca University, a full-service distance learning provider. It is a Canadian public-accredited undergraduate and graduate institution. Another example is Unexus University (1999), established in New Brunswick as a virtual institution and later named Landsbridge University, the only private, secular, and degree-granting university in Canada with Distance and Educational Training Council (DETC) accreditation (Landsbridge 2006). Such institutions deliver a breadth of well-integrated distance learning opportunities and support services designed from the beginning to meet a variety of student needs. Distance learners are the primary if not exclusive consumers, and program designs are conceived with that assumption in mind.

The *complementary* distance model is the most common in Canadian colleges and universities. Unlike an exclusive approach, this model focuses primarily on proximate campus-based learning, with supplemental offerings through distance options. The emphasis of academic programs at these institutions is on serving the residential student, with an extension of services through distance technologies. Such institutions often serve distance learners as adjunct enrollees in already well-established on-campus programs, and in doing so mostly adapt materials and delivery modes designed initially with a different assumption. For example, syllabi created for in-class courses might simply be reformatted digitally for access through various Web-based systems (e.g., Blackboard).

A third approach, the *integrative* distance model, is found in each of several types of Canadian higher education. First is a Canadian-grown consortium of public-accredited universities sharing a common credit-transfer system. The Canadian Virtual University (CVU), for example, includes a group of accredited Canadian institutions that offer complete degrees, diplomas, and certificates online and through distance education. In 2009, this particular collaborative consisted of twelve institutions and featured a catalogue of over 2,500 courses and 350 complete programs. However, it does not grant degrees independently but rather facilitates the programs of participating institutions through distance technologies. Its website describes a preliminary list of services to students, including career planning and financial aid information, and highlights institutions that have services specially designed for First Nations learners and international students. In a similar arrangement and by way of another example, at the provincial/ territorial level, in Manitoba there is a "consortium of Manitoba's public post-secondary institutions. It serves as a conduit to provide access to college and university courses and programs for Manitobans through distributed learning mechanisms, including the Internet. Campus Manitoba supports students by providing services that remove barriers and enable the achievement of educational goals" (Campus Manitoba). This commitment is exemplified by one of its newest services, an online math centre. A second type of integrative model includes institutions that are largely home-based in other countries that have campuses in Canada (e.g., DeVry Institute, University of Phoenix, Jones International University, Herzing College). Like the complementary approach, these institutions offer both campus-based and distance opportunities, but emphasize the latter more. Most recently, though, a third type of global consortium has emerged – U21Global. This is a joint venture between Universitas 21 (an international network of leading research-intensive universities) and Thomson Learning, in partnership with McGill University and the University of British Columbia, to create an "eUniversity" with programs designed to excel in shaping leaders for the global economy. Services provided to students vary with each model and institution; however, for the purposes of this chapter, we focus primarily on those provided through the complementary and exclusive models.

There appears to be no single template for student services in the complementary model. The norm is the creation of distance courses, with service components added later, focusing on administrative and technical support (e.g., registration, book purchases, library resources, fee collection, exam schedules) independently within the campus, with emphasis on delivery to the on-campus student. Consequently, student services functions relatively independent of the distance delivery system, which appears to be more of an afterthought connected to the domains of traditional student services providers.

In comparison, services in the exclusive distance model parallel those provided in mainstream student services. For example, at Athabasca University, students are provided with academic advising for program and course planning, as well as referral to professional counselling staff for personal matters. Students can avail themselves of memberships in their home community facilities, such as fitness centres, as an outreach service offered in partnership with the university. These self-directed services are provided through websites and service email databases that allow students to control their inquiries. In addition, services around finance and payments, and the ordering of textbooks and other course materials, are available online.

Much of the delivery of student services for distance learners has developed from a business-based "customer service" standard. With services boasting a twenty-four hour, seven-days-a-week support system, such savvy has become even more significant with the rapid expansion to worldwide Internet course offerings. As a result, many of the new distance delivery practices have begun to raise the bar for on-campus student services to become more efficient and accessible. Specifically, students have come to expect higher levels of customer service: 24/7 online technical support, a twenty-four-hour turnaround on email inquiries, immediate response self-directed services, and an online "two-click rule" to locate service and obtain a quick response.

### Organization of Distance Student Services

A typical organizational chart of a distance education department features a manager of student services reporting directly to a director. The manager usually holds a master's degree, with a background in student services, humanities, or business. Such a position entails working with a multi-faceted team with expertise in course production, finance, advertising, marketing, and communications. Often the manager has a staff of four to five people (sample ratio 1:1000 students). Usually, staff either have a clerical background and/or possess a university degree with a background in student services, education, business, or human services. Previous experiences as student leaders and mainstream student services providers are also assets brought by staff. A business orientation is helpful because distance education is often strongly influenced by a revenue-generation mandate. Typical staff development initiatives focus on cross-training in student services counselling, advising, empathy, stress, and conflict management and mediation. Overall, in distance learning operations, teamwork and "translation" skills complement technical savvy. In fact, the ability to "translate" service needs from students to a technical support team is valued more than in-depth technical knowledge. However, the debate continues as to whether the system or the students should drive the services. Best practice models would emphasize the latter. Thus, the student services manager in a distance organization must assume a major leadership role in translating how traditional services and institutional agendas can be more responsive to the needs of distance learners.

The organizational operating structure of distance education departments must support student success and requires continual attention in order to be most effective. For example, the organizational structure at Memorial

University of Newfoundland is embedded in a database system that ensures student questions are answered quickly by all staff at all levels. Accordingly, any student request not answered within twenty-four hours is escalated up the organizational hierarchy to the next individual in charge. As a result, the organizational press is toward solving the problem at its lowest level, most likely at the point at which service is initiated.

## Institutional Models

Services to distance students in Canada fall into three categories, related to: pre-enrolment needs, entering courses/programs, and accessing learning support throughout the program. Using Athabasca University and the Saskatchewan Institute of Applied Science and Technology (SIAST) as exemplars, the most important services reported by students are those "early" in the process, such as orientation programs that include information about courses and expected learning formats. Students value information on ordering textbooks, advice on course selection, information on specific distance education formats, and help in learning more about how distance education can impact their families. According to Potter (1998), students who are beginning their programs most often desire communication with their instructor, with other learners, and for tutoring assistance with course material. Learner support and retention appear linked to a "one-stop shopping" approach that is characterized as timely and accurate. Thus, for example, learner support at Athabasca University includes, among other features, the ability to request services such as transcripts and financial transactions electronically, online mentoring programs, learning service tutorials, online ID services, and exam stress assessments. An interesting partner in these developments has been the federal government, which now offers support and online guides to distance learners, along with various tools, such as an online learning quiz to test students' suitability for online learning (Service Canada). Among the supports, for example, is an explanation of the traditional role of student services in the pre-enrolment phase.

## Best Practices in Distance Services

Best practice models for distance learning programs are emerging quickly in the development of computer-mediated learning environments. Early models included descriptions of service levels and categories. For example, three key components that should be considered when developing services are (a) front-end communication and problem solving, (b) follow-up service assessment and satisfaction, and (c) back-end problem assessment and planning. Evolving rapidly are services that concentrate on tracking email communication and responses and that guarantee quick response rates through implementation of various ticketing and control systems. Services are developed to maximize accessibility and responsiveness twenty-four hours a day. Such trends reflect the needs of an expanding international market in distance education that requires the introduction of shift work for responders and partnerships with call centre personnel. In the distance learning environment online features permeate all service interactions.

Typical services focus on: supporting technology failures, providing academic and personal advice, and accessing administrative functions such as ordering textbooks and other course materials. Counselling for personal and career issues are offered through desktop media streams and telephone sessions. Service websites must be interactive and linked to institutional resources and employ standards and protocols that extend quick and concise service to the distance learner. However, this new service environment creates an expectation of immediacy that can only be satisfied by an automatic response. Whether this remains realistic, it nonetheless reflects the expectations of learner-customers growing accustomed to high service standards.

Athabasca University maintains its status as a leader and innovator in student services at a distance with two distinct approaches to service development. First is their strategic emphasis on measurement, evaluation, and the continuous improvement of services through surveys, assessments, and personalized communications. Second are their designs and implementation of services using innovative electronic communication techniques, such as websites, emails, blogs, and various learning platforms (e.g., Web CT, Desire To Learn). Athabasca has also field-tested the development of the first email-driven interactive service database, providing students access to immediate and concise responses to inquiries. Their innovation continues with initiatives such as the first ever "e-magazine" for students, online career path assessments, and virtual counselling. Finally, Athabasca excels in recognizing the consumer and market needs of the distance learner. Their priority placed on profiling learners to understand the locations in which they study (e.g., from home and the office, while commuting and travelling) has led to the design of services and programs that are more flexible and self-directed. Such practices are now being emulated throughout other traditional institutions providing distance opportunities. For example, Memorial University of Newfoundland features an online writing and disability support service. The Saskatchewan Institute of Applied Science and Technology (SIAST) provides distance education leadership at the college level. With the development of the SIAST Virtual Campus, the institution has created an online learning environment that is as innovative as it is unique. Commencing in 1997, SIAST realized the need to connect learners, province-wide, in the evolving online environment. Their goals included: (a) increasing virtual instruction capability, (b) providing instructor training in connecting to the learner, (c) developing and maintaining the Virtual Campus infrastructure while moving toward complete Virtual Campus offerings, and (d) achieving sustainable and predictable funding. A highlight of its Virtual Campus includes a "greenhouse room," that is, a Web-based environment that supports innovation in course development and service.

## ISSUES AND CHALLENGES

Advances in technology have dramatically changed the functions of colleges and universities (Moneta 1997). The "Wired Young Canadians" report (Rotermann 2001) indicating that 85 per cent of fifteen- to twenty-four-year-old Canadians use the Internet set the stage for a number of emerging challenges to educators and services providers in higher education. Continued support of students in computer mediated distance learning environments entails a further understanding of (a) the philosophical underpinnings and purposes of student services, (b) the evolving profile of distance learners, (c) student expectations for timely accessibility and support for their queries, (d) the logistics of mixed learning schedules, (e) the need for continued evaluation of the distance learning experience relative to retention, and (f) the preparation of professional distance services providers. Each of these concerns gives pause regarding many of the assumptions that currently inform the design and delivery of student services in higher education, with an eye toward their improvement and applicability in a rapidly changing learning environment.

### Philosophical Underpinnings and Purposes

Arriving at a consensus as to what defines "service" to distance education students is difficult. Devonshire and Crocker (1999, 4) suggest that the aim of student services is to enhance "academic outcomes achieved through participation in distance experiences." Their perspective is not incorrect and probably reflects the general approach to student services found in most institutions. However, services development and assessment in a distance learning environment is quite different. Practitioners of campus-based student services report a common error in the transferral of traditional services to distance learners with an assumption that "services are services" no matter what the learning platform. For instance, a study of best practices of distance education in remote Canadian Aboriginal communities (McMullen and Rohrbach 2003) identified on-site support as an integral component of student success in such programs. Other features identified include incorporation of the local culture and socioeconomic environment in the design of programs, prompt feedback, student relationship building, flexibility

relative to assignment topics and completion times, access to reliable technology, a welcoming environment for students, and the availability of
government support.

### Evolving Profile of Distance Learners

The development and delivery of distance education has been useful in
reducing and removing barriers to post-secondary education for many.
Issues related to geography, class scheduling, child care, and parking can
be reduced through distance education (Cochrane 2000; Potter 1998; Sewart
1993). Some universities have also created distance education programs to
increase access to students who would not otherwise be able to participate
in post-secondary education (Phillips, Scott, and Fage 1998). However,
some students simply prefer distance education because of the independence
and flexibility offered (Bartolic-Zlomislic and Bates 2000; Cahoon 1998;
Daugherty and Funke 1998). In addition, from an institutional perspective,
Devonshire and Crocker (1999) viewed distance education as an opportunity
to be more responsive to flexible styles of student learning.

Potter (1998) profiled distance students at three Canadian universities
(University of Victoria, University of Manitoba, and Memorial University
of Newfoundland), noting their ages ranged from twenty-five to fifty years
old, that four out of five were women, and that many were employed in
the health and education fields. Full-time students were younger and single,
while older students tended to be married with children and attended classes
part-time. The younger single, full-time students reported that they registered for distance courses because of the flexibility this medium offered.
Forty-four per cent of students surveyed lived over 200 kilometers from
the institution, reporting that distance education was the only option available to them for participating in post-secondary education. Forty per cent
had completed a university or community college program prior to enrolling.
When asked, over one-half stated that they preferred traditional on-campus
educational opportunities to the distance learning option.

Modern economic contexts also make it difficult for individuals to take
time away from work to attend school (Bates 1997a). Yet there is a growing trend of learners registering for post-secondary programs who are
part-time, over twenty-five, working, interested in career advancement,
and residing off campus (Eastmond 1998). This trend is further supported
in Canada through the introduction of online graduate programs. For
example, at Royal Roads University, the typical student is forty years old,
and institutions like Scotland's Heriot-Watt University "is reported to have
2000 Canadian students in its MBA program" (Frank 2000, 12). Likewise,
distance education is also becoming an increasingly attractive option for
doctoral level studies.

## Student Expectations for Access and Support

In addition to distance learners, on-campus students are also seeking access to their educational institution 24/7 and expect to have their needs met when the time is convenient for them (Moneta 1997). With continued growth of computer-mediated learning options through distance education, student services continues to make a fundamental shift in its delivery of services. Administrators might consider questions such as the following when offering services and courses dependent on computer-mediated technology (Bates 1997a): Can students ask questions? Who answers these questions? Who assists with technological problems? When is this help available? Bates (1997b) and Barolic-Zlomislic and Bates (2000) of the University of British Columbia recommend a more careful examination of access and student support issues. They remind services providers that students need to be psychologically and financially prepared to embrace this type of learning and the services that support their success. They list the various necessities for modern distance education programs: (a) computer modem with sufficient speed for downloading course materials, (b) a telephone line that can be dedicated to students' online time, (c) Internet service with an accessible help line, and (d) financial resources to pay for long distance and high speed costs. Often best practices in distance student services are grounded in a business model of customer service. Although controversial, this approach attempts to first be responsive to student needs. Toward such a goal, institutions like Memorial University of Newfoundland have claimed the title of the first distance education unit in Canada to be certified to the International Organization for Standardization (ISO) by achieving ISO 9001:2000 Quality Management System designation. This framework provides for, "organizational effectiveness, consistency in products and services and increasing client satisfaction" (Griffin 2008).

## Logistics of Mixed Learning Schedules

With the development of computer-mediated systems, students no longer need to come to campus, for instance, to access library catalogues and journals, pay tuition, or register for courses. This change has heightened student expectations and opened up the learning environment considerably. It is not uncommon, for example, for traditional on-campus students to pursue a percentage of their courses through the option of distance education. More often than not, distance education as a self-directed learning opportunity allows students the flexibility to accommodate other course demands, part–time employment schedules, commuting in inclement weather conditions, family or personal commitments, and enhanced lifestyles. As increasing numbers of learners are mixing their learning schedules, it can no longer be assumed that online students live at a distance. This may require a rethinking of the purposes of distance learning programs and those whom they are intended to serve.

## Continued Evaluation Relative to Retention

The importance of student services for the development and academic success of on-campus residence students has been well documented (Pascarella and Terenzini 1991, 2005). While it is tempting to utilize these established institutional services to gauge individual needs of distance education students, Gibson and Gibson (1995) warn against treating the needs of distance education students in the same manner as those of traditional students. Further research such as that of Powell, Conway, and Ross (1990), which identified nine characteristics of students significantly related to their success in distance education, has begun to capture these differences.

Administrations must determine supports to help distance education respond appropriately to the diverse needs of its students while maintaining an effective off-campus learning environment. Learning to ask relevant questions at the appropriate times and taking decisive action are essential to maximizing student retention. For example, that type of Canadian research on distance education in remote Aboriginal communities has yielded best practices for programs interested in developing distance courses for this population (McMullen and Rohrbach 2003).

Best practices in this context are often evaluated in terms of "customer satisfaction." The reality is that best practices can be discerned through the tools that a customer relationship model provides. Satisfaction surveys, focus groups, and assessment tools can provide institutions with excellent benchmarks on services and the quality of their academic program. Again, Athabasca University, a leader in the distance education field, rigorously applies assessment tools to the pre- and post-experiences of students enrolled in their courses and programs. Data are meticulously examined in an effort to identify gaps, weaknesses, and strengths of the programs and services. Through this process, Athabasca has built a reputation for quality, and the growth of their enrolment and services in the past four decades projects a distinctive leadership image in such programs. This reputation is well supported by the numerous best practices attributed to the institution. Reviews also suggest that high satisfaction with services generates return students who continue their lifelong learning with a dedication to the Athabasca process.

## Preparation of Professionals

Distance education services have evolved over the years, for the most part, from the student services profession. Traditionally, services providers have been professionals who have "fallen" into distance services roles. However, heightened expectations of effective distance programs have challenged student services professionals to look carefully at the preparation and training required to provide services at a level of excellence.

Preparation of student services staff continues to evolve in Canadian higher education, with two current programs at the master's level. This emphasis on advanced training suggests a tilt toward certification of a new and emerging field of professionals, for example, in international services, academic advising, and distance education. While traditional literature and resources apply, more and more training and support materials are coming from the World Wide Web, through online journals such as *Student Affairs On-line* (http://www.studentaffairs.com/ejournal/Spring_2006/), the *Chronicle of Higher Education* (http://chronicle.com/index.htm), and other resources.

Although in student services the emphasis remains on traditional models, the focus shifts in the training of professionals, who must be able to creatively apply those practices through electronic media to meet student customer needs.

The preparation of individual student services professionals for distance education has benefited recently from partnering within a number of organizations that have also focused resources on increasing expertise in this area. The Canadian Association for Distance Education (CADE) now includes services providers in partnership with academic members of the organization. Likewise, the Canadian Association for University Continuing Education (CAUCE) partners with services professionals and highlights relevant research and services projects within the organization. In addition, the Canadian Association of College and University Student Services (CACUSS) facilitates the training of services professionals who have moved into non-traditional areas such as distance education and international student services. Through these organizations' inter-association networks, journal research is disseminated and links to distance providers are highlighted and utilized through national conferences and joint work projects. All indicators point to the continuing evolution of student services professionals in this new realm.

## CONCLUSION

Successful distance learning is driven by the quality of support services (Tait 2000) that recognize the challenges of linking the two very different worlds of the learner – the personal and the institutional (Ludwig-Hardman and Dunlap 2003; Potter 1998). The typical student profile in distance education is that of the self-motivated and self-directed learner who has chosen the distance option as a strategy because of (a) lifestyle choices, (b) financial expedience, (c) the challenge of learning, and (d) the excellence of the academic product. This extends naturally into an expectation that the learner will receive excellent service, so standards of service such as response turnaround times are scrutinized. The bottom line is that learners expect quick and exact responses. Therefore, unlike traditional models, the logistics of such services necessitate special consideration to account for differences of time zones, electronic connectivity, political and social demands, health concerns, and challenges of travel.

Although a relatively new dimension of Canadian higher education, distance student services has solid roots in earlier forms of extension, correspondence, and distance programs. It is clear that online learning is a growing reality for post-secondary education and students expect and require significant support services to successfully engage in such opportunities. In the Information Age, technology will continue to play an essential role in higher education. Establishing systems to support student success in this new digital environment can be complex and challenging for both students and staff (Devonshire and Crocker 1999).

Continuing effectiveness in this domain will depend much on its capacity to address the complementary relationship between the needs of distance education students and student services delivery models designed on their behalf. This is a topic of great significance for the future of higher education and one that warrants additional campus-specific and national research.

# PART FOUR
# Achieving Student Success: Conclusion

Although the term *student services* is used frequently in this analysis to refer to a collection of offices, programs, and practices found on all post-secondary campuses in Canada, any implication that this field functions from a clear consensus of professional identities is probably an over-statement at this point in its history. Perhaps more accurate is the impression that, while each of the services outlined and discussed in the previous chapters identifies with its respective domain (e.g., counselling or enrolment management), the degree of common affinity of such services for any foundational core of professional understandings is only just now beginning to emerge.

There was a time when our identity was solidly grounded in the field of counselling. However, the student services field in Canada has evolved today to such an extent that its specialized divisions and subunits are both necessary and desirable in order to deliver the level of services expected with the degree of expertise demanded. Consequently, professional circles have focused as much, if not more, on various specialties within the field than they have on the purposes and goals that in the end define them all. Thus we began this analysis with our focus on student success as the most compelling purpose and goal of all that we do in student services.

We now conclude with a similar focus on helping students achieve their educational goals. Despite the professional segmentation that has characterized much of this work on our campuses in recent decades, the descriptions of each of these student services and contexts contain the seeds of a professional identity that transcends all of these specializations, in the form of several key tenets that, if not explicit, are at least implied in the work done. In this final chapter, we draw some conclusions about the underlying principles we think might identify the contributions these various units make to student success. There are lessons to be learned from one another about best practices in responding to students' needs: chapter 17 features what we believe to be some of the highlights of those lessons.

# 17

# Principles and Strategies of Good Practice in Student Services

## C. CARNEY STRANGE AND DONNA HARDY COX

The emergence in recent decades of a more *professional* model of student services in Canadian higher education has been a significant development in the success of Canada's college and university students. In terms of the quality of overall experience, it has been those in student services who have welcomed, oriented, housed, engaged, and supported students in the process of their development as they have pursued the best of what higher learning has to offer. From enrolment management and admissions to career employment and lifelong learning, student services has contributed in complementary and holistic ways, such that graduates are not only adept at their chosen disciplines but also capable of attending to the many challenges of life's questions and opportunities.

Ultimately, students who succeed in higher learning do so by immersing themselves in the college or university experience, both in and out of the classroom, to effect a sense of personal competence, identity, and direction that will serve them well after convocation. It is the programs, policies, and facets of the student services described herein that continue to shape an infrastructure of support and success for many in Canada's post-secondary system. Learning from their many contributions implicates a set of principles or strategies those in the field may wish to emulate when considering how to proceed. We've identified eight key principles/strategies in all:

1 Centring practices in student needs
2 Expecting individual differences
3 Being flexible in our approaches
4 Responding to needs appropriately and on time
5 Anticipating needs rather than reacting to them
6 Applying resources efficiently and sustainably
7 Focusing on outcomes and results
8 Designing and implementing services integratively

## PRINCIPLES AND STRATEGIES

There is certainly enough evidence in the preceding pages to suggest that these eight principles/strategies, although not an exhaustive list, offer important operational ideas. We address each (in no order of importance), exploring its essence and considering its potential effect through examples embedded in the services it illustrates. Some principles (e.g., principle 3) are quite obvious and apply universally in any attempt to organize and manage resources responsive to others' needs. Some (e.g., principle 5) are worth re-stating because, in the press of expediency, we sometimes overlook or, frankly, forget them. Finally, others (e.g., principle 7) extend from our core mission as educators, as human resource providers, and as student services professionals committed to the success of students.

### Student-centred Practices

If ever there were a first principle that frames both *what* we do and *why* we do what we do as student services professionals, this would be it. We are defined by students; we exist to serve students. So our practices begin with two fundamental questions: How do students learn, develop, and grow? and How do the policies and programs we fashion enhance that transformative process? Evidence of the student-centred nature of our work is seen, for example, in a traditional health services setting (See chapter 10), where links between wellness programming and brain health support students' overall well-being. The mission, philosophy, values, and organizational structures of student services on each campus guide the specific approach to such responsive practices (See chapters 14 and 15).

### Individual Differences

Engaging in the endless varieties of human experience, as we do in higher education and student services, we are not surprised that individual differences manifest themselves in a myriad of ways. Some students come seemingly fully formed, ready to take on the world. We are amazed at their independence and bravado, and inclined to just turn them loose and let them chart their own paths. We often point to them as archetype examples for others to admire and we fear that, if not careful, we might get in their way or burden their momentum. We've all known such "stars" and we jump at the opportunity to run with the best of them. More often, though, students come to us in various lesser stages of development. Regardless of the need, our task becomes creating or re-establishing a basic sense of personal agency so that self-direction will someday be part of their lives. Such is the moment of student success.

When we consider that students come from so many different circumstances and with so many different expectations and preferences, engaging individual differences becomes a critical standard in the metrics of achievement. The temptation is to "treat them all the same and let the chips fall where they may." Although less labour intensive, such an approach might be deemed "sufficient," with any failures relegated to "experimental error" or lack of effort on the part of students. "One size fits all" is a fiction of practice that serves no one well. Illusions of uniformity are also sometimes reinforced by an overreliance on aggregate reports, claims, and even stereotypes that serve to mask our best intentions when we fail to consider the unique context of each student. Responding to individual differences, on the other hand, is demanding and comes at a significant cost of staff time and resources. However, creative uses of technology and more judicious application may hold promise for resolving this conundrum.

The uniformity of Web pages describing services and providing self-guided information options can offer timely and relevant resources, twenty-four hours a day and seven days a week, to all students looking for specific information on particular topics (See chapter 16). Increasing reliance on such resources to respond to general routine inquiries frees up staff time to deal more carefully with individual matters. Assuming a more proactive programmatic stance might also provide relief. For example, Shea describes the creation of the Student Work and Services Program (See chapter 11) in response to the career development needs of single parents. From the start, its delivery and allocation systems were built upon inherent knowledge of single parents' realities and the kind of supports they required. Similarly, Mirwaldt (See chapter 10) reinforces the importance of understanding the range of personal health conditions and circumstances of various student subgroups (e.g., GLBT, first-generation, and international students) in the design of campus health services. Finally, as illustrated by McGrath (See chapter 12) in response to supporting students with disabilities, diverse needs can often be anticipated proactively through statistical benchmarks that implicate various services and programs and that offer information to educate institutions regarding such support.

## Flexible Approaches

Related to the above two principles is the wisdom of offering a range of flexible service options that cater to a variety of needs and possibilities. Just as students differ one from another, so too should our approaches and practices in serving them. Flexible alternatives increase the potential of a service responding to the unique circumstances and changes in the lives of students. Rules, standards, and systems are important for consistency and accountability, but adaptability is equally important in tailoring services to support the needs of students. For example, in describing the "technology imperative," Neuman (See chapter 3) recognizes the service commitment required in the design and maintenance of systems that respond in a timely manner to students' inquiries and expectations. For instance, telephone and online registration systems have enabled students to register for courses from the comfort of home, while improving the overall delivery of services.

## Appropriate Responsiveness

Being responsive is a basic feature of any good service. It means listening carefully to the presenting need or situation and responding in an empathic and timely manner. Clearly, it is a challenge to meet all concerns in this manner, given the ebb and flow of workload in the academic cycle and the fact that many students may wait until the very last moment to appear with urgency at our door. Nonetheless, good service is both appropriately designed and on time. Lessons on this principle have been gained perhaps most acutely from services designed for distance students (See chapter 16), where the combination of access and accountability has created an environment of immediacy that elevates responsiveness to a higher standard for all. Perhaps integrating new technologies and self-monitoring systems might hold the most promise for managing these growing demands without forfeiting the degree of personalization that hallmarks our best work. Another example of responsiveness is found in Russel's description (See chapter 9) of the level of mental health services made possible by an on-campus outreach and peer referral partnership program that promotes early recognition and crisis mode referrals to appropriate individuals.

## Proactive Versus Reactive

Anticipating student needs is perhaps the best antidote to the press of demands that more often characterizes our work. In examining trends and looking ahead, and drawing on the knowledge base that informs students' learning, growth, and development, student services professionals can expect increased demands for certain programs and services at predictable intervals throughout the academic year. For example, as explained by Mason (See chapter 5), orientation and first-year programs frontload many of their services to accompany students in the matriculation process, when issues of adjustment and transition are paramount in their lives. Failure to do so would likely jeopardize students' chances of success just as they are beginning their post-secondary journey. Murray (See chapter 4) also suggests that a similar strategy benefits the institution that anticipates student and parent concerns about financial assistance long before they arrive on campus.

## Efficient and Sustainable

The efficient and sustainable use of resources is an administrative mandate linked to institutional funding which, in turn, is strongly influenced by public expectations and governmental accountability measures. Efficiency implies the very best outcome or product for the least amount of cost. For example, Lane Vetere (See chapter 6) explores this notion with reference to the capital-intensive nature of student housing and the value-added residence life programs. Sustainability refers to the renewable qualities of the resources used. Achieving both goals is especially important in a competitive environment that judiciously monitors all expenses as a hedge against a shrinking resource base. Such goals also support an administrative environment intent on achieving its ends with maximum effect (See chapters 13, 14, and 15).

Related to such considerations is the role of professional standards, designed to identify the essential components and benchmarks of various student services. For example, the enrolment management function has taken on greater importance in higher education as population trends shift and demographics evolve. Neuman (See chapter 3) describes the range of intersecting factors that have influenced the increased marketing and recruitment efforts of Canadian universities in response to their public ratings and data inputs. Efficiency demands that colleges and universities consider more carefully the student profile best served by the programs each institution offers. Another example of the press toward efficient use of resources is apparent in the delivery of student health services on campus, where expectations of a universal health care system in Canada demand that campus professionals be knowledgeable of current trends and patterns (See chapter 10). Thus, the increasing use of surveys has been helpful in understanding and sorting through a range of student health issues likely to affect student success (e.g., alcohol use, sexual activity, dysfunctional sleep patterns, and body image projections).

## Results-oriented Effectiveness

The ultimate question any service provider must satisfy is: Did this program, intervention, or assistance work? Or more specifically: Did it lead to the desired effect, either (or both) from the perspective of the provider and/or the consumer? We cannot afford to stop at reporting only on the input effort for a particular service, with no accounting of the outcome(s) from that service. Ultimately, the effectiveness of a service is a measure of its contribution to the overall learning mission of the institution.

Since the early 1990s, a number of measures have been developed in response to questions about the effectiveness of various student services.

Some focus on the specific services appropriate to a particular unit (e.g., CAS), while others (e.g., National Study of Student Engagement, Canadian University Survey Consortium) examine the outcomes of broader institutional purposes to which some areas of student services might contribute (e.g., student leadership and involvement programs). Such assessments are critical for conveying the purpose and effect of student services on campus and the role it plays in supporting students' success.

## Integrative Services

It must be recognized that student services and the programs and interventions it sponsors are not entities unto themselves, but rather complementary and significant components of the broader post-secondary experience for students. A focus on student learning and development requires that all units consider how they contribute collectively to these goals. For example, services of a campus career development and employment office (See chapter 11) clearly supplement the choices of students to pursue particular academic majors (and vice versa), and thereby support the overall goal of assisting students in achieving a sense of purpose in their vocational and avocational interests. This, in turn, contributes to their retention and ultimate sense of success in their post-secondary experience. Another illustration of this principle is apparent in Robinson's discussion (See chapter 7) of the potential for leadership development from student involvement in campus clubs and societies, as well as in community, provincial/territorial, and national opportunities. Such programs provide students with the knowledge and skills to take an active and informed role in student life, in addition to developing linkages for post-graduation civic engagement. Similarly, Eerkes (See chapter 8) highlights the importance of the creation of educational and preventative programs in relation to judicial affairs in upholding the institutional academic integrity mission. In a final example, an integrative organizational structure is recognized as the hallmark of effective enrolment management (See chapter 3), where admission and registrarial services are combined through individualized portals to offer students a "one-stop shop" approach to institutional access.

## PROFESSIONALIZING OUR FUTURE

We conclude this analysis recognizing that, although the student services field in Canadian post-secondary education has made significant strides in its quest for professional status in the colleges and universities it serves, further development requires serious attention to the kinds of resources, motivations, and rewards that can sustain such a status. Certainly, the emergence of professional organizations and specialties over the past fifty years has brought the field a long way toward that end in Canada, but these are only periodic investments, personally driven and dependent on conference attendance and continuous organizational membership. As satisfying as that may be for generating enthusiasm and renewal in our work, it fails to address the more fundamental long-term question of professional preparation and competence. It is our belief that the kinds of understandings, insights, and strategies associated with the programs and practices reflected in the above chapters require that practitioners in this field be prepared more systematically and at a level that reflects the professional standards of their work.

A typical pattern that presently characterizes the entry-level student services career path in many Canadian institutions is the completion of a bachelor's degree (in most any major) following some significant out-of-class leadership experience in areas such as orientation, residence associations, or student governance. A position is then secured at the same institution with the expectation that one's career would advance there over time through gradual extension of one's portfolio and level of responsibility. This pattern generally reflects an emphasis on job training rather than planned institutional leadership development. Nonetheless, an increasing number of professionals are pursuing graduate studies in this area, primarily from personal motivation rather than from any requirements or rewards of the job. In addition, it is rare that such efforts are acknowledged or supported through professional leave opportunities and financial incentives. Further evidence of this predicament is found in the observation that most advanced leadership roles in student services (e.g., director, dean, AVP) are assumed more often by senior academics, with a minimum of a master's or doctorate in any number of fields, and a demonstrated propensity toward students and administrative matters. While such credentials might be sufficient to maintain division activities, they probably fall short in the professional grounding required to lead and advance its mission.

Canadian higher education holds a rich natural resource in its dedicated and experienced student services leaders. Tapping into this wealth of vast and varied practice experience calls for continued innovation, such as the many insights and ideas the authors in this foundational book offer. Such initiatives will continue to secure student services as an integral partner in student success in higher education. Nonetheless, the student services field in Canadian higher education cannot afford to become overly dependent on "on-the-job training" and must seek a common conceptual framework for identifying and communicating its purposes and for understanding the effects of what it does. Thus, we conclude our survey of these principles and strategies with a call for a new commitment and investment in the professional preparation support of student services practitioners in Canada. More specifically, we are recommending the development of additional programs at the graduate level (master's and doctoral studies), through distance learning and on-campus opportunities, to prepare leaders in the various student services specialties. By way of preparation, topics concentrating on post-secondary education are suggested, such as:

- History of Canadian higher education
- History and philosophy of student services
- Budget and resource management
- Governance and organizational management
- Diversity of Canadian higher education systems
- Student development theory
- Demographics of Canadian students
- Outcomes of post-secondary education
- Counselling theories and practices
- Group dynamics and processes
- Organizational dynamics and change
- Leadership theories and practices
- Student services functions and practices
- Professional values and ethics
- Selection, supervision, and evaluation of personnel
- Functions and issues of select student services
- Legal issues and procedures in higher education
- Research applications in higher education
- Characteristics of diverse student populations
- Assessment of campus environments
- Assessment of student outcomes
- Program evaluation methods and practices
- Collaboration with student governments

Implicit in this list is the existence of a body of knowledge that informs the general practice of student affairs educators and the particulars of specific student services. It is expected that anyone claiming expertise in this field should understand the parameters of Canadian post-secondary education and how the various facets of student services contribute to its ends. Furthermore, any leadership position (e.g., director or AVP) should require additional, in-depth preparation in these areas at the doctoral level, to support a strategic vision about their development in the context of institutional mission. Achievement of the doctorate would also prepare student services leadership to interact with others, such as faculty and academic administrators, perhaps more from the position of a peer rather than a supportive staff. The goal is to infuse colleges and universities with an understanding of how students learn, develop, and grow, and how institutional environments, within and beyond the classroom, can enhance the developmental processes already underway among its students.

## CONCLUSION

It is our hope that the expanding knowledge base reflected in these chapters has established a baseline understanding of the student services field, its culture, and its contributions to Canadian higher education. We expect that it will further encourage the cross-fertilization of ideas and the professional development of practitioners committed to its insights and aims. Ultimately, embracing of these ideas, under the leadership of educators who understand their import, can only serve to enhance the post-secondary experience for all students and, in the end, secure their success.

# References

FOREWORD

Keeling, Richard, ed. 2004. *Learning reconsidered: A campus-wide focus on the student experience.* Washington, DC: National Association of Student Personnel Administrators and American College Personnel Association.
Keeling, Richard, ed. 2006. *Learning reconsidered 2: A practical guide to implementing a campus-wide focus on the student experience.* Washington, DC: American College Personnel Association, Association of College and University Housing Officers–International, Association of College Unions International, National Academic Advising Association, National Association for Campus Activities, National Association of Student Personnel Administrators, National Intramural-Recreational Sports Association.

CHAPTER ONE

Atlantic Association of College and University Student Services (AACUSS). The story of AACUSS. http://www.aacuss.ca/about/const_hist.html, accessed 27 April 2009.
Canadian Association of Disability Service Providers in Post-Secondary Education (CADSPPE). https://www.cacuss.ca/en/divisions/cadsppe/overview.htm, accessed 30 April 2009.
The Canadian Encyclopedia. http://www.thecanadianencyclopedia.com/index.cfm?PgNm=TCESubjects&Params=A1, accessed 5 May 2009.
Canadian University Survey Consortium (CUSC). http://edudata.educ.ubc.ca/Data_Pages/12-PSE/Undergrad.htm, accessed 27 April 2009.
Hardy Cox, Donna, Dennis Dominie, and Eric McKee. 1998. Canadian undergraduate survey consortium. Paper presented at the annual conference of the Canadian Institutional Research and Planning Association, 18–20 October, in St. John's, Canada.

Hatcher, Albert. Memorial University of Newfoundland College Report of the President for the Year 1937-38. http://web.archive.org/web/20070810211818/http://www.mun.ca/mundays/30s/report38.html, accessed 10 August 2007.

Hatcher, Albert. Memorial University of Newfoundland College Report of the President for the Year 1938-39, 6 June 1939. http://web.archive.org/web/20070810114213/http://www.mun.ca/mundays/30s/report39.html, accessed 10 August 2007.

Hoskin, Thomas, Ivan Melhuish, and Robert Wagner. 1969. *A history of the university career planning association 1946-1969*. n.p.: University Career Planning Association.

Jones, Glen. ed. 1997. *Higher education in Canada: Different systems, different perspective*. New York: Garland Publishing.

National Aboriginal Student Services Association (NASSA). https://www.cacuss.ca/en/divisions/nassa/overview.htm, accessed 30 April 2009.

President Paton Report 1926-27. Memorial University of Newfoundland. http://web.archive.org/web/20070810221654/http://www.mun.ca/mundays/20s/report27.html, accessed 10 August 2007.

Paton, John. *Memorial University College Report 1925-1926*. http://web.archive.org/web/20070810121935/http://www.mun.ca/mundays/20s/report26.html, accessed 10 August 2007.

Paton, John. *Memorial University College Report 1926-1927*. http://web.archive.org/web/20070810121935/http://www.mun.ca/mundays/20s/report26.html, accessed 10 August 2007.

Queen's Encyclopedia. *Deans of women*. http://qnc.queensu.ca/Encyclopedia/d.html#DeanofWomen, accessed 29 April 2009.

Queen's Encyclopedia. *Student strikes*. http://qnc.queensu.ca/Encyclopedia/s.html#Strikes, accessed 29 April 2009.

Smith, Stewart. 1991. *Report Commission of inquiry on Canadian university education*. Ottawa: Association of College and University Student Services.

Sontag, Maynard. 1999. *Saskatchewan's Minister of Post-Secondary Education and Training*. Regina, Saskatchewan: Government of Saskatchewan.

## CHAPTER TWO

American College Personnel Association (ACPA). 1994. *The student learning imperative: Implication for student affairs*. Washington, DC: Author.

Astin, Alexander. 1985. *Achieving educational excellence: A critical assessment of priorities and practices in higher education*. San Francisco: Jossey-Bass Publishers.

Atkinson, Donald, George Morten, and Derald Sue. 1983. *Counseling American minorities: A cross-cultural perspective* (2nd ed.). Dubuque, IA: Brown.

Banning, James, and Sharon Bartels. 1993. A taxonomy for physical artifacts: Understanding campus multiculturalism. *The Campus Ecologist* 11(3): 2-3.

Baxter Magolda, Marcia. 1992. *Knowing and reasoning in college: Gender-related patterns in students' intellectual development*. San Francisco: Jossey-Bass Publishers.

Carnegie Foundation for the Advancement of Teaching. 1990. *Campus life: In search of community*. Princeton, NJ: Author.

Cass, Vivienne. 1979. Homosexual identity formation: A theoretical model. *Journal of Homosexuality* 4:219-235.

Chickering, Arthur, and Linda Reisser. 1993. *Education and identity* (2nd ed.). San Francisco: Jossey-Bass Publishers.

Cross, William, Jr. 1995. The psychology of nigrescence: Revising the Cross model. In *Handbook of multicultural counseling*, ed. Joseph G. Ponterotto, J. Manuel Casas, and Charlene M. Alexander, 93-122. Thousand Oaks, CA: Sage.

Dewey, John. 1933. *How we think: A restatement of the relation of reflective thinking to the educative process*. New York: D.C. Heath.

DuBois, William. 1903. *The souls of black folk*. Chicago: A.C. McClurg and Co.

Gilligan, Carol. 1982. *In a different voice: Psychological theory and women's development*. Cambridge, MA: Harvard University Press.

Hage, Jerald. 1980. *Theories of organizations: Form, process, and transformation*. New York: Wiley.

Hage, Jerald, and Michael Aiken. 1970. *Social change in complex organizations*. New York: Random House.

Helms, Janet, ed. 1993. *Black and white racial identity: Theory, research, and practice*. Westport, CT: Praeger.

Holland, John. 1973. *Making vocational choices: A theory of careers*. Englewood Cliffs, NJ: Prentice Hall.

Josselson, Ruthellen. 1987. *Finding herself: Pathways to identity development in women*. San Francisco: Jossey-Bass Publishers.

King, Patricia, and Karen Kitchener. 1994. *Developing reflective judgment: Understanding and promoting intellectual growth and critical thinking in adolescents and adults*. San Francisco: Jossey-Bass Publishers.

Kohlberg, Lawrence. 1969. Stage and sequence: The cognitive developmental approach to socialization. In *Handbook of socialization theory and research*, ed. David A. Goslin, 347-480. Chicago: Rand McNally.

Kolb, David. 1983. *Experiential learning: Experience as the source of learning and development*. Englewood Cliffs, NJ: Prentice-Hall.

Kuh, George, John Schuh, Elizabeth Whitt, and Associates. 1991. *Involving colleges: Encouraging student learning and personal development through out-of-class experiences*. San Francisco: Jossey-Bass Publishers.

Levinson, Daniel, and Judith Levinson. 1996. *The seasons of a woman's life*. New York: Ballantine Books.

Lewin, Kurt. 1939. *Principles of topological psychology*. New York: McGraw-Hill.

Lewin, Kurt. 1951. *Theory in social science*. New York: Harper and Row.

Maslow, Abraham. 1968. *Toward a psychology of being.* New York: Van Nostrand.

Mehrabian, Albert. 1981. *Silent messages* (2nd ed.). Belmont, CA: Wadsworth.

Michelson, William. 1970. *Man and his urban environment: A sociological approach.* Reading, MA: Addison-Wesley.

Moos, Rudolf. 1979. *Evaluating educational environments.* San Francisco: Jossey-Bass Publishers.

Moos, Rudolf, and Edison Trickett. 1974. *Classroom environment scale manual.* Palo Alto, CA: Consulting Psychologists Press.

Myers, Isabel. 1980. *Gifts differing.* Palo Alto, CA: Consulting Psychologists Press.

Palmer, Parker. 1987. Community, conflict, and ways of knowing. *Change* September/October: 20-5.

Perry, William. 1970. *Forms of intellectual and ethical development in the college years: A scheme.* New York: Holt, Rinehart, and Winston.

Piaget, Jean. 1950. *The psychology of intelligence.* Trans. M. Piercy and D.E. Berlyne. London: Routledge and Kegan Paul.

Price, James. 1972. *Handbook of organizational measurement.* Lexington: D.C. Heath.

Schein, Edgar. 1992. *Organizational culture and leadership* (2nd ed.). San Francisco: Jossey-Bass Publishers.

Schlossberg, Nancy. 1981. A model for analyzing human adaptation to transition. *Counseling Psychologist* 9(2): 2-18.

Smart, John, Kenneth Feldman, and Corinna Ethington. 2000. *Academic disciplines: Holland's theory and the study of college students and faculty.* Nashville: Vanderbilt University Press.

Stern, George. 1970. *People in context: Measuring person-environment congruence in education and industry.* New York: Wiley and Sons.

Stern, Robert. 1986. *Pride of place: Building the American dream.* New York: Houghton Mifflin.

Strange, C. Carney. 2003. Dynamics of campus environments. In *Student services: A handbook for the profession* (4th ed.), ed. Susan R. Komives, Dudley B. Woodard, Jr., and Associates, 297-316. San Francisco: Jossey-Bass Publishers.

Strange, C. Carney. 1994. Student development: The evolution and status of an essential idea. *Journal of College Student Development* 35:399-412.

Strange, C. Carney, and James Banning. 2001. *Educating by design: Creating campus learning environments that work.* San Francisco: Jossey-Bass Publishers.

Sturner, William. 1973. The college environment. In *The future in the making,* ed. Dychman W. Vermilye, 71-86. San Francisco: Jossey-Bass Publishers.

Thelin, John, and James Yankovich. 1987. Bricks and mortar: Architecture and the study of higher education. In *Higher education: Handbook of theory and research No. 3,* ed. John C. Smart, 57-83. New York: Agathon Press.

Wicker, Allan. 1984. *An introduction to ecological psychology.* Cambridge: Cambridge University Press.

## CHAPTER THREE

Association of Registrars of the Universities and Colleges of Canada (ARUCC) Advisory Committee. 2004. Program and course calendars in Canadian colleges and universities: A review of current practices and issues and lessons learned and some recommendations. Paper presented at the annual conference of ARUCC, 27-30 June, in Ottawa, Canada. http://arucc2004.centennialcollege.ca/documents/D3.pdf, accessed 6 May 2009.

Association of Registrars of the Universities and Colleges of Canada (ARUCC). 2003. National transcript guide for use in Canadian post-secondary institutions. http://www.arucc.com/documents/transc.pdf, accessed 6 May 2009.

Association of Registrars of the Universities and Colleges of Canada. Statement of purpose. http://www.arucc.ca/, accessed 6 May 2009.

Atlantic Association of Registrars and Admissions Officers (AARAO). AAROA best practices guidelines. http://www.unb.ca/aarao/documents/BestPractices Guidelines.pdf, accessed 6 May 2009.

Canadian Education Centre (CEC). http://www.cecnetwork.ca/, accessed 29 April 2009.

CONTACT Newsletter Archives. http://www.arucc.ca/, accessed 29 April 2009.

CUMREC – A Higher Education Administrative Technology Conference. Annual Conference. http://net.educause.edu/content.asp?page_id=3089&bhcp=1, accessed 29 April 2009.

Gladwell, Malcolm. 2000. *The tipping point: How little things can make a big difference.* Boston: Little, Brown.

Howe, Neil, and William Strauss. 2000. *Millennials rising: The next great generation.* New York: Vintage Books.

McMaster University. 2007. Brand standards manual. http://www.mcmaster.ca/opr/html/opr/mcmaster_brand/visual_identity/McMaster_brand_manual.pdf.

Ontario Universities' Fair. http://www.ouf.ca/, accessed 29 April 2009.

Shared hierarchical academic research network. http://www.sharcnet.ca/, accessed 29 April 2009.

Western Association of Registrars of the Universities and Colleges of Canada (WARUCC). WARUCC news archives 2000-08. http://www.warucc.ca/newsletters.htm, accessed 29 April 2009.

## CHAPTER FOUR

Anisef, Paul, and Robert Sweet. 2002. Financial planning for post-secondary education: A social-demographic profile of Canadian families. Pacific Demographics: Vancouver.

Astin, Alexander. 1984. Student involvement: A developmental theory for higher education. *Journal of College Student Personnel* 25:297-308.

Baker, Murray. 2008. *The debt free graduate: How to survive college or university without going broke* (8th ed.). Vancouver: MoneySmarts Publishing.

Canadian Association of University Business Officers (CAUBO). 2008. Financial information of universities and colleges 2006-2007. Ottawa: Author. http://www.caubo.ca/pubs/documents/CAUBO_2006_2007_FINANCIAL_INFORMATION_OF_UNIVERSITIES_AND_COLLEGES.pdf, accessed 29 April 2009.

Dundes, Lauren, and Jeff Marx. 2006. Balancing work and academics in college: Why do students working 10-19 hours per week excel? *Journal of College Student Retention* 8(1): 107-20.

Gucciardi, Franca. 2004. *Recognizing excellence? Canada's merit scholarships.* Montreal: Canada Millennium Scholarship Foundation.

Ontario Student Assistance Program. Student access guarantee. https://osap.gov. on.ca/eng/not_secure/Access_Guarantee_12.htm, accessed 29 April 2009.

Statistics Canada. *University Tuition Fees (2006-2007).* http://www.statcan.gc.ca/daily-quotidien/060901/dq060901a-eng.htm, accessed 29 April 2009.

Somers, Patricia. 1993. Are 'mondo' scholarships effective? *Journal of Student Financial Aid* 23(2): 37-8.

University of British Columbia Board of Governors. 2005. Access to the University of British Columbia (Policy No. 72). Vancouver: University of British Columbia. http://www.universitycounsel.ubc.ca/policies/policy72.pdf, accessed 29 April 2009.

## CHAPTER FIVE

Adams, Michael. 2000. *Better happy than rich? Canadians, money, and the meaning of life.* Toronto: Penguin Books.

Adams, Michael. 1997. *Sex in the snow: Canadian values at the end of the millennium.* Toronto: Penguin Books.

Association of Universities and Colleges of Canada. 2001. *Trends in higher education.* Ottawa: Author.

Beloit College. Beloit College's annual "Class of" Mindset List®- MindSet list for the class of 2012. http://www.beloit.edu/mindset/2012.php, accessed 1 May 2009.

Bibby, Reginald. 1995. *The Bibby report: Social trends Canadian-style.* Toronto: Stoddart.

Bibby, Reginald. 2001. *Canada's teens: Today, yesterday, and tomorrow.* Toronto: Stoddart.

Brooks II, James, and David DuBois. 1995. Individual and environmental predictors of adjustment during the first year of college. *Journal of College Student Development* 36(4): 347-60.

Brown, Louise. 2003. Boomers' anxiety high for college-bound kids. *Toronto Star*, 3 August, A.04.

Christie, Nancy, and Sarah Dinham. 1991. Institutional and external influences on social integration in the freshman year. *Journal of Higher Education* 62:412-36.

Coburn, Karen, and Madge Treeger. 1988. *Letting go: A parents' guide to today's college experience*. Bethseda, Maryland: Adler and Adler.

Forbes, Karen. 2001. Students and their parents. Where do campuses fit in? *About Campus* September/October: 11-17.

Gilbert, Sid, Judy Chapman, Peter Dietsche, Paul Grayson, and John Gardner. 1997. *From best intentions to best practices: The first-year experience in Canadian post secondary education, Monograph 22*. Columbia, SC: National Resource Center for the Freshman Year Experience and Students in Transition, University of South Carolina.

Horowitz, Helen. 1987. *Campus life: Undergraduate cultures from the end of the eighteenth century to the present*. New York: Alfred A. Knopf.

Howe, Neil, and William Strauss. 2000. *Millennials rising: The next great generation*. New York: Vintage Books.

Johnson, Helen E. Educating parents about college life, *Chronicle of Higher Education*, 9 January 2004

Levine, Arthur, and Jeanette Cureton. 1998. *When hope and fear collide: A portrait of today's college student*. San Francisco: Jossey-Bass Publishers.

National Resource Center for the First-Year Experience and Students in Transition. http://www.sc.edu/fye/center/index.html, accessed 1 May 2009.

National Resource Center. 22nd International Conference on The First-Year Experience. http://www.sc.edu/fye/, accessed 29 April 2009.

Sanford, Nevitt. 1962. Developmental status of the entering freshman. In *The American college*, ed. Nevitt Sandford, 253-82. New York: Wiley.

Schlossberg, Nancy, Elinor Waters, and Jane Goodman. 1995. *Counseling adults in transition* (2nd ed.). New York: Springer.

University of Guelph. *ST@RT Online*. http://www.startonline.ca, accessed 29 April 2009.

Upcraft, M. Lee, John Gardner, and Associates. 1990. *The freshman year experience: Helping students survive and succeed in college*. San Francisco: Jossey-Bass Publishers.

University of Guelph. Guide for parents and families. http://www.studentlife.uoguelph.ca/parents/studentexperience.cfm, accessed 29 April 2009.

## CHAPTER SIX

Chickering, Arthur, and Linda Reisser. 1993. *Education and identity* (2nd ed.). San Francisco: Jossey-Bass Publishers.

Komives, Susan R. 1994. Increasing student involvement through civic leadership education. In *Realizing the educational potential of residence halls*, ed. Charles C. Schroeder and Phyllis Mable, 218-40. San Francisco: Jossey-Bass Publishers.

Leafgren, Fred. 1993. Wellness as a comprehensive student development approach. In *Student housing and residence life*, ed. Roger B. Winston, Jr. and Scott Anchors, 443-60. San Francisco: Jossey-Bass Publishers.

Levine, Arthur. 1994. Guerrilla education in residential life. In *Realizing the educational potential of residence halls*, ed. Charles C. Schroeder and Phyllis Mable. 93-106. San Francisco: Jossey-Bass Publishers.

Pascarella, Ernest, and Patrick Terenzini. 1991. *How college affects students*. San Francisco: Jossey-Bass Publishers.

Pascarella, Ernest, Patrick Terenzini, and Gregory Blimling. 1994. The impact of residential life on students. In *Realizing the educational potential of residence halls*, ed. Charles Schroeder, Phyllis Mable, and Associates, 22–52. San Francisco: Jossey-Bass Publishers.

Schroeder, Charles. 1994. Developing learning communities. In *Realizing the educational potential of residence halls*, ed. Charles C. Schroeder and Phyllis Mable, 165-89. San Francisco: Jossey-Bass Publishers.

Schroeder, Charles, Phyllis Mable, and Associates. 1994. *Realizing the educational potential of residence halls*. San Francisco: Jossey-Bass Publishers.

Shapiro, Nancy, and Jodi Levine. 1999. *Creating learning communities: A practical guide to winning support, organizing for change, and implementing programs*. San Francisco: Jossey-Bass Publishers.

Strange, C. Carney, and James Banning. 2001. *Educating by design: Creating campus learning environments that work*. San Francisco: Jossey-Bass Publishers.

Upcraft, M. Lee. 1994. Organizational and administrative approaches. In *Student housing and residence life*, ed. Roger B. Winston Jr. and Scott Anchors, 189-202. San Francisco: Jossey-Bass Publishers.

Upcraft, M. Lee, John Gardner, and Associates. 1990. *The freshman year experience: Helping students survive in college*. San Francisco: Jossey-Bass Publishers.

Winston, Roger, Jr., Scott Anchors, and Associates. 1993. *Student housing and residential life: A handbook for professionals committed to student development goals*. San Francisco: Jossey-Bass Publishers.

Zeller, William, ed. 2008. *Residence life and the new student experience (3rd ed.), Monograph 5*. Columbia, SC: National Resource Center for the First-Year Experience and Students in Transition.

## CHAPTER SEVEN

Altbach, Philip, and Robert Cohen. 1990. American student activism: The post-sixties transformation. *The Journal of Higher Education* 61:32-49.

Ansley, Fran, and John Gaventa. 1997. Research for democracy and democratizing research. *Change* 29:46-53.

Astin, Alexander, and Helen Astin. 2001. *Leadership reconsidered: Engaging higher education in social change.* Battle Creek, MI: W.K. Kellogg Foundation.

Astin, Alexander, Lori Vogelgesang, Elaine Ikeda, and Jennifer Yee. 2000. *How service learning affects students.* Los Angeles: Higher Education Research Institute, University of California, Los Angeles.

Bringle, Robert, and Julie Hatcher. 1996. Implementing service learning in higher education. *Journal of Higher Education* 67:221-39.

Canadian Alliance of Student Associations (CASA). http://www.casa.ca/, accessed 29 April 2009.

Canadian Alliance for Community Service–Learning. http://www.community servicelearning.ca, accessed 29 April 2009.

Canadian Federation of Students (CFS). http://www.cfs-fcee.ca/, accessed 29 April 2009.

Hudson, Helen, Tom Keefer, Lana Rabkin, and Andrew Thompson, eds. 1997. *When campus resists: The politics of space, power, and the culture of resistance in the Guelph occupation movement.* Guelph, Canada: Occupation Press.

Jones, Glen. 2002. The structure of university governance in Canada: A policy network approach. In *Governing higher education: National perspectives on institutional governance*, ed. Alberto Amaral, Glen A. Jones, and Berit Karseth, 213-34. Boston: Kluwer.

Jones, Glen. 1995. Student pressure: A national survey of Canadian student organizations. *Ontario Journal of Higher Education,* 93-106.

Jones, Glen and Michael Skolnik. 1997. Governing boards in Canadian universities. *The Review of Higher Education* 20:277-95.

Knopf, Gordon. 1960. *College student government.* New York: Harper and Brothers.

Komives, Susan, Nancy Lucas, and Tim McMahon. 1998. *Exploring leadership: For college students who want to make a difference.* San Francisco: Jossey-Bass Publishers.

Kouzes, James, and Barry Posner. 2005. *The student leadership practices inventory (LPI).* San Francisco: Jossey-Bass Publishers.

Kuh, George, John Schuh, Elizabeth Whitt, and Associates. 1991. *Involving colleges: Encouraging student learning and personal development through out-of-class experiences.* San Francisco: Jossey-Bass Publishers.

McGrath, Earl. 1970. *Should students share the power? A study of their role in college and university governance.* Philadelphia: Temple University Press.

Meinhard, Agnes, and Mary Foster. 1998. *Community service programs in Toronto's secondary schools.* Toronto: Ryerson Centre for Voluntary Sector Studies.

Morison, Robert. 1970. The President's Commission on Student Involvement in Decision-Making. The Chairman's Report. Washington, DC: Public Affairs Press.

Ontario Undergraduate Student Alliance. 1994. Our new responsibility: Meeting the guidelines for the new ministry of education and training

policy on compulsory ancillary fees. http://web.archive.org/web/
20050220111420/http://www.ousa.on.ca/docs/pdf/pub0894.pdf, accessed
20 May 2009.

Prentice, Mary, and Rudy Garcia. 2000. Service learning: The next generation in
education. *Community College Journal of Research and Practice* 24:19-26.

Robinson, Nona. 2003a. Student affairs and student service delivery: A comparison of the American and Canadian models. Master's course paper, OISE/
University of Toronto.

Robinson, Nona. 2003b. Undergraduate student association by-laws. Master's
course paper, OISE/University of Toronto.

Robinson, Vanda Wenona. 2004. The experience of elected undergraduate
student leaders in Canada. MA thesis, University of Toronto.

University of British Columbia. 2005. Leadership and involvement program.
http://students.ubc.ca/leadership/, accessed 9 February 2005.

University of Guelph. 2005. Citizenship and leadership education. http://www.
studentlife.uoguelph.ca/citizenleader/, accessed 9 February 2005.

Zuo, Bing, and Eugene Ratsoy. 1999. Student participation in university governance. *The Canadian Journal of Higher Education* 29:1-26.

## CHAPTER EIGHT

Adams, Michael. 2003. *Fire and ice: The United States and Canada and the
myth of converging values.* Toronto: Penguin.

Bertram Gallant, Tricia. 2008. Academic Integrity in the twenty-first Century:
A teaching and learning imperative. *ASHE Higher Education Report* 33 no. 5
(20 March): 1-143. http://www3.interscience.wiley.com/journal/117944722/
issue, accessed 4 September 2008.

Birchard, Karen. Cheating is rampant at Canadian colleges. *Chronicle of Higher
Education* 53, 8(13 October) http://chronicle.com/weekly/v53/i08/08a05302.
htm, accessed 9 November 2006.

Bohun, Jim, Chris Fukushima, Tracey Mason-Innes, and Chris Hackett. 2007.
Web 2.0 and post-secondary discipline. Paper presented at the Canadian
Association of College and University Student Services Conference, 10-13 June,
in Saskatoon, Canada.

Canadian Centre for Substance Abuse(CCSA). http://www.ccsa.ca/ENG/Pages/
Home.aspx, accessed 6 May 2009.

Center for Academic Integrity. 1999. *The fundamental values of academic
integrity.* (Brochure). Des Plaines, IL: Author. http://www.academicintegrity.org/
fundamental_values_project/pdf/FVProject.pdf, accessed 23 September 2008.

Christensen Hughes, Julia, and Donald McCabe. 2006. Academic misconduct
within higher education in Canada. *Canadian Journal of Higher Education*
36(2): 1-21.

Christensen Hughes, Julia, and Donald McCabe. 2006. Understanding academic
misconduct. *Canadian Journal of Higher Education* 36(1): 9-63.

Dannells, Michael. 1997. *From discipline to development: Rethinking student conduct in higher education.* ASHE-ERIC Higher Education Report 25(2). Washington, DC: George Washington University, Graduate School of Education and Human Development.

Devine, Sheila. 2006. Administrative law: The importance of process and a case Study. Lecture presented at the University Management Course offered by the Centre for Higher Education Research and Development, 5-12 May, in Banff, Canada.

Foxman, Stuart. 2006. But everybody cheats! *Reader's Digest Canada* October 2006. http://www.readersdigest.ca/mag/2006/10/everybody_cheats.php, accessed 24 July 2007.

Gulli, Cathy, Nicholas Kohler, and Martin Patriquin. 2007. The great university cheating scandal. *MacLean's,* 9 February. http://www.macleans.ca/article.jsp?content=20070212_140680_140680&source=srch, accessed 30 July 2008.

Hannah, David. 1998. *Post-secondary students and the courts in Canada: Cases and commentary from the common law provinces,* The Higher Education Administration Series, ed. Donald D. Gehring and D. Parker.Young. Asheville, NC: College Administration Publications.

Hoekema, David. 1994. *Campus rules and moral community: In place of* in loco parentis. Lanham, MD: Rowman and Littlefield.

Kibler, William, Elizabeth Nuss, Brent Paterson, and Gary Pavela. 1988. *Academic integrity and student development: legal issues, policy perspectives.* The Higher Education Administration Series, ed. Donald D. Gehring and D. Parker Young. Asheville, NC: College Administration Publications.

Lancaster, James, and Associates. 2006. *Exercising power with wisdom: Bridging legal and ethical practice with intention.* The Higher Education Administration Series, ed. Donald D. Gehring and D. Parker Young. Asheville, NC: College Administration Publications.

Martin, Elizabeth. 1997. *Oxford dictionary of law* (4th ed.). Oxford: Oxford University Press.

Pavela, Gary. 2000. New research on academic integrity: The success of modified honor codes. *Synfax Weekly Report,* 00.17, no. 975, (15 March). Asheville, NC: College Administration Publications.

Shea, Robert, and Peggy Patterson. 2007. Both sides of the coin: An exploration of realities and myths about faculty life. Paper presented at the annual Canadian Association of College and University Student Services conference, 10-13 June, in Saskatoon, Canada.

Smith, Lynn. Personal email communication to author, 13 June 2007.

Smith, Lynn. 1998. *Procedural fairness for university and college students.* *Canadian Association of College and University Student Services, Monograph Series No.* 3. Kingston, ON: Canadian Association of College and University Student Services.

Utgoff, Dima. Personal conversation with author, Edmonton, AB, August 2005.

## CHAPTER NINE

Astin, Alexander. 1975. *Preventing students from dropping out.* San Francisco: Jossey-Bass Publishers.

Axelson, John. 1999. *Counseling and development in a multicultural society* (3rd ed.). Pacific Grove, CA: Brooks/Cole.

Benton, Sherry, John Robertson, Wen-Chih Tseng, Fred Newton, and Stephen Benton. 2003. Changes in counselling centre client problems across 13 years. *Professional Psychology: Research and Practice* 34:66-72.

Bertolino, Bob. 2004. Maximizing therapeutic effectiveness with challenging clients: Collaborative, change-oriented therapy. Paper presented at the American Counselling Association Learning Institute, 1 April, in Kansas City, MO.

Bolles, Richard. 2002. *What color is your parachute? 2003: A practical manual for job-hunters and career-changers.* Berkeley, CA: Speed Press.

Canadian University and College Counselling Association (CUCCA). 2005. History of CUCCA. https://www.cacuss.ca/en/divisions/CUCCA/information.htm, accessed 29 April 2009.

Chiste, Paola, and Melanie Rathgeber. 1998. *First year attrition at the university of Saskatchewan, office of student affairs and services.* Saskatoon: University of Saskatchewan.

Comprehensive student survey 2002. 2002. University Planning Office, Ryerson University, Toronto, Ontario. http://www.ryerson.ca/upo/reports/#compsurvey02, accessed 29 April 2009.

Coniglio, Connie, G. McLean, and T. Mueser. 2005. *Personal counselling in a Canadian post-secondary context.* Kingston, ON: Canadian University and College Counselling Association.

Crozier, Sharon, and Nancy Willihnganz. 2005. *Canadian counselling centre survey.* Canadian University and College Counselling Association. https://www.cacuss.ca/en/divisions/CUCCA/resources/2005.htm, accessed 29 April 2009.

Duenwald, Mary. 2004. The dorms may be great, but how's the counseling? *New York Times,* 26 October.

Gerdes, Hilary, and Brent Mallinckrodt. 1994. Emotional, social, and academic adjustment of college students: A longitudinal study of retention. *Journal of Counseling and Development* 72:281-8.

Gordon, Sheldon. 2003. Reaching out to students. *University Affairs* 44(10): 22-5.

Gordon, Virginia. 1998. Career decidedness types: A literature review. *The Career Development Quarterly* 6:386-403.

Heslop, Joanne. 2004. Undergraduate student survey: Report of findings. Burnaby, British Columbia: Simon Fraser University Office of Analytical Studies. http://www.sfu.ca/analyticalstudies/ugss/2004/ugss2004report, accessed 10 February 2005.

Hoyt, Jeff, and Bradley Winn. 2004. Understanding retention and college student bodies: Differences between drop-outs, stop-outs, opt-outs, and transfer-outs. NASPA *Journal* 41:395-400.

Hubble, Mark, Barry Duncan, and Scott Miller, ed. 1999. *The heart and soul of change: What works in therapy*. Washington, DC: American Psychological Association.

Khanna, Arunima, and Susan Qadeer. 2005. Counselling international and minority students. Kingston, ON: The Canadian Association of College and University Student Services Conference.

Kitzrow, Martha. 2003. The mental health needs of today's college students: Challenges and recommendations. NASPA *Journal* 41:165-79.

Lambeth, Gregory, and Marybeth Hallett. 2002. Promoting healthy decision making in relationships: Developmental interventions with young adults on college and university campuses. In *Counselling across the lifespan: Prevention and treatment*, ed. Cindy L. Juntunen and Donald R. Atkinson, 209-226. London: Sage Publications.

Levine, Arthur, and Jeanette Cureton. 1998. *When hope and fear collide: A portrait of today's college student*. San Francisco: Jossey-Bass Publishers.

Miner, John. 2003. Local mental health facilities in desperate state, officials say. *London Free Press* (London, Ontario), 8 May.

Morgan, Tracy, and David Ness. 2003. Career decision-making difficulties of first-year students. *The Canadian Journal of Career Development* 2:33-9.

Niles, Spencer, and JoAnn Harris-Bowlsbey. 2002. *Career development: Interventions in the 21st century*. Upper Saddle, NJ: Pearson, Inc.

Pledge, Deanna, Richard Lapan, Paul Heppner, Dennis Kivlighan, and Helen Roehlke. 1998. Stability and severity of presenting problems at a university counseling centre: A 6-year analysis. *Professional Psychology: Research and Practice* 29:386-9.

Polanksy, Joan, John Horan, and Christine Hanish. 1993. Experimental construct validity of the outcomes of study skills training and career counselling as treatment for the retention of at risk students. *Journal of Counseling and Development* 71:488-92.

Shale, Doug. 2004. *Fact Book* 2003-2004. Office of Institutional Analysis, University of Calgary, Calgary Alberta.

Sharkin, Bruce. 2004. College counselling and student retention: research findings and implications for counselling centres. *Journal of College Counseling* 7:99-107.

Stone, Gerald, and James Archer. 1990. College and university counseling centers in the 1990s: Challenges and limits. *Counseling Psychologist*, 18: 539–607.

Sue, Derald, Patricia Arredondo, and Roderick McDavis. 1992. Multicultural counseling competencies and standards: A call to the profession. *Journal of Counseling and Development*, 70:477-86.

Surtees Paul, Nicholas Wainwright, and Paul Pharoah. 2000. *Student mental health, use of services and academic attainment: A report to the review committee of the University of Cambridge Counselling Service*, Cambridge, England. http://www.brookes.ac.uk/student/services/osmhn/researchers/review.html#cambridge, accessed 29 April 2009.

Titley, Robert, and Bonnie Titley. 1980. Initial choice of college major: Are only the "undecided" undecided? *Journal of College Student Personnel* 21:293-8.

Turner, Andrew, and Thomas Berry. 2000. Counseling center contributions to student retention and graduation: A longitudinal assessment. *Journal of College Student Development* 41:627-36.

Western Facts, 2004. Office of Institutional Planning and Budgeting, University of Western Ontario. http://www.ipb.uwo.ca/facts.php, accessed 29 April 2009.

Whitehead, Alfred. 1929. *The aims of education and other essays*. New York: McMillan Co.

Wyckoff, Sarah. 1999. The academic advising process in higher education: History, research, and improvement. *Recruitment and Retention in Higher Education* 13:1-3.

## CHAPTER TEN

Adlaf, Edward, and Anca Ialomiteanu. 2002. Centre for Addictions and Mental Health, Research Report. http://www.camh.net/Research/Research_publications/Research_AR_2002/population_lifecourse_rar2002.html, accessed 29 April 2009.

American College Health Association (ACHA). 1999. Guidelines for a college health program. Baltimore: Author.

American College Health Association (ACHA). 2002. Healthy campus 2010: Making it happen. Baltimore: Author.

American College Health Association (ACHA). 2008. Reference group executive summary. Baltimore: Author.

American College Health Association(ACHA). 2004. Standards of practice for health promotion in higher education. http://www.acha.org/info_resources/sphphe_statement.pdf, accessed 29 April 2009.

Banning, James, and Leland Kaiser. 1974. An ecological perspective and model for campus design. *Personnel and Guidance Journal* 52:372-5.

Berman, Alan, David Jobes, and Morton Silverman. 2006. *Adolescent suicide: Assessment and intervention* (2nd ed.). Washington, DC: American Psychology Association.

Burrage, Hollie. 2001. UBC nurse in residence program. Paper presented at the annual meeting of the Canadian Association of College and University Student Services (CACUSS), 20 June, in Montreal, Canada.

Caulfield, Stephen. 2007. Student health: Supporting the academic mission. *Student Health Spectrum* February: 3-19. http://www.aetnastudenthealth.com/uploads/documents/spectrum/2007%20Winter%20-%20Student%20Health%20Supporting%20The%20Academic%20Mission.pdf, accessed 6 May 2009.

Crozier, Sharon, and Nancy Willihnganz. 2005. Canadian counseling centre survey. *Coast to Coast with CUCCA* 7(2): 4-7. https://www.cacuss.ca/content/documents/fileItemController/CoastToCoastSpring2005.pdf, accessed 29 April 2009.

Ehlinger, Ed. 2006. Assessment in college. Student health spectrum (June). http://
www.aetnastudenthealth.com/uploads/documents/spectrum/2006%20Summer
%20-%20Assessment%20of%20College%20Health.pdf, accessed 6 May 2009.

Fairservice, Julie, Pam Komonoski, Patricia Mirwaldt, and Ben Tan. 2007. Building immunization standards for health science students: Is it possible? Paper
presented at the annual conference of the Canadian Association of College
and University Student Services, 13 June, in Saskatoon, Canada. http://cacuss.
usask.ca/schedule/, accessed 29 April 2009.

Fitzgerald, Corinna, Desmond Pouyat, and Phil Wood. 2008. Collaborative
approaches to dealing with difficult behaviour: Adding voluntary withdrawal
in the student code of conduct at McMaster. Paper presented at the annual
conference of the Canadian Association of College and University Student
Services, 22-25 June, in St. John's, Canada.

Hildebrand, Glenn. 2006. College's successful hand washing campaign expands.
RN Journal: 31–32. http://cms.tng-secure.com/file_download.php?fFile_id=261,
accessed 6 May 2009.

Hoban, Mary, and E. Victor Leino. 2006. American College Health Association
national college health assessment (ACHA-NCHA): Spring 2005 reference group
data report (abridged). Journal of American College Health 55(1): 5–16.

Jed Foundation. Framework for developing institutional protocols for the acutely
distressed or suicidal college student. http://www.jedfoundation.org/, accessed
29 April 2009.

Kadison, Richard, and Theresa Foy DiGeronimo. 2005. College of the
overwhelmed: The campus mental health crisis and what to do about it.
San Francisco: Jossey-Bass Publishers.

Kezar, Adrianna. 2007. Creating and sustaining a campus ethos encouraging
student engagement. About Campus 11(6): 13-18.

Mirwaldt, Patricia, Sara Taman, and Kandi McElary. 2007. Partnering to create
a Canadian student health data set: A tool to build bridges on our campuses.
Paper presented at the annual conference of the Canadian Association of
College and University Student Services, 10–13 June, in Saskatoon, Canada.

Mirwaldt, Patricia, and Marsha Trew. 2008. National college health assessment.
University of British Columbia Student Health Centre. Unpublished.

National Advisory Committee on Immunization (NACI).www.atlantique.phac.
gc.ca/naci-ccnn/index-eng.php, accessed on 1 May 2009.

National Association of Student Personnel Administrators. Leadership for a
healthy campus, health education and leadership program. http://www.longwood.
edu/Health/aboutus/docs/leadership_for_a_healthy_campus.pdf, accessed
29 April 2009.

National Survey on Student Engagment(NSSE). www.NSSE.org, accessed
29 April 2009.

Public Health Agency of Canada. 2008. Statement on influenza vaccination for
the 2008-2009 season. http://www.phac-aspc.gc.ca/publicat/ccdr-rmtc/08vol34/
acs-3/index-eng.php, accessed 29 April 2009.

Sedgwick, Whitney, Cheryl Washburn, Christie Newton, and Patricia Mirwaldt. 2008. Shared care depression Collaborative model: From project inception to outcome data. *Canadian Journal of Community Mental Health* 27(2): 219–32.

University of British Columbia. *Academic concession.* http://www.students.ubc.ca/calendar/print.cfm?tree=3,48,0,0, accessed 29 April 2009.

World Health Organization. http://www.who.int/suggestions/faq/en/index.html, accessed 19 May 2009.

## CHAPTER ELEVEN

Axelrod, Paul, and John Reid. 1989. *Youth, university and Canadian society: Essays in the social history of higher education.* Montreal: McGill-Queen's University Press.

Canadian Association of Career Educators and Employers. http://www.cacee.com, accessed 19 May 2009.

Cobban, Alan. 1975. *The medieval universities: Their development and organization.* London: Methuen & Co. Ltd.

Conference Board of Canada. Employability skills 2000+. http://www.conferenceboard.ca/Libraries/EDUC_PUBLIC/esp2000.sflb

The Counselling Foundation of Canada. 2002. *A coming of age: Counselling Canadians for work in the twentieth century.* Toronto: Ginger Press.

Crozier, Sharon, Jack Dobbs, Kathy Douglas, and Jeanette Hung. 1999. Career counselling position paper. Kingston: Canadian University and College Counselling Association.

Dennison, John. 1995. *Challenge and opportunity: Canada's Community colleges at the crossroads.* Vancouver: University of British Columbia Press.

Dennison, John, and Paul Gallagher. 1986. *Canada's community colleges: A critical analysis.* Vancouver: University of British Columbia Press.

Gaffield, Chad, Lynne Marks, and Susan Laskin. 1989. Student populations and graduate careers: Queens University, 1895-1900. In *Youth, university and Canadian society: Essays in the social history of higher education,* ed. Paul Axelrod and John Reid, 3-25. Montreal: McGill-Queen's University Press.

Gallagher, Paul, and Ann Kitching. 2003. Canada's community colleges and alternation. In *Integrating school and workplace learning in Canada: Principles and practices of alternation education and training,* ed. Hans G. Schuetze and Robert Sweet, 156-74. Toronto: McGill-Queen's University Press.

Levin, John. 2001. *Globalizing the community college: Strategies for change in the twenty-first century.* New York: Palgrave.

McGill University. *Program for the Advancement of Career Exploration.* http://caps.mcgill.ca/programs/pace/, accessed 20 May 2009.

Mellor, Julie. 1990. Co-ordinating the re-organization of ruling relations: Management's use of human resources development for the New Brunswick community colleges. In *Education for work, education as work: Canada's changing community colleges*, ed. Jacob Muller, 69–89. Toronto: Garamond Press.

Ryerson University. *Tri-mentoring program*. http://www.ryerson.ca/trimentoring, accessed 20 May 2009.

Schuetze, Hans, and Robert Sweet. 2003. *Integrating school and workplace learning in Canada: Principles and practices of alternation education and training*. Montreal: McGill-Queen's University Press.

Smith, Dorothy, and George Smith. 1990. Re-organizing the job-skills training relation: From 'human capital' to 'human resources.' In *Education for work, education as work: Canada's changing community colleges*, ed. Jacob Muller, 171–96. Toronto: Garamond Press.

University of Victoria. *The Applied Career Transitions Program*. http://career services.uvic.ca/alumni/act.html, accessed 29 April 2009.

York University. *Career Centres' Strategic Planning*. http://www.yorku.ca/careers/ strategicPlanning/, accessed 29 April 2009.

## CHAPTER TWELVE

Allen, Walter. 1992. The color of success: African-American college student outcomes at predominantly White and historically Black public colleges and universities. *Harvard Educational Review* 62:26-44.

Anderssen, Erin, and Michael Valpy. 2003. Face the nation: Canada remade. *The Globe and Mail*, 7 June, A8-A9.

Astin, Alexander, and Helen Astin. 2000. *Leadership reconsidered: Engaging higher education in social change*. Battle Creek, MI: Kellogg Foundation.

Bennett, Christine. 1995. Research on racial issues in American higher education. In *Handbook of research on multicultural education*, ed. by James A. Banks and Cherry A. McGee Banks, 663-682. New York: Macmillan.

*Canadian charter of rights and freedoms*. 1982. http://laws.justice.gc.ca/en/ charter/, accessed 29 April 2009.

Cass, Vivienne. 1979. Homosexual identity formation: A theoretical model. *Journal of Homosexuality* 4:219-235.

Chickering, Arthur, and Linda Reisser. 1993. *Education and identity* (2nd ed.). San Francisco: Jossey-Bass Publishers.

Cross, William, Jr. 1971. The Negro-to-Black conversion experience: Toward a psychology of Black liberation. *Black World* 20:13-27.

Dalhousie University. http://web.archive.org/web/20050405152347/http://student services.dal.ca/services_2666.html, accessed 5 April 2005.

Feagin, Joe, Hernan Vera, and Nikitah Imani. 1996. *The agony of education: Black students at white colleges and universities*. New York: Routledge.

Gentile, Mary. 2005. Stepping up to the challenge: Recruiting and retaining for diversity. Presented at Symposium Recruiting and Retaining for Diversity. University of Toronto, May 11, in Toronto, Canada.

Howe, Neil, and William Strauss. 2000. *Millennials rising: The next great generation.* New York: Vintage Books.

Jones, Susan, and Marylu McEwen. 2000. A conceptual model of multiple dimensions of identity. *Journal of College Student Development* 41:405-14.

Josselson, Ruthellen. 1973. Psychodynamic aspects of identity formation in college women. *Journal of Youth and Adolescence* 2:3-52.

Looker, E. Dianne, and Graham Lowe. 2001. *Post-secondary access and student financial aid in Canada: Current knowledge and research gaps.* Canadian Policy Research Networks Workshop on Post-Secondary Access and Student Financial Aid. Ottawa: Canadian Millennium Scholarship Foundation.

McGill University handbook on student rights and responsibilities. 2003. http://upload.mcgill.ca/deanofstudents/greenbookenglish.pdf, accessed 29 April 2009.

Parkin, Andrew, and Matthew Mendelsohn. 2003. *A New Canada: An identity shaped by diversity.* Montreal: Centre for Research and Information on Canada.

Pascarella, Ernest, and Patrick Terenzini. 2005. *How college affects students: A third decade of research.* San Francisco: Jossey-Bass Publishers.

Statistics Canada. 2005. *Report of the Pan-Canadian education indicators program.* http://www.statcan.ca/english/freepub/81-582-XIE/2006001/highlights.htm, accessed 29 April 2009.

The University of British Columbia. Access & Diversity. http://students.ubc.ca/access/about.cfm, accessed 29 April 2009.

University of Manitoba. Aboriginal Student Centre. http://umanitoba.ca/student/asc/, accessed 29 April 2009.

## CHAPTER THIRTEEN

American College Personnel Association (ACPA). (1994). *The student learning imperative: Implications for student affairs.* Washington, DC: Author.

Andres, Lesley, and Finola Finlay. 2004. *Student affairs: Experiencing higher education.* Vancouver: University of British Columbia Press.

Barr, Margaret, and Associates. 1993. *The handbook of student affairs administration.* San Francisco: Jossey-Bass Publishers.

Brand, Stewart. 1999. *The clock of the long now: Time and responsibility.* New York: Basic Books.

Bresciani, Marilee, Carrie Zelna, and James Anderson. 2004. *Assessing student learning and development: A handbook for practitioners.* Washington, DC: National Association of Student Personnel Administrators.

British Columbia Council on Admissions and Transfer. 2008. 2006 *mobility of transfer students in British Columbia.* http://www.bccat.bc.ca/pubs/rr_july07.pdf, accessed 29 April 2009.

British Columbia Council on Admissions and Transfer. 2003. *The class of 1996 five years after graduation. http://www.bccat.bc.ca/pubs/rr_may03.pdf, accessed 29 April 2009.*

Canadian Association of College and University Student Services (CACUSS). *The mission of student services.* https://www.cacuss.ca/en/services/publications/mission.htm, accessed 6 May 2009.

Davenport, Paul. 2006. Engaging the future: Final report of the task force on strategic planning. London, Ontario: University of Western Ontario. http://www.uwo.ca/pvp/strategic_plan/report/01.htm, accessed 29 April 2009.

Eastman, Julia. 2003. *Strategic management of universities?* CSSHE Professional File, Canadian Society for the Study of Higher Education, No. 24, Fall.

Ellis, Shannon. 2003. *Dreams, nightmares, and pursuing the passion: Personal perspectives on college and university leadership.* Washington, DC: National Association of Student Personnel Administrators.

Fanshawe College. *Strategic plan* 2008-09. http://www.fanshawec.ca/assets/pas/plan2008.pdf, accessed 29 April 2009.

Fullan, Michael. 2001. *Leading in a culture of change.* San Francisco: Jossey-Bass Publishers.

Gilbert, Sid, Judy Chapman, Peter Dietsche, Paul Grayson, and John Gardner. 1997. *From best intentions to best practices: The first-year experience in Canadian post secondary education, Monograph 22.* Columbia, SC: National Resource Center for the Freshman Year Experience and Students in Transition, University of South Carolina.

Hamrick, Florence, Nancy Evans, and John Schuh. 2002. *Foundations of student affairs practice: How philosophy, theory, and research strengthen educational outcomes.* San Francisco: Jossey-Bass Publishers.

Harvey-Smith, Alicia. 2005. *The seventh learning college principle: A framework for transformational change.* Washington, DC: National Association of Student Personnel Administrators.

Hirt, Joan. 2006. *Where you work matters: Student affairs administration at different types of institutions.* Lanham, MD: University Press of America.

James, Ted. 1999. *Learner support and success: Determining the educational support needs of learners into the 21st century.* http://www.bccat.bc.ca/pubs/learner.pdf, accessed 13 December 2008.

Keeling, Richard, ed. 2004. *Learning reconsidered: A campus-wide focus on the student experience.* Washington, DC: National Association of Student Personnel Administrators and American College Personnel Association.

Komives, Susan, Dudley Woodard, Jr., and Associates. 2003. *Student services: A handbook for the profession* (4th ed.). San Francisco: Jossey-Bass Publishers.

Love, Patrick, and Sandy Estanek. 2004. *Rethinking student affairs practice.* San Francisco: Jossey-Bass Publishers.

Manning, Kathleen, Jillian Kinzie, and John Schuh, ed. 2006. *One size does not fit all.* New York: Routledge.

Mount Allison University. 2007. *A strategic statement for 2007-2016.* http://www.mta.ca/governance/president/thestrategicstatement.pdf, accessed 29 April 2009.

Ryerson University. *Shaping our future: Academic plan for 2008-2013.* http://www.ryerson.ca/senate/academicplan.pdf, accessed 29 April 2009.

Sandeen, Arthur. 1996. Organization, functions, and standards of practice. In *Student services: A handbook for the profession* (3rd ed.), ed. Susan R. Komives, Dudley B. Woodard, Jr., and Associates, 435-457. San Francisco: Jossey-Bass Publishers.

Strange, C. Carney, and James Banning. 2001. *Educating by design: Creating campus learning environments that work.* San Francisco: Jossey-Bass Publishers.

TD Bank Financial Group. 2004. *Time to wise up on post-secondary education in Canada.* TD Economics Special Report, 15 March. http://www.td.com/economics/special/dd0304_pse.pdf, accessed 29 April 2009.

United Nations Educational, Scientific and Cultural Organization (UNESCO). 2002. *The role of student affairs and services in higher education.* Paris: Author. http://unesdoc.unesco.org/images/0012/001281/128118e.pdf, accessed 29 April 2009.

University of Alberta. 2008. 2007-2011 *University Plan: Update* 2008. http://www.uofaweb.ualberta.ca/strategic//pdfs/UPlan2008_Final.pdf, accessed 29 April 2009.

University of Guelph Senate. 1987. *Aims and objectives report.* Guelph, ON: Author.

University of Toronto. 2005. *Measuring up.* Toronto: Author

Upcraft, M. Lee, and John Schuh. 1996. *Assessment in student affairs: A guide for practitioners.* San Francisco: Jossey-Bass Publishers.

Whitt, Elizabeth. 2006. Are all of our educators educating? *About Campus* 10(6): 2-9.

Whitt, Elizabeth. 1999. *Student learning as student affairs work: Responding to our imperative.* Washington, DC: National Association of Student Personnel Administrators.

## CHAPTER FOURTEEN

Adams, Michael. 1998. *Sex in the snow: Canadian social values at the end of the millennium.* Toronto: Penguin Books.

Alberta Learning. 2002. *Alberta's post-secondary education system: Developing the blueprint for change.* Edmonton, AB: Adult Learning Division. http://advancededandtech.alberta.ca/pubstats/AdultLearn/PostSecIssues.pdf, accessed 29 April 2009.

Allen, Mary, Shelley Harris, and George Butlin. 2003. Finding their way: A profile of young Canadian graduates, Research Paper No. 81-595-MIE–003. Ottawa: Statistics Canada. http://publish.uwo.ca/~dkerr/81-595-MIE2003003.pdf, accessed 29 April 2009.

Andres, Lesley. 1998. *Investigating transfer project. Phase II: Community college students.* Paper prepared for the British Columbia Council on Admission and

Transfer. http://eric.ed.gov:80/ERICDocs/data/ericdocs2sql/content_storage_01/0000019b/80/16/6d/4e.pdf, accessed 29 April 2009.

Andres, Lesley. 2001. Transfer from community college to university: Perspectives of British Columbia students. *Canadian Journal of Higher Education* 31(3): 35-74.

Andres, Lesley, and Finola Finlay. 2004. *Student affairs: Experiencing higher education*. Vancouver: University of British Columbia Press.

Ansari, Arif, and Debbie Bruckner. 2004. I am committed to your success. *Communique* 4(2): 16.

Association of Canadian Community Colleges (ACCC). *The National and International Voice of Canada's Colleges*. www.accc.ca, accessed 6 May 2009.

Association of Canadian Community Colleges (ACCC). 1997. *100% success: Just say 'yes' to student success*. Ottawa: Association of Canadian Community Colleges Task Group on Student Success and Retention.

Association of Canadian Community Colleges (ACCC). 2005. Meeting the needs of Aboriginal learners: An overview of current programs and services, challenges, opportunities, and lessons learned. Toronto: Author.

Asuncion, Jennison, Mai Nguyen, Marie-Eve Landry, Maria Barile, and Catherine Fichten. 2005. Promoting academic success of all students: Including those with disabilities. *Communiqué* 6(1): 14-15.

Barr, Robert. 1998. Obstacles to implementing the learning paradigm: What it takes to overcome them. *About Campus* 2(3): 18-25.

Barr, Robert, and John Tagg. 1995. From teaching to learning: A new paradigm for undergraduate education. *Change* November/December: 13-25.

Beales, Joseph. 1998. *Professional counselling in the BC college, university college, and institute system*. Report prepared for the BC Ministry of Education, Skills and Training and the Centre for Curriculum, Transfer and Technology. Victoria, BC.

Beatty-Guenter, Patty. 1988. Systems for student success. Research report. Victoria, BC: Camosun College.

Belbin, Bruce. 2003. Would you like fries with that? The emergence of students as customers. *Communiqué* 3(3): 10-11.

Boutilier, Sue. 2001. Supporting student success. *Communiqué* 2(1): 22-23.

British Columbia Ministry of Skills, Training and Labour (BCMSTL). 1995. *Intervention strategies and student retention in British Columbia public post-secondary institutions*. Victoria, BC: Author.

British Columbia Outcomes Working Group (BCOWG) and Centre for Education Information Standards and Services. 1999. *BC college and institute student outcomes report*.

British Columbia Student Services Advisory Committee (BCSSAC). 1981. *A student services model for British Columbia: A discussion paper*. Monograph.

Cairns, Sharon. 2006. Self-harm behaviour: How to assess and effectively intervene. Paper presented at the annual conference of the Canadian Association of College and University Student Services, 18–21 June, in Hamilton, Canada.

Canadian Association of College and University Student Services (CACUSS). *Statement of guiding principles*. www.cacuss.ca, accessed 7 May 2009.

Campbell, Jean. 1998. Redefining student success: Learning from nontraditional learners. PhD diss., University of Victoria, British Columbia.

Clark, Burton. 1960. The "cooling out" function in higher education. *American Journal of Sociology* 65(6): 569-76.

Coaldrake, Peter. 2001. Responding to changing student expectations. *Higher Education Management* 13(2): 75-92.

COMPAS, Inc. 2005. *Post-secondary education: Cultural, scholastic and economic drivers*. Report prepared for the Canada Millennium Scholarship Foundation, Montreal, QC. http://www.millenniumscholarships.ca/images/Publications/PSE_Drivers-en.pdf, accessed 6 May 2009.

Conley, David. 2005. *College knowledge: What it really takes for students to succeed and what we can do to get them ready*. San Francisco: Jossey-Bass Publishers.

Conrad, John. 2005. College student services: The challenges faced by the service provider: an Ontario perspective. *Communiqué* 5(2): 14.

Consensus Canada. 1996. ISO 9001: For St. Lawrence College, the golden rule. http://www.qnet.mb.ca/resources/iso9_journart.htm, accessed 29 April 2009.

Corman, June, Lynn Barr, and Tullio Caputo. 1992. Unpacking attrition: A change of emphasis. *The Canadian Journal of Higher Education* 22(3): 14-27.

Cross, Carol. 2000. Cyber-counselling, virtual registration, and student self-service: Student services in the information age. In *Taking a big picture look @ technology, learning, and the community college*, ed. Mark D. Milliron and Cindy L. Miles, 131-61. Mission Viejo, CA: League for Innovation in the Community College.

Dennison, John, ed. 1995. *Challenge and opportunity: Canada's community college at the crossroads*. Vancouver: University of British Columbia Press.

Dennison, John. 1992. The university college idea: A critical analysis. *Canadian Journal of Higher Education* 22(1): 109-24.

Dennison, John, and Paul Gallagher. 1986. *Canada's community colleges: A critical analysis*. Vancouver: University of British Columbia Press.

Dennison, John, and Hans Schuetze. 2004. Extending access, choice, and the reign of the market: Higher education reforms in British Columbia. *Canadian Journal of Higher Education* 34(3): 29-35.

Dennison, John, Alex Tunner, Gordon Jones, and Glen Forrester. 1975. *The impact of community colleges: A study of the college concept in British Columbia*. Vancouver: BC Research. http://eric.ed.gov:80/ERICDocs/data/eric docs2sql/content_storage_01/0000019b/80/31/6f/e7.pdf, accessed 29 April 2009.

Dietsche, Peter. 1995. Attrition research: Implications for quality in community colleges. *Community College Journal of Research and Practice* 19:423-436.

Dietsche, Peter. 1990. Freshman attrition in a college of applied arts and technology of Ontario. *Canadian Journal of Higher Education* 20(3): 65-84.

Dietsche, Peter. 2006. Results of the HRSDC-ACCC pan-Canadian study of college students and the college experience. HRSDC briefing report given 24 September in Hull, QC.

Dietsche, Peter. 1999. Student needs and college services: Can we make the match? *Communiqué* 9(3): 1-2.

Dippo, Don. 1994. The enigma of choice in career development materials. In *Sociology of education in Canada: Critical perspectives on theory, research, and practice,* ed. Lorna Erwin and David MacLennan, 203-16. Toronto: Copp Clark Longman.

Doucette, Don. 1998. *Business not as usual in our colleges and universities.* Paper presented at *Connections '98: Bridging the Gap* Conference, 11 May, in Vancouver, Canada.

Douglas College. 2005. "Students first! A shared vision to support learning and services." Internal planning document. New Westminster, BC. http://www.douglas.bc.ca/__shared/assets/students_first38430.pdf, accessed 29 April 2009.

Drea, Catherine. 2003. Access for success: Ontario's accessibility policies and the consequences for Ontario college students between 1965 and 1995. *College Quarterly* 6(1).

Drucker, Peter. 1992. *Managing for the future: The 1990s and beyond.* New York: Dutton.

Earwaker, John. 1992. *Helping and supporting students.* Buckingham: Open University Press.

Engstrom, Cathy, and Vincent Tinto. 2000. Developing partnerships with academic affairs to enhance student learning. In *The handbook of student affairs administration* (2nd ed.), ed. Margaret J. Barr, Mary K. Dresler, and Associates, 425–52. San Francisco: Jossey-Bass, Publishers.

Erland, Racine. 2003. Student-defined success in post-secondary education. MA thesis, Royal Roads University, British Columbia.

Finnie, Ross. 2000. Holding their own: Employment and earnings of post-secondary graduates. *Education Quarterly Review* 7(1).

Fishman, Steve, and Lisa Decandia. 2006. SUCCESS @ Seneca: Facilitating student and staff success. *College Quarterly* 9(2).

Freed, Jann, and Marie Klugman. 1997. *Quality principles and practices in higher education: Different questions for different times.* Phoenix: Oryx Press.

Freeland, Elizabeth. 2006. Getting engaged, keeping engaged, staying connected. Paper presented at the annual conference of the Canadian Association of College and University Student Services, 18-20 June, Hamilton, Canada.

Gallagher, Paul. 1995. Promise fulfilled, promise pending. In *Challenge and opportunity: Canada's community colleges at the crossroads,* ed. John D. Dennison, 256-74. Vancouver: University of British Columbia Press.

Gilbert, Sid, Judy Chapman, Peter Dietsche, Paul Grayson, and John Gardner. 1997. *From best intentions to best practices: The first-year experience in Canadian post secondary education, Monograph* 22. Columbia, SC: National

Resource Center for the Freshman Year Experience and Students in Transition, University of South Carolina.

Gilbert, Sid, and Ian Gomme. 1986. Future directions in research on voluntary attrition from college and universities. *College and University* 61(3): 227-38.

Goho, Jim, Ray Hoemsen, and Ken Webb. 2005. How can colleges and institutes achieve NSERC institutional eligibility (E/SI). Paper presented at the annual meeting of the Association of Canadian Community Colleges, 7 June, in Moncton, Canada.

Gomme, Ian, and Sid Gilbert. 1984. Paying the cost: Some observations on the problem of post-secondary student attrition. *Canadian Journal of Higher Education* 23(3): 18-35.

Grayson, J. Paul, and Kyle Grayson. 2003. *Research on retention and attrition.* Report prepared for the Canada Millennium Scholarship Foundation, Montreal, QC. http://www.millenniumscholarships.ca/images/Publications/retention_final. pdf, accessed 6 May 2009.

Hampton, Mary, and Joan Roy. 2002. Strategies for facilitating success of first nations students. *The Canadian Journal of Higher Education* 32(3): 1-28.

Harvey-Smith, Alicia. 2003. The adoption of the learning paradigm in student affairs divisions in Vanguard community colleges. PhD diss., University of Maryland.

Holgerson, Ronald. 2005. Marketing the college brand in Ontario. *College Quarterly* 8(4). http://www.senecac.on.ca/quarterly/2005-vol08-num04-fall/ holgerson.html, accessed 29 April 2009.

Holmes, David. 2005. *Embracing differences: Post-secondary education among Aboriginal students, students with children, and students with disabilities.* Montreal: Canada Millennium Scholarship Foundation.

Holmes, Jeffrey. 1992. Programs. In *Higher education in Canada,* ed. Alexander D. Gregor and Giles Jasmin, 59-65. Ottawa: Ministry of Supply and Services.

James, Ted. 1999. *Learner support and success: Determining the educational support needs for learners into the 21st century.* Report prepared for the British Columbia Senior Educational Officers Committee and Senior Instructional Officers Committee. www.bccat.bc.ca/pubs/learner.pdf, accessed 29 April 2009.

James, Ted. 2005. The learning college concept and its compatibility with student affairs. In *The seventh learning college principle: A framework for transformational change,* ed. Alicia B. Harvey-Smith, 27-48. Washington, DC: National Association of Student Personnel Administrators.

James, Ted. 2002. No longer Cinderella: The future of student development services. Paper presented at the annual meeting of the American Association of Community Colleges, April, in Seattle, USA.

Jensen, Blaine. 2002. New initiatives integrate and renew student services at SIAST. *Communiqué* 2(2): 17-18. Jones, Glen, ed. 1997. *Higher education in Canada: Different systems, different perspectives.* New York: Garland Press.

Jones, Glen. 2004. Ontario higher education reform, 1995-2003: From modest modifications to policy reform. *Canadian Journal of Higher Education* 34(3): 39-54.

Jones, Glen, Patricia McCarney, and Michael Skolnik. 2005. *Creating knowledge, strengthening nations: The changing role of higher education.* Toronto: University of Toronto Press.

Keeling, Richard, ed. 2004. *Learning reconsidered: A campus-wide focus on the student experience.* Washington, DC: American College Personnel Association and National Association of Student Personnel Administrators.

Keeling, Richard, ed. 2006. *Learning reconsidered 2: A practical guide to implementing a campus-wide focus on the student experience.* Washington, DC: American College Personnel Association and National Association of Student Personnel Administrators.

Keith, John. 2005. Customer service in Ontario's colleges. *College Quarterly* 8(4). http://www.senecac.on.ca/quarterly/2005-vol08-num04-fall/keith.html, accessed 29 April 2009.

Kershaw, Paul. 1998. Addressing the concerns of student-parents and campus child care services: A critical examination of the British Columbia child care subsidy system. Paper prepared for the Campus Child Care Association of British Columbia.

Kilbride, Kenise, and Lucy D'Arcangelo. 2002. Meeting immigrant community college students' needs. *The Canadian Journal of Higher Education* 32(2): 14-26.

Kilian, Crawford. 1995. 2020 *visions: The futures of Canadian education.* Vancouver: Arsenal Pulp Press.

Kirby, Dale. 2000. Investigating college student attrition: A report of an internship at the College of the North Atlantic with an analysis of first-semester student attrition. MA thesis, Memorial University of Newfoundland.

Knowles, Janet. 1995. A matter of survival: Emerging entrepreneurship in community colleges in Canada. In *Challenge and opportunity: Canada's community colleges at the crossroads,* ed. John D. Dennison, 184-207. Vancouver: University of British Columbia Press.

Krakauer, Renate. 2001. A learning college for health care: The applicability of learning-centred education to the Michener Institute for Applied Health Sciences. EDD diss., University of Toronto.

Krakauer, Renate. 2005. When do you know you have a learning college? In *Establishing and sustaining learning-centered community colleges,* ed. Christine J. McPhail, 181-96. Washington, DC: American Association of Community Colleges.

Leary, Tamara. 2006. "Student success" from buzzword to reality. *Communiqué* 6(2): 23.

Levin, John. 2001. *Globalizing the community college: Strategies for change in the twenty-first century.* New York: Palgrave.

Losak, John. 1986. What constitutes student success in the community college? *Community College Journal for Research and Planning* 5:2.

Mathews, Rachel, and Elizabeth Freeland. 2006. Increasing access at Ontario colleges. Paper presented at the annual conference of the Canadian Association of College and University Student Services, 18-21 June, Hamilton, Canada.

Maw, Jennifer. 2005. The facilitation of student success: Incorporating affective, behavioural, and cognitive factors into first-year experience programs. PhD diss., University of Manitoba.

McElary, Kandi. 2006. Optimal therapies: Injury prevention and rehabilitation complementary wellness service. Paper presented at the annual conference of the Canadian Association of College and University Student Services, 18-21 June, in Hamilton, Canada.

McKeown, Brent, Allan, Macdonell, and Charles Bowman. 1993. The point of view of the student in attrition research. *Canadian Journal of Higher Education* 23(2): 65-85.

McLaren, Laurie, and Roger Chum. 2006. Is this Cree country? Paper presented at the annual conference of the Canadian Association of College and University Student Services, 18-21 June, in Hamilton, Canada.

McWilliams, John. 1998. Effects of a student success course on achievement, self-efficacy, and locus of control. MEd thesis, University of Regina.

Millar, Erin. 2007. Not all degrees are created equal. *Macleans,* 2 April. http://www.macleans.ca/article.jsp?content=20070402_104057_104057, accessed 28 May 2009.

Miller, Jaynn. 2006. Establishing a student success culture: Finding a "magic formula." Paper presented at the annual conference of the Canadian Association of College and University Student Services, 18-21 June, in Hamilton, Canada.

Miller, Thomas, Barbara Bender, John Schuh, and Associates. 2005. *Promoting reasonable expectations: Aligning student and institutional views of the college experience.* San Francisco: Jossey-Bass Publishers.

Miner, Rick. 2004. Access to success: Individual, institutional, and societal considerations. Paper presented at the annual meeting of the Association of Canadian Community Colleges, 29-31 January, in Vancouver, Canada.

Moore, David. 2004. A framework for preparing students to design their own learning strategies. *College Quarterly* 7(4).

Noam Eli. 1996. Electronics and the dim future of the university. *Science* 270: 247–9.

O'Banion, Terry. 1997. *A Learning college for the 21st century.* Phoenix: Oryx Press.

Pendleton, Sham, and Ashley Lambert-Maberly. 2006. *Undergraduate student survey on student satisfaction and engagement: Transfer student experience vs. direct entry student experience.* Paper prepared for British Columbia Council on Admissions and Transfer, Vancouver, British Columbia. http://www.bccat.bc.ca/pubs/ubcengagement05.pdf, accessed 29 April 2009.

PRA, Inc. 2003. *Summary report: 2003 Canadian college student survey.* Report prepared for the Canada Millennium Scholarship Foundation, 26 November.

Reed, Alex. 2006. Student services opportunities or challenges for Canada's polytechnic institutions? Paper presented at the annual conference of the Canadian Association of College and University Student Services, 18-21 June, in Hamilton, Canada.

Rekar Munro, Carolin. 2005. "Best practices" in teaching and learning: Challenging current paradigms and redefining their role in education. *College Quarterly* 8(3).

Rhatigan, James. 2000. The history and philosophy of student affairs. In *The handbook of student affairs administration,* ed. Margaret Barr and Mary Desler, 3–24. San Francisco: Jossey-Bass Publishers.

Robinson, M. 1999. Proactive documentation and evaluation of a counselling service: Accountability vs. complacency. *Communiqué* 9(3): 10.

Rowley, Daniel, Lujan, Herman, and Michael Dolence. 1998. Strategic choices for the academy: How demand for lifelong learning will re-create higher education (Jossey-Bass Higher and Adult Education Series). San Francisco: Jossey-Bass Publishers.

Roueche, John and George Baker. 1987. *Access and excellence: The open-door college*. Alexandria, VA: AACJC Publications.

Tagg, John. 2003. *The learning paradigm college*. Bolton, MA: Anker Publishing.

Tinto, Vincent. 1987. *Leaving college: Rethinking the causes and cures of student attrition*. Chicago: University of Chicago Press.

Tinto, Vincent. 2004. Taking student learning seriously. Paper presented at the annual meeting of the Association of Canadian Community Colleges, 29-31 January, in Vancouver, Canada.

Tysick, Kim. 2004. The Quebec model: System-wide approach. Paper presented at the annual meeting of the Association of Canadian Community Colleges, 29-31 January, in Vancouver, Canada.

Uhl, Norman, and Anne Marie MacKinnon. 1992. Students. In *Higher education in Canada*, ed. Alexander D. Gregor and Giles Jasmin, 47-57. Ottawa: Ministry of Supply and Services.

Unger, Sheldon. 1980. The retention problem: An analysis of enrolment attrition at a Canadian college. *Canadian Journal of Higher Education* 10(1): 50-74.

University College of the Fraser Valley (UCFV). 1992. *Systems for student success*. Internal planning document.

Warkentin, Joy. 2005. Student success report. Presentation to Board of Governors, Fanshawe College, 22 September.

Willms, J. Douglas, and Patrick Flanagan. 2003. *Ready or not? Literacy skills and post-secondary education*. Report prepared for the Canada Millennium Scholarship Foundation, Montreal, QC. http://www.millenniumscholarships.ca/images/Publications/ready_en.pdf, accessed 29 April 2009.

Zmetana, Katherine. 2002. Reflections on change: A community college faculty perspective. EDD diss., Oregon State University.

## CHAPTER FIFTEEN

Abraham, Jimmie, and Bill Wagnon. 1992. Helping students ease into college. *Planning for Higher Education* 21:32-6.

Astin, Alexander. 1984. Student involvement: A developmental theory for higher education. *Journal of College Student Personnel* 25:297-308.

Bacon, Jean. 2002. Promoting community through citizenship and service. In *Creating campus community: In search of Ernest Boyer's Legacy*, ed. William McDonald and Associates, 121-44. San Francisco: Jossey-Bass Publishers.

Blimling. Greg. 1993. New challenges and goals for residential life programs. In *Student housing and residential life,* ed. Roger B. Winston, Jr., Scott Anchors, and Associates, 1-20. San Francisco: Jossey-Bass Publishers.

Bridwell, Margaret, and Stanley Kinder. 1993. Confronting health issues. In *The handbook of student affairs administration,* ed. Margaret J. Barr and Associates, 481-92. San Francisco: Jossey-Bass Publishers.

Cameron, David. 1997. The federal perspective. In *Higher education in Canada: Different systems, different perspective,* ed. Glen A. Jones. New York: Garland Publishing.

Creamer, Don. 1993. Conflict management skills. In *The handbook of student affairs administration,* ed. Margaret Barr and Associates, 313-26. San Francisco: Jossey-Bass Publishers.

Dixon, Benjamin. 2001. Student affairs in an increasingly multicultural world. In *The professional student affairs administrator: Educator, leader, manager,* ed. Roger B. Winston, Jr., Don G. Creamer, Ted K. Miller, and Associates, 65-80. Lillington, NC: Taylor and Francis.

Dungy, Gwen. 2003. Organizations and functions of student affairs. In *Student services: A handbook for the profession* (4th ed.), ed. Susan R. Komives, Dudley B. Woodward, Jr., and Associates, 339-557. San Francisco: Jossey-Bass Publishers.

Gardner, John, Gretchen Van der Veer, and Associates. 1998. *The senior year experience: Facilitating integration, reflection, closure, and transition.* San Francisco: Jossey-Bass Publishers.

Gordon, Virginia. 1989. Origins and purpose of the freshman seminar. In *The freshman year experience: Helping students survive and succeed in college,* ed. M. Lee Upcraft, John L. Gardner, and Associates, 183-97. San Francisco: Jossey-Bass Publishers.

Hanson, Gary, and Ursula Delworth, eds. 1980. *Student services: A handbook for the profession.* San Francisco: Jossey-Bass Publishers.

Jacoby, Barbara, and Associates. 1996. *Service-learning in higher education.* San Francisco: Jossey-Bass Publishers.

Jewler, A.J. 1989. Elements of an effective seminar: The university 101 program. In *The freshman year experience: Helping students survive and succeed in college,* ed. M. Lee Upcraft, John L. Gardner, and Associates, 198-215. San Francisco: Jossey-Bass Publishers.

Johnson, Cynthia. 1989. Mentoring programs. In *The freshman year experience: Helping students survive and succeed in college,* ed. M. Lee Upcraft, John L. Gardner, and Associates, 118-28. San Francisco: Jossey-Bass Publishers.

Jones, Glen, ed. 1997. *Higher education in Canada: Different systems, different perspectives.* New York: Garland Publishing.

Keeling, Richard, ed. 2004. *Learning reconsidered: A campus-wide focus on the student experience.* Washington, DC: American College Personnel Association and National Association of Student Personnel Administrators.

Keeling, Richard, ed. 2006. *Learning reconsidered 2: A practical guide to implementing a campus-wide focus on the student experience.* Washington, DC: American College Personnel Association and National Association of Student Personnel Administrators.

Komives, Susan, John Dugan, Julie Owen, Craig Slack, eds. 2006. *Handbook for student leadership programs.* College Park: National Clearinghouse for Leadership Programs.

Kramer, Gary, and Robert Spencer. 1989. Academic advising. In *The freshman year experience: Helping students survive and succeed in college,* ed. M. Lee Upcraft, John L. Gardner, and Associates, 95-107. San Francisco: Jossey-Bass Publishers.

Kuh, George, John Schuh, Elizabeth Whitt, and Associates. 1991. *Involving colleges: Encouraging student learning and personal development through out-of-class experiences.* San Francisco: Jossey-Bass Publishers.

Lenning, Oscar, Kenneth Sauer, and Phillip Beal. 1980. *Student retention strategies.* AAHE-ERIC/Higher Education Research Report No. 8. Washington, DC: American Association for Higher Education.

McClellan, Melanie, Tony Cawthon, and Gene Tice. 2001. Why university housing philosophy matters. *Journal of College and University Student Housing* 30:3-9.

Perigo, Donald, and M. Lee Upcraft. 1989. Orientation programs. In *The freshman year experience: Helping students survive and succeed in college,* ed. M. Lee Upcraft, John L. Gardner, and Associates, 82-94. San Francisco: Jossey-Bass Publishers.

Roberts, Dennis. 2003. Community building and programming. In *Student services: A handbook for the profession* (4th ed.), ed. Susan R. Komives, Dudley B. Woodward, Jr., and Associates, 539-54. San Francisco: Jossey-Bass Publishers.

Roper, Larry, and Susan Longerbeam. 2002. Modeling community through campus leadership. In *Creating campus community: In search of Ernest Boyer's Legacy,* ed. William McDonald and Associates, 69-92. San Francisco: Jossey-Bass Publishers.

Sandeen, Arthur. 1991. *The chief student affairs officer: Leader, manager, mediator, educator.* San Francisco: Jossey-Bass Publishers.

Sandeen, Arthur. 1993. Developing effective campus and community relationships. In *The handbook of student affairs administration,* ed. Margaret J. Barr and Associates, 300-12. San Francisco: Jossey-Bass Publishers.

Schroeder, Charles. 2003. Using the lessons of research to develop partnerships. In *Student services: A Handbook for the profession* (4th ed.), ed. Susan R. Komives, Dudley B. Woodward, Jr., and Associates, 618-36. San Francisco: Jossey-Bass Publishers.

Strange, C. Carney, and James Banning. 2001. *Educating by design: Creating campus learning environments that work.* San Francisco: Jossey-Bass Publishers.

Tinto, Vincent. 1993. *Leaving college: Rethinking the causes and cures of student attrition* (2nd ed.). Chicago: The University of Chicago Press.

Upcraft, M. Lee, and Margaret Barr. 1990. Identifying challenges for the future in current practice. In *New futures for student affairs,* ed. Margaret J. Barr, M. Lee Upcraft, and Associates, 3-21. San Francisco: Jossey-Bass Publishers.

Widmar, Gary. 1994. Supplemental instruction: From small beginnings to a national program. *New Directions for Teaching and Learning* 60:3-10. San Francisco: Jossey-Bass Publishers.

Winston, Roger Jr., and Scott Anchors. 1993. New challenges and goals for residential life programs. In *Student housing and residential life,* ed. Roger B. Winston, Jr., Scott Anchors, and Associates, 25-64. San Francisco: Jossey-Bass Publishers.

## CHAPTER SIXTEEN

Anderson, Terry, and Fathi Elloumi. 2004. *Theory and practice of online learning* (2nd ed.). http://cde.athabascau.ca/online_book/, accessed 29 April 2009.

Bartolic-Zlomislic, Sylvia, and Tony Bates. 2000. Investing in online learning: potential benefits and limitations. Vancouver: University of British Columbia [Online]. http://bates.cstudies.ubc.ca/investing.html, accessed 29 April 2009.

Bates, Anthony. 1997a. The impact of technological change on open and distance learning. *Distance Education* 18:93-109.

Bates, Anthony. 1997b. Restructuring the university for technological change. Paper presented at *The Carnegie Foundation for the Advancement of Teaching. What Kind of University?* on 18–20 June, in London, England. http://bates.cstudies.ubc.ca/carnegie/carnegie.html, accessed 8 May 2009.

Bates, Anthony. 2000. In *Strategies for the future.* http://bates.cstudies.ubc.ca/paper2.html, accessed 29 April 2009.

Brindley, Jane, and Maxim Jean-Louis. 1990. Student support services: The case for a proactive approach. *Journal of Distance Education* 5(1): 66-70.

Cahoon, Brad. 1998. Adult learning and the internet: Themes and things to come. In *New Directions for Adult and Continuing Education, No.78,* ed. Brad Cahoon, 71-6. San Francisco: Jossey-Bass Publishers.

Campus Manitoba. http://www.campusmanitoba.com/, accessed 29 April 2009.

Canadian Virtual University. http://www.cvu-uvc.ca, accessed 29 April 2009.

Cochrane, Clive. 2000. The reflections of a distance learner 1977-1997. *Open Learning* 15(1): 17-34.

Daugherty, Martha, and Barbara Funke. 1998. University, faculty, and student perceptions of web-based instruction. *Journal of Distance Education* 13(1): 21-39.

Devonshire, Elizabeth, and Ruth Crocker. 1999. Making choices about the correct mix of academic support for postgraduate distance learners: A balancing act? Paper presented at the Annual International Conference of the Higher Education Research and Development Society of Australasia (HERDSA), 12-15 July, in Melbourne, Australia. http://www.herdsa.org.au/wp-content/uploads/conference/1999/pdf/Devonsh.PDF, accessed 29 April 2009.

Eastmond, Daniel. 1998. Adult learners and internet-based distance education. In *Adult learning and the internet, New Directions for Adult and Continuing Education, No.78*, ed. Brad Cahoon, 33-41. San Francisco: Jossey-Bass Publishers.

Frank, Tema. 2000. Universities compete for a presence online. *University Affairs*, 10-14 October.

Gibson, Chere Campbell, and Terry Gibson. 1995. Lessons learned from 100+ years of distance learning. *Adult Learning* September/October: 7, 15.

Granger, Daniel, and Meg Benke. 1995. Supporting students at a distance. *Adult Learning* 7(1): 22-3.

Griffin, Courtenay. 2008. DELT celebrates Canadian first. *Gazette*. 3 July. www.mun.ca/gazette, accessed 6 May 2009.

Haughey, Denis. 1994. Towards a changing profile of the adult learner. In *University continuing education in Canada: Current challenges*, ed. Michael Brooke and Mark Waldron, 124-32. Toronto: Thompson Educational Publishing.

Landsbridge. 2006. http://www.lansbridge.edu/general/index.php?mnu=ABOUT_News&p=news, accessed 29 April 2009.

Ludwig-Hardman, Stacey, and Joanna Dunlop. 2003. Learner support services for online students: Scaffolding for success. *The International Review of Research in Open and Distance Learn*ing 4(1). http://www.irrodl.org/index.php/irrodl/article/view/131/602, accessed 6 May 2009.

McMullen, Bill, and Andreas Rohrbach. 2003. *Distance education courses in remote Aboriginal communities across Canada: Barriers, learning styles, and best practices*. Prince George, BC: College of New Caledonia Press.

Miller, Gary. 1996. Technology, the curriculum and the learner: Opportunities for open and distance education. In *Supporting the learner in open and distance learning*, ed. Roger Mills and Allan Tait, 34-42. London: Pittman.

Moneta, Larry. 1997. The integration of technology with the management of student services. In *Using technology to promote student learning: New Directions for Student Services, No. 78*, ed. Cathy M. Engstrom and Kevin W. Kruger, 5-16. San Francisco: Jossey–Bass Publishers.

Mugridge, Ian, and David Kaufman, eds. 1986. *Distance education in Canada*. Beckenham, Kent: Croom Helm.

Pascarella, Ernest, and Patrick Terenzini. 1991. *How college affects students.* San Francisco: Jossey-Bass Publishers.

Pascarella, Ernest, and Patrick Terenzini. 2005. *How college affects students: A third decade of research.* San Francisco: Jossey-Bass Publishers.

Paul, Ross, and Jane Brindley. 1996. Lessons from distance education for the university of the future. In *Supporting the learner in open and distance learning,* ed. Roger Mills and Allan Tait, 43-55. London: Pittman.

Phillips, Marion, Peter Scott, and Judith Fage. 1998. Towards a strategy for the use of new technology in student guidance and support. *Open Learning* 13(2): 52-8.

Potter, Judith. 1998. Beyond access: Student perspectives on support service needs in distance learning. *Canadian Journal of University Continuing Education* 24:59-82.

Potter, Judith. 1994. Improving support services for adult learners. In *University continuing education in Canada: Current challenges,* ed. Michael Brooke and Mark Waldron, 26-35. Toronto: Thompson Educational Publishing Incorporated.

Powell, Richard, Christopher Conway, and Lynda Ross. 1990. Effects of student predisposing characteristics on student success. *Journal of Distance Education* 5(1): 5-19. http://www.jofde.ca/index.php/jde/article/view/368/259, accessed 6 May 2009.

Rotermann, Michelle. 2001. Wired young Canadians. *Canadian social trends, statistics Canada, catalogue no.* 11-008. http://www.statcan.ca/english/studies/11-008/feature/star2001063000s4a01.pdf, accessed 11 July 2006.

Selman, Gordon. 1994. Continuing education and the Canadian Mosaic. In *University continuing education in Canada: Current challenges,* ed. Michael Brooke and Mark Waldron, 4-17. Toronto: Thompson Educational Publishing Incorporated.

Service Canada. Training and Careers - Online Learning. http://www.jobsetc.ca/pieces.jsp?category_id=348&crumb=11&crumb=608, accessed 29 April 2009.

Sewart, David. 1993. Student support systems in distance education. *Open Learning* 8: 3-12.

Srivastava, Manjulika. 2002. A comparative study on the trends in distance education in Canada and India. *Turkish Online Journal of Distance Education* 3(4). http://tojde.anadolu.edu.tr/tojde8/articles/srivastava.htm, accessed 29 April 2009.

Tait, Alan. 2000. Planning student support for open and distance learning. *Opening Learning* 15(3):287-99.

Thompson, Gordon. 1989. The provision of student-support services in distance education. In *Policies, procedures and priorities: Post-secondary distance education in Canada,* ed. Robert Sweet, 34-50. Alberta: Athabasca University and the Canadian Society of Studies and Education.

Volery Thierry, and Deborah Lord. 2000. Critical success factors in online education. *International Journal of Educational Management* 14:216-23.

University of Waterloo. Daily Bulletin. http://www.bulletin.uwaterloo.ca/2000/
jul/21fr.html, accessed 29 April 2009.

Wagner, Ellen. 1995. Distance education success factors. *Adult Learning* 7:18-19.

## WEB RESOURCES

### GENERAL STUDENT SERVICES

American College Personnel Association (ACPA). http://www.acpa.nche.edu/

Association of Canadian Community Colleges (ACCC). www.accc.ca

Association of University and Colleges of Canada (AUCC). www.aucc.ca

Atlantic Association of College and University Student Services (AACUSS).
http://www.aacuss.ca/

Association of Atlantic Universities (AAU). http://www.atlanticuniversities.ca/

Canadian Association of College and University Student Services (CACUSS).
http://www.cacuss.ca

Canadian Council for the Advancement of Education (CCAE). http://www.ccae
canada.org/

NASPA: Student Affairs Administrators in Higher Education. http://www.naspa.org/

The Student Life Education Company. http://www.studentlifeeducation.com/

### ENROLMENT MANAGEMENT/REGISTRAR

Association of Registrars of the Universities and Colleges of Canada (ARUCC).
http://www.arucc.com/

Atlantic Association of Registrars and Admissions Officers (AARAO). http://www.
unb.ca/aarao/

Canadian Bureau for International Education (CBIE). http://www.cbie.ca/
index_e.htm

Committee of Registrars, Admissions and Liaison Officers (CRALO). http://www.
cralo.ca/

Conference of Rectors and Principals of Québec Universities (CREPUQ). http://
www.crepuq.qc.ca/

Ontario Universities Registrars' Association (OURA). http://www.oura.ca/

Western Association of Registrars of the Universities and Colleges of Canada
(WARUCC). http://www.warucc.ca/

### FINANCIAL AID

Canadian Association of Financial Aid Administrators (CASFAA). www.casfaa.ca

Canadian Merit Scholarship Foundation (CMSF). www.cmsf.ca

Canadian Millennium Scholarship Foundation. www.millenniumscholarships.ca

CANLEARN. www.canlearn.ca

DebtFreeGrad. www.debtfreegrad.com

Scholarships Canada. www.scholarshipscanada.com

Student Awards. www.studentawards.com

ORIENTATION

Environics Research Group (ERG). http://erg.environics.net/
National Orientation Directors Association (NODA). http://www.nodaweb.org
National Resource Centre for the First-Year Experience and Students in Transi-
tion. http://www.sc.edu/fye/index.html

HOUSING & FOOD SERVICES

Association of College and University Housing Officers – International
(ACUHO-I). www.acuho-i.org
Association of Physical Plant Administrators (APPA). www.appa.org
Canadian College and University Food Services Association (CCUFSA).
www.ccufsa.on.ca
Ontario Association of College and University Housing Officers (OACUHO).
www.oacuho.com
Resident Assistant and Residence Life Resources Online. www.residentassistant.com

STUDENT LEADERSHIP AND UNIONS

Canadian Alliance of Student Associations (CASA). http://www.casa.ca/
Canadian Federation of Students (CFS). http://www.cfs-fcee.ca/

JUDICIAL AFFAIRS AND ACADEMIC INTEGRITY

Association for Student Judicial Affairs (ASJA). http://www.asjaonline.org/
Bill Taylor's letter to his students regarding academic integrity. http://www.
academicintegrity.org/pdf/Letter_To_My_Students.pdf
Canadian Academic Integrity and Student Judicial Affairs (CAISJA). https://www.
cacuss.ca/en/divisions/CAISJA/overview.htm
Center for Academic Integrity (CAI). http://www.academicintegrity.org
Council on Law in Higher Education (CLHE). http://www.clhe.org/
Education Law Reporter: http://www.edlawcanada.com
McGill University. http://www.mcgill.ca/integrity/
National Center for Higher Education Risk Management (NCHERM). http://www.
ncherm.org/
Purdue University Online Writing Lab (OWL). http://owl.english.purdue.edu/owl/
resource/589/01/
Ryerson University. http://www.ryerson.ca/academicintegrity/
University of Alberta. http://www.uofaweb.ualberta.ca/tie
University of Saskatchewan. http://www.usask.ca/university_secretary/honesty/
University of Toronto. http://www.utoronto.ca/academicintegrity/
Wilfrid Laurier University. http://www.wlu.ca/academicintegrity
York University. http://www.yorku.ca/academicintegrity/

ACADEMIC INTEGRITY CODES

Bishop's University Code of Student Conduct. http://www.ubishops.ca/
administration/CHARTER.htm

Brock University Code of Student Conduct and Disciplinary Procedures in Non-Academic Matters. http://www.brocku.ca/atyourservice/studentconduct.php

Carleton University Information on How the University Deals with Student Non-Instructional Misconduct. http://www.carleton.ca/secretariat/policies/Non_Instructional_Conduct.html

Concordia University Code of Rights and Responsibilities. http://secretariat.concordia.ca/policies/bd/en/BD-3.pdf

Grant MacEwan College Academic Integrity Policy. http://www.macewan.ca/web/ims/client/upload/Policy%20C1000%20-%20Academic%20Integrity.pdf

Grant MacEwan College Student Discipline Policy. http://www.macewan.ca/web/services/ims/client/upload/E3102%20Student%20Discipline.pdf

King's College, University of Western Ontario Code of Student Conduct. http://www.uwo.ca/kings/pdf/code_of_conduct_2003.pdf

Lakehead University Code of Student Behaviour and Disciplinary Procedures. http://policies.lakeheadu.ca/policy.php?pid=60

Malaspina University-College Student Conduct Code. http://www.mala.ca/policies/policy.asp?rdPolicyNumber=99.01

McMaster University Academic Integrity Policy. http://www.mcmaster.ca/univsec/policy/AcademicIntegrity.pdf

McMaster University Student Code of Conduct. http://www.mcmaster.ca/univsec/policy/StudentCode.pdf

Queen's University Code of Conduct. http://www.queensu.ca/secretariat/senate/policies/code2008.pdf

Queen's University Non-academic Discipline System. http://www.queensu.ca/secretariat/senate/policies/nonacad.html

Ryerson University Student Code of Non-Academic Conduct. http://www.ryerson.ca/senate/policies/pol61.pdf

Simon Fraser University Code of Student Conduct. http://www.sfu.ca/policies/teaching/t10-01.htm

University College of the Fraser Valley Student Conduct Policy. http://www.ucfv.ca/calendar/2008_09/General/RegulationsAndPolicies.htm#StudentConduct

University of Alberta Code of Student Behaviour. http://www.uofaweb.ualberta.ca/GFCPOLICYMANUAL/policymanualsection30.cfm

University of Guelph Student Rights and Responsibilities. http://www.uoguelph.ca/studentaffairs/home/documents/Brochure2005.pdf

University of Lethbridge Principles of Student Citizenship. http://www.uleth.ca/ross/policies/student_citizenship.pdf

University of Lethbridge Student Discipline Policy. http://www.uleth.ca/ross/calendar/part04.pdf

University of Manitoba Inappropriate or Disruptive Student Behaviour Policy. http://umanitoba.ca/admin/governance/governing_documents/students/279.htm

University of Manitoba Student Discipline Bylaw. http://www.umanitoba.ca/admin/governance/governing_documents/students/868.htm

University of New Brunswick Student Disciplinary Code. http://www.unb.ca/current/disciplinary_code/partB.html

University of Northern British Columbia Undergraduate Regulations and Policies. http://www.unbc.ca/calendar/undergraduate/general/regulations.html

University of Regina Regulations Governing Discipline for Academic and Non-Academic Misconduct. http://www.uregina.ca/presoff/vpadmin/policymanual/Academic%20Regulations/DisciplinaryRegulations.pdf

University of Toronto Code of Student Conduct. http://www.governingcouncil.utoronto.ca/policies/studentc.htm

University of Western Ontario Code of Student Conduct. http://www.uwo.ca/univsec/board/code.pdf

University of Windsor Student Code of Conduct. http://www.uwindsor.ca/units/senate/main.nsf/982foe5fo6b5c9a285256d6eoo6cff78/631cc46c9f9oeec3852570070054cf23!OpenDocument

Wilfrid Laurier University Student Code of Conduct Discipline. https://www.wlu.ca/page.php?grp_id=158&p=8383&pv=1Discipline

York University Student Code of Conduct. http://www.yorku.ca/scdr/CodeOfConduct.html

## SERVICE LEARNING

Canadian Alliance for Community Service-Learning (CACSL). http://www.communityservicelearning.ca

## COUNSELLING

Canadian University and College Counselling Association (CACUSS). https://www.cacuss.ca/en/divisions/CUCCA/resources/2005.htm

## HEALTH AND WELLNESS

American College Health Association (ACHA). http://www.acha.org/.

American College Health – National College Health Assessment. http://www.acha-ncha.org/

Canadian Organization of University and College Health (COUCH). https://www.cacuss.ca/en/divisions/COUCH/overview.htm

## CAREER AND EMPLOYMENT

Canadian Association For Co-operative Education (CAFCE). www.cafce.ca.

Canadian Association of Career Educators and Employers (CACEE). http://www.cacee.com.

Canadian Education and Research Institute for Counselling (CERIC). www.ceric.ca.

ContactPoint: An online source of information for career practitioners. www.contactpoint.ca

Dalhousie University Cooperative Education. http://architectureandplanning.dal.ca/coop/arch_coop.shtml

Dalhousie University DalTech's Cooperative Education. http://technical
    cooperativeeducation.dal.ca/index.html
McGill University's P.A.C.E. program. http://caps.mcgill.ca/programs/pace/
Monster. An international website dedicated to job postings. http://www.monster.ca/
Ryerson University's Tri-Mentoring program. http://www.ryerson.ca/trimentoring/
School of Business Administration Career Centre, Dalhousie University. http://
    sba.management.dal.ca/
University of Toronto Career Centre. http://www.careers.utoronto.ca/
University of Victoria Career Services ACT Program. http://careerservices.uvic.ca/
    alumni/act.html
Workopolis. A website for job postings with a specific focus on university
    graduates. http://www.workopolis.com/
York University Career Centre Cyberguide. http://www.yorku.ca/careers/
    cyberguide/main.html
York University's Career Planning Centre-Strategic Plan. http://www.yorku.ca/
    careers/strategicPlanning/

DIVERSITY
Association of Higher Education and Disability (AHEAD). http://www.ahead.org/
Canadian Association of Disability Service Providers in Post-Secondary Education
    (CADSPPE). https://www.cacuss.ca/en/divisions/CADSPPE/overview.htm
National Aboriginal Student Services Association (NASSA). https://www.cacuss.ca/
    en/divisions/NASSA/overview.htm

DISTANCE LEARNERS
Canadian Network for Innovation in Education (CNIE). http://www.cnie-rcie.
    ca/?q=node
Centre for the Advancement of Distance Education (CADE). http://www.uic.edu/
    sph/cade/

STUDENT SERVICES RESEARCH
Canadian University Survey Consortium (CUSC). http://www.cusc-ccreu.ca/home.
    htm
National Survey of Student Engagement (NSSE). www.nsse.org

# Contributors

MURRAY BAKER is the author of the best-selling *The Debt-Free Graduate*, a financial survival guide for students, and brings expertise on student finance and debt. Having previously coordinated first-year programs at the University of Western Ontario, focusing on transition and financial issues, he now lectures internationally on student finance, and is a consultant, researcher, and writer for various financial and educational publications.

BRUCE BELBIN is associate vice-president of student services at the Northern Alberta Institute of Technology. He has served in leadership roles as president of the Atlantic Association of College and University Student Services and as a board member of the Canadian Association of College and University Student Services.

DEBORAH EERKES is director of the Office of Student Judicial Affairs at the University of Alberta. She has been a member of the board of directors and, subsequently, the advisory board for the Center for Academic Integrity in the United States, and is the first president of Canadian Academic Integrity and Student Judicial Affairs, a division of the Canadian Association of College and University Student Services.

DONNA HARDY COX is associate professor in the School of Social Work, with cross-appointments to the Faculty of Education and the Centre for Collaborative Health Professional Education at Memorial University of Newfoundland. She is also honorary research associate in the School of Graduate Studies at the University of New Brunswick. She was founding director of student development at Memorial University and the Canadian Institute in Student Affairs and Services and past president of the Canadian Association of College and University Student Services, the Atlantic

Association of College and University Student Services, and the Student Affairs Division (Student Affairs & Services Association).

TED JAMES is dean, student development at Douglas College, an urban, comprehensive institution in New Westminster, British Columbia. He has served on the board of the Canadian Association of College and University Student Services and as Canadian board member for the National Council on Student Development (USA).

HEATHER LANE VETERE is vice provost, students at Ryerson University. She has been dean of students at the University of Toronto and executive director of student housing at the University of Guelph. Active in professional organizations, she has served on the boards of the Ontario Association of College and University Housing Officers, the Council for the Advancement of Standards in Higher Education, and as president of the Canadian Association of College and University Student Services.

CHRIS MCGRATH is assistant dean of student affairs at the University of Toronto and has served on the executive boards of several professional associations in Canada, including the Student Affairs and Services Association. He is pursuing doctoral studies in higher education, exploring the experiences of diverse students and their capacity to effect social change in colleges and universities.

ROBERTA MASON is vice-president (acting), university relations at Royal Roads University in British Columbia. She has more than twenty years of experience in university administration gained at the University of Guelph, Simon Fraser University, North Island College, and Royal Roads University. The Roberta Mason Award at the University of Guelph acknowledges her contributions there to student life.

PATRICIA MIRWALDT is director of the Student Health Service at the University of British Columbia. She trained in family and community medicine at the University of Manitoba, where she was director of the University Health Service and associate dean for Admissions and Student Affairs. She has played a leadership role in the Canadian Organization of University and College Health.

BONNIE NEUMAN is vice-president (student services) at Dalhousie University. Over the past twenty years she has served as vice-president (students) at York University; associate vice-president (student services) at Brock University; director of admissions, University of Alberta; and director of student records,

University of Alberta. She is a member of the board for the Canadian Bureau of International Education.

MICHEL OUELLETTE served as the director of housing and student life and associate faculty at Cochise College (Arizona). His past experiences included residence life coordinator and residence life programming manager at the University of Alberta and the first director of residential life and conference services at the University of New Brunswick. He was the Canadian district representative with the Association of College and University Housing Officers-International and an active contributor to the Canadian Association of College and University Student Services.

C. CARNEY STRANGE is professor of higher education and student affairs at Bowling Green State University in Ohio where, since 1978, he has taught graduate courses on student development and the design and impact of campus environments. An ACPA Senior Scholar and NASPA Faculty Fellow, he was selected as a Diamond Honoree (1999) and Pillar of the Profession (2006) respectively by each organization. He publishes widely in the field and is senior author of *Educating by Design: Creating Campus Learning Environments That Work*. He also serves on the board of trustees of Saint Xavier University (IL).

NONA ROBINSON is dean of students at University College, University of Toronto. She is pursuing doctoral studies in higher education at the Ontario Institute for Studies in Education. A former editor and frequent contributor to *Communiqué*, she shares an interest in the values of Canadian student affairs practitioners and the experiences of elected undergraduate student leaders.

JACK RUSSEL is a psychotherapist, career counsellor, adjunct professor in the graduate Faculty of Education, and instructor in the Department of Psychology at the University of Western Ontario. He has served on boards of the Canadian University and College Counselling Association and the Canadian Association of College and University Student Services.

ROBERT SHEA is an assistant professor (post-secondary and adult educa-tion) at Memorial University of Newfoundland. He is past president of the Canadian Association of College and University Student Services and of the Canadian Education and Research Institute for Counselling, founding director of the Canadian Journal of Career Development, and former direc-tor of the Departments of Career Development and Experiential Learning and of Student Development at Memorial University.

BRIAN SULLIVAN is vice-president, students at the University of British Columbia. He has served on the board of the Canadian Association of College and University Student Services and is past director of the National Association of Student Personnel Administrators' Steven's Institute for Senior Student Affairs Officers.

# Index